From Soul to Mind

From Soul to Mind

The Emergence of Psychology
from Erasmus Darwin to William James

Edward S. Reed

Yale University Press   New Haven and London

Printed in the United States of America.

Library of Congress
Cataloging-in-Publication Data
Reed, Edward (Edward S.)
From soul to mind: the emergence
of psychology, Erasmus Darwin to William
James / Edward S. Reed.
p. cm.
Includes bibliographical references (p.   )
and index.
ISBN 0-300-06967-7 (cloth)
0-300-07581-2 (paper)

1. Psychology—History—19th Century.
I. Title.
BF103.R44   1997
150'.9'034—dc21   96-49051
CIP

A catalogue record for this book is available
from the British Library.

The paper in this book meets the guidelines for
permanence and durability of the Committee on
Production Guidelines for Book Longevity
of the Council of Library Resources.

10 9 8 7 6 5 4 3 2

If the labours of men of Science should ever create any material revolution, direct or indirect, in our condition, and in the impressions which we habitually receive, the Poet will sleep then no more than at present, but he will be ready to follow in the steps of the Man of Science, not only in those general indirect effects, but he will be at his side, carrying sensation into the midst of the objects of the Science itself.

William Wordsworth, Preface to *Lyrical Ballads*

Contents

Preface / ix

CHAPTER 1
In Search of Psychology / 1

CHAPTER 2
The Impossible Science / 22

CHAPTER 3
Frankenstein's Science / 38

CHAPTER 4
The Breakdown in the Concert of European Ideas / 60

CHAPTER 5
The Brief Life of Natural Metaphysics / 81

CHAPTER 6
1848 and All That / 109

CHAPTER 7
The Three Unconsciousnesses and How They Grew / 127

CHAPTER 8
The Apotheosis of Positivism / 144

CHAPTER 9
The Anomalous Mr. Darwin / 168

CHAPTER 10

The Generation of 1879, or How Philosophy
Emerged from Psychology / 184

CHAPTER 11

William James: Psychology as a Science of Experience / 201

Bibliographic Essay / 221
Index / 273

PREFACE

Students of psychology often ask why the psychological insights of novelists and other creative writers tend to be overlooked by those who call themselves scientific psychologists. Surely Dostoevsky or Proust—to name two obvious examples—have much to tell us about the human psyche. This is a better question than most students realize, for it opens up a historical problem of the greatest significance: the parallel emergence of modern psychology and the modern novel. In the late nineteenth century these two important aspects of modernist culture appeared, and they have gained power in the twentieth century, during which time experimental and clinical psychologists have become extremely numerous and the novel has held, until recently, pride of place in Western culture. In the early nineteenth century, psychological issues were more likely to be explored in the poetry of Shelley or Wordsworth than in the novels of Scott or Balzac. At the same time, the few scientists who were exploring the psyche were likely to be physicians or physiologists, and of course there were no clinical psychologists at all.

The curious student's question about why scientific psychologists shun the insights of creative writers thus leads to the more pointed question of what happened during the 1800s to segregate science from literature. What historical transformation encouraged people to define themselves as psychologists rather than writers, or vice versa? In many ways this is a fundamental question for historians of psychology, because both modern psychological theories and the social institutions in which psychology is practiced grew out of the process of segregation. Yet it is on this question that the existing literature is surprisingly silent.

This unhelpful reticence in histories of psychology, as well as in related histories of philosophy, is largely the result of a series of avoidances that has characterized the history of science in general and that of psychology in particular. These avoidances have kept the history of science isolated from other areas of historical work and have undermined its utility for helping us understand the emergence of the modern—even though modern culture is inextricably bound up with advances in science and technology.

From Soul to Mind begins the ambitious task of telling a new story about the development of psychology. I start from the realization that we do not actually know what constituted psychology in the eighteenth and early nineteenth centuries. Most histories devote extensive space to theorists but give short shrift to experimentalists. This bias makes it easy to tell the old story about a "scientific psychology" that emerged from centuries of "mere speculation"—but of course it doesn't do anything to validate the truth of that old fable; quite the opposite. Historians of psychology have avoided what should be one of their central tasks: to explain the history and origins of ideas concerning what should and should not be counted as psychology.

Historians of psychology have also ignored the ideas that later proved mistaken. Luigi Galvani and Alessandro Volta, for example, appear in most histories of psychology as physiologists who discovered the electrical basis of neural transmission, not as researchers into the nature of vital and mental forces. This despite the fact that neither Galvani nor Volta would have wished to be called a physiologist, had such a term been available in their day. Neither believed that what they had discovered was electricity in our sense of the word, nor did either have anything approaching a concept of neural transmission. They thought they were studying the relation between electricity and the life force ("vital force"). By ignoring what Galvani and Volta actually thought (and characterizing their ideas in an anachronistic and inaccurate way), modern histories make it impossible to understand the power of the concept of force (animate and mental, as well as electrical or caloric) in the first half of the nineteenth century. The intimate connection between theories of animal magnetism, animal electricity, animal heat, mesmerism, and phrenology and the first serious attempts to "physiologize" the association of ideas will never be understood unless we overcome the reluctance of historians of science to study the "fringe" elements in the origin of modern scientific thinking.

In trying to understand the growth of modern psychology, we must not overlook the historical development of the career of "being a psychologist." As late as 1900 there were few career psychologists, whereas a century later psychology is among the largest of the scientific professions. When we study earlier periods, we should not be surprised to find doctors, academics, preachers, writers, and quacks all actively engaged in the practice of psychology. Yet historians of psychology have rarely looked beyond a narrowly defined group—primarily the canonical "theorists of the mind" found in histories of philosophy, plus the "nerve physiologists" from histories of physiology—in identifying their protagonists. Neither Kierkegaard nor the Combe brothers (who combined phrenology with Protestant ministry) stand a chance of inclusion, given this blinkered perspective. The blindness to all but a small number of historical actors is an egregious error, I argue here, because at the beginning of the nineteenth century the most important European psychologist was a medical doctor and poet, Erasmus Darwin. Students of literature have long known this, but Erasmus Darwin has received little serious attention within histories of psychology or philosophy. I hope that the present account will begin to restore the elder Darwin to his important place in the history of the science of the mind.

Late-twentieth-century developments in the historiography of science do not offer much help for those of us who wish to revise the history of psychology. This history, at least in English, has been excessively "internalist" and "presentist." History of psychology, like history of science in general, has suffered from its attempt to read the past primarily in terms of present concerns. Unfortunately, the "externalist" historians of science who have come forth to oppose this tendentious reading have not so much solved the problems as created new ones.

Externalists have argued—rightly, in my opinion—that history of psychology should make contact with other areas of history. We should examine how scientists in a given era related to the social forces and institutions of their day. There is no doubt, for instance, that the friendship between Erasmus Darwin and the early industrialist Josiah Wedgwood is of historical significance. But externalists must also be internalists, for scientific controversy often concerns interpretations of facts and experiments. It matters that Joseph Priestley, who was acquainted with both Darwin and Wedgwood, did not accept, as Darwin did, Antoine Lavoisier's theory of oxygen. Neither externalism nor internalism alone produces satisfactory history of science. We need to know why the man who isolated what we call oxygen (Priestley, although the term was coined by Darwin) nonetheless could never admit that such a thing existed, and this surely requires us to understand Priestley's thinking, as well as his social status. The dichotomy between externalism and internalism is false and pernicious. Historians of psychology need to be open to a wider array of questions and approaches than they have been. But we cannot simply replace existing internalist histories of psychology with externalist versions of the same story, peopled by the same characters, for this will not advance our understanding.

The career of Robert Whytt (1711–66) offers a good illustration of why it is necessary to appreciate a scientist's career in context. Whytt was a physician who taught at the prestigious medical school of the University of Edinburgh, offering theories somewhat at variance with those of the dominant faculty members (the Cullen family) or the later, and somewhat notorious, Robert Brown. Unlike these other doctors, Whytt was a brilliant experimentalist who demonstrated, among other things, the basic mechanism of spinal reflexes in vertebrates. In the context of these experiments Whytt invented both the idea and the term *stimulus,* by which he meant a brief application of a physical energy (light, heat, mechanical energy, electricity) to a nerve. Whytt argued that nerves could somehow bring the impression of that stimulus to the spinal cord, where the organism would, in some way, "feel" the stimulus and begin the process of responding to it. Whytt's conceptual emphasis on stimuli to the nervous system became the basis of virtually all later psychophysical research and had immense influence during the next century and a half. But Whytt has never been given credit by internalist historians for his fundamental breakthrough, because although he was the first to get the physiological mechanisms "right," he interpreted them in terms of what he called the "sentient principle" (which he explicitly suggested was a sort of subordinate soul) in the spinal cord—an idea that was eliminated from "scientific" psychology in the second half of the nineteenth century. Yet externalist historians have not reevaluated Whytt's place in history. Indeed, they are in no position to do so. Strictly speaking, an externalist historian cannot acknowledge that an earlier thinker's contribution might have been overlooked or misinterpreted, because the strict externalist has committed him- or herself to tracing the actual unfolding of power and prestige within scientific institutions. In this regard, what matters about the Edinburgh school is who dominated it and its influence on other schools of thought and practice. Externalist history thus treats Whytt as a collateral figure. My claim that Whytt's influence was pervasive but unacknowledged is, for externalists, a contradiction in terms: nobody can be influential but unacknowledged.

From Soul to Mind had its origin some twenty years ago as I was trying to trace Whytt's influence and becoming increasingly frustrated by the inability of historians to understand what, exactly, he had done and therefore feeling confused about his place in history. Time and again, I found that psychologists toward the end of the 1800s would restate Whytt's ideas in the language of the *mind* rather than the *soul,* without crediting him. In fact, Charles Sherrington, to whom the modern reflex theory is due, followed Whytt's ideas closely in everything except the language in which they were expressed, receiving credit for a good bit of the work Whytt had done a century and a half earlier. (Not that Sherrington needed Whytt's credit, as his own original work was of the greatest importance.)

Whytt argued that sensory impulses to the spinal cord are felt by a sentient principle that then reacts selectively and adaptively by contracting muscles in a specific way. According to Whytt, the true soul (in the brain) can by itself cause equivalent sensory impulses to occur and thereby activate the body. Sherrington argued that sensory impulses to the spinal cord "communicate" to the cord, making contact with other signals, a process that results, ultimately, in a selective choice of outgoing signals that contract specific muscles. According to Sherrington, the mind (in the brain) can selectively activate or inhibit the same signals, thus causing the body to move (or resist motion). Whytt's soul-like sentient principle was thus replaced by Sherrington's telegraph-like communications system, superimposed on what is now said to be a mind, not a soul.

Why, I wondered, did it take the transition from soul to mind for the theory of spinal reflexes to gain acceptance? The basic phenomenon of the vertebrate reflex was clearly and definitively established by Whytt's experiments of the 1740s and his controversy with Albrecht von Haller over the matter in the 1750s. Yet this work was not widely understood or accepted until Sherrington's largely linguistic revision around 1900. Why should what seems to us little more than a change in wording have proved so powerful? And why did both scientists and later historians of science show such an inability to "read through" Whytt's theoretical vocabulary to the details of his experiments —especially considering that these experiments were and still are acknowledged to be classic?

All these questions took me far afield, away from Sherrington and Whytt (to whom I plan on returning). The more I looked into the nineteenth-century reception of earlier ideas about psychology, the more intrigued I became. I was especially struck by the widespread tendency of nineteenth-century thinkers to narrow down their field of study, to resist the broad reach of such earlier theorists as Whytt and Erasmus Darwin. With a few important exceptions, psychologists after 1850 consistently avoided developing the ontological implications of their work; moreover, those who, like Gustav Fechner, did take these ontological implications seriously, found their ontological claims ignored in favor of narrower aspects of their work. *From Soul to Mind* tells the story of this progressive narrowing of focus, the story of how psychology became a science, divorced itself from literature, and invented that most modern of concepts, the mind. In two related books, I have offered suggestions for how modern psychology might overcome its legacy of narrowness. In *Encountering the World: Toward an Ecological Psychology* (1996), I argue that the mind lies not in the brain but in the relation of organism to environment. And in *The Necessity of Experience* (1996), I contend that a revamped concept of experience is needed to open psychology up from its current narrowness. In *From Soul to Mind* I trace the history behind that constriction, suggesting some of the reasons that have led to it and some possible ways of opening psychology up to a wider notion of experience.

My research on Whytt and his influence was supported by a Drexel University Research Grant, while bibliographical research on nineteenth-century psychology was supported by the Franklin and Marshall College faculty research fund. And I received a grant from the John Simon Guggenheim Memorial Foundation while writing this book. I thank all these agencies for their kind help, without which *From Soul to Mind* would not exist.

I also thank a number of colleagues for advice and information: Joel Eigen, Howard Kaye, and Fred Owens at Franklin and Marshall College; Mike Montgomery and Rob Wozniak for bibliographic leads; Sherry Anders for research assistance and preparation of the index; and Stuart Shanker for suggesting I write up my ideas on the nineteenth century. At Yale University Press I had invaluable help from Gladys Topkis, Susan Abel, and Susan Laity. I thank them all for intelligent editing and a cheerful attitude, both of which improved the book and its author.

From Soul to Mind

I

In Search of Psychology

Smack in the middle of the nineteenth century, on February 12, 1850, seven United States senators — among them Sam Houston, Henry Clay, and Daniel Webster — invited a psychologist to speak in the Hall of Representatives in Washington, D.C. Their choice was the Universalist minister John Bovee Dods (1795–1872), who duly provided a series of lectures on "electrical psychology." Published that spring, Dods's lectures were so popular that they went through several printings, and a revised and augmented edition appeared in the fall.

Dods's lectures offer the modern reader a convenient microcosm of nineteenth-century psychology. Beginning with a teleological view of "man" as an "intellectually progressive being" and keeping one eye firmly fixed on the established religious verities, Dods offered his psychology as a new science which he believed would become queen among the sciences because of the insights it would provide into the most important aspects of life: human beings' relation to nature, to other people, and to the deity. These insights could not be derived from the Bible or even from natural religion; they would come from the difficult work of good, hard science. Dods devoted the entirety of his second lecture to showing how his psychology was modeled on the latest and most relevant sciences of human nature — phrenology and mesmerism.

For Dods, as for the majority of nineteenth-century proponents of science, to be pro-science was most assuredly not to be antireligious or to denigrate religion in any way. In the nineteenth century, almost all proponents of science went out of their way to explain how modern science was an important ally of religion. Indeed, for Dods as for most other psychologists, psychology was a queenly science precisely because it was the most effective scientific means of buttressing religion. "The brain is invested with a living spirit," Dods assured his auditors, "which, like an enthroned deity, presides over and governs . . . all the voluntary motions of this organized corporeal universe; while its living presence, and its involuntary self-moving powers cause all the involuntary functions of life" (p. 53).

Throughout the first half of the nineteenth century, psychology was considered the fundamental science by many philosophers, theologians, and educated laypeople because, like Dods, they saw it as the science best suited to preserve religion in an increasingly scientific modern world. The metaphor of the human being as a microcosm of the universe, with the soul as its principal organizing agent, held great sway in a century in which even some of the most "advanced" and "radical" of scientists endorsed the use of science to support the notion of God as the organizer of the universe. Psychology as the science of the soul thus occupied an important place in intellectual life. But this science of the soul also at times gave rise to concerns: Might it contain the seeds of ideas that would undermine religion? Although attacks against orthodoxy were few (or were hushed up, as we shall see), worries about heterodoxy were omnipresent. One of Germany's most distinguished philosophers, Rudolf Hermann Lotze (1817–81), hit the nail on the head: "As the growing farsightedness of astronomy dissipated the idea that the great theater of human life was in direct connection with divinity, so the further advance of mechanical science begins to threaten with similar disintegration the smaller world, the microcosm of man."

Charles Darwin's attack on the theocentric science of nature (see Chapter 9) led to an unprecedented intellectual war against him and his science. It is crucial for modern readers to understand that this war against Darwin's ideas was largely successful in re-establishing many elements of the theocentric worldview among educated elites at the end of the century. Throughout the nineteenth century, and even after Darwin's work had become widely known, psychology was viewed through that microcosmic lens, and even those varieties of psychological thought that were not directly associated with religious orthodoxy and ruling elites—spiritualism, phrenology, and mesmerism—tended to align themselves along a fixed deistic axis.

What distinguished the psychology of 1890 from that of 1815, besides the change of name from *moral philosophy* to *psychology*, was primarily the way in which psychology was used to support religious ideas. Early in the century, psychology was considered to be a science of the soul. By the end of the century, psychology had more or less abandoned the soul and replaced it with the mind. Nevertheless, as I hope to show, most psychologists still expected this science of the mind to reinforce important religious beliefs.

It is dangerous, however, for readers at the end of the twentieth century to succumb to temptation and dismiss these philosophers and psychologists as mere apologists for a reigning set of beliefs. Modern historians of ideas, writing from an agnostic perspective, have tended to overlook the religious differences that animated a great deal of nineteenth-century scientific work, especially in fields like psychology. The "scientific" debates over mind, body, and soul in the 1800s are inseparable from the religious debates concerning these matters—it is, in fact, anachronistic to separate the two. Much of nineteenth-century psychological thought emerged from religious apologists' efforts to justify specific views of the deity or the soul.

Dods's lectures offer an excellent example of this kind of creative apologetics. His science of electrical psychology amounted to an attempt to show that the connection between soul and body is electromagnetic. He pieced together ideas and occasional facts from the work of mesmerists (students of what Dods still called animal magnetism or animal electricity) and phrenologists with a vague inkling of the then-novel idea of the interchangeability of physical forces. In several lectures aimed at showing that all disease, psychological or physical, results from an imbalance in electrical forces within the body, he elaborated an account of voluntary behavior that—shorn of the electrical metaphysics—was soon to dominate physiological psychology. Spiritual activity in the brain, Dods said, created or excited electrical impulses, which became nerve force; this in turn caused muscle contractions and, ultimately, human action. In the next four decades countless physicians were to stimulate their patients electrically in order to make their muscles contract and thereby to release nervous or psychological tension, supposedly curing a whole range of diseases. (William James, whose degree was in medicine, recommended such electrotherapy to his sister, Alice, for her "nervous condition" and increasingly relied on this treatment when his own health failed.) Shortly after the introduction of these clinical procedures, researchers like Gustav Fritsch and Edward Hitzig in Germany, and soon thereafter David Ferrier in Britain, electrically stimulated the exposed brains of dogs and primates and demonstrated that such central excitation elicits movements of the animal's body. To many, this seemed to provide proof that thought was, at least in part, the electrical activity of the brain.

But which came first, the mind or the brain, the thought or the electric spark? To someone already convinced that the brain, like the rest of the body, is an instrument or tool of the immortal soul, these demonstrations proved that the mind acts in and through certain special regions of matter. And, surprising as it may sound to a modern reader, this doctrine of the soul's using the body dominated European scientific and medical thought between 1848 and 1890—the period when modern experimental psychology proudly announced its arrival on the scene. Hence, the typical understanding of the emergence of modern experimental psychology and its allied neurophysiological disciplines —and specifically the assumption that progressive thinkers in these fields placed all causality in the brain—is seriously misguided.

Psychology as Secular Theology

Most scientists and philosophers actively involved in the construction and reception of the "new psychology" at the end of the 1800s did not assume that the new discipline was materialist in its inspiration or goals, and regularly defended their work against the charge that it tended to promote materialism. The twentieth-century notion that new sciences were hostile to religion has blinded us to the intimate alliance between modern psychology and liberal Protestant thought. We easily assume that the late-nineteenth-century propensity for placing the mind in the brain is a stepping stone to a secular materialist worldview and therefore is opposed to, or at least independent of, any religious view of human nature. But this assumption is wrong.

First of all, it is possible to locate the soul in the spinal cord as well as in the cerebrum. The Scottish physician Robert Whytt, who discovered spinal reflexes in the 1740s, produced a strong and influential argument for this position: How can the spinal cord regulate all the intricate bodily functions (breathing, heartbeat, sexual movements, and so on) if it does not contain the soul? Unless the soul resides in the spinal cord, how can one explain the adaptive characteristics evident in many reflexive activities, such as the scratching or wiping reflexes by which animals use their legs to remove such skin irritants as fleas or ticks? The idea of a soul or mind that is distributed throughout the spine and perhaps even throughout the body (as opposed to being locked inside the skull) forms a kind of counterpoint to mainstream psychological and physiological thought, at least until the writings of George Henry Lewes in the 1860s and 1870s (see Chapter 8).

This view of the distributed soul serves to undermine the Cartesian separation of soul and body, especially the key Cartesian assumption that the mind is in contact only with states of the brain. For many nineteenth-century thinkers, this theory of the distributed soul placed it dangerously close to the "animal" aspects of the world and tended to make the soul indistinguishable from our viscera. (It also seemed to suggest that even simple animals had souls and thus to demote human beings from their position as the undisputed lords of God's creation.) Certainly, Whytt's position engendered fierce opposition wherever and whenever it was proposed. Thus, the "cerebralists," who situated the mind in the brain, saw themselves not as materialists but as defenders of the soul (that is, they were saving the soul from being "naturalized"), attackers of Whyttian infidels, and defenders of liberal Protestantism's separation of sin from self. True evil, the new psychology affirmed, is an external force with regard to the soul, capable of corrupting human nature from without, but not intrinsic to human nature and certainly not ineradicable.

In keeping with the theological underpinnings of the new psychology, many of the first reports on it published in North America appeared in the liberal Protestant periodicals of the time, such as the *New Andover Review*. A good example comes from the pen of one of the most respected early scientific psychologists in North America, James Mark Baldwin. In 1887 he wrote in the *Presbyterian Review:* "To say that the soul is natural is not to say that it is mechanical, nor is it to say that there is continuity of law in the natural and spiritual worlds; on the contrary, it is to say that nature is intelligent and that the laws of thought are the laws of things." Three years later, explicitly referring to the new "scientific psychology," Baldwin added: "It is spiritualism and not materialism which is profiting by the advances of science." Nor were the Americans alone in seeing in scientific psychology a defense of a spiritual worldview. The important German neo-Kantian philosopher Friedrich A. Lange published a three-volume *History of Materialism* in the 1860s with the goal of showing how the new physiological psychology undermined the materialist worldview.

Thus, Dods's lectures, for all their simplicity, represent a genuine trend within the discipline of psychology. Indeed, my purpose in the present book is to argue that this trend was the dominant one throughout the second half of the nineteenth century. To put it simply, psychology succeeded in becoming a science in large part because of its defense of a theological conception of human nature typically associated with liberal Protestant theology. In this conception of human nature, genuine evil and irrationality are considered to be external to the core self. Within science the defense of this position involved a strategic retreat: the earlier Galenic concept of the soul as a balance of the attributes of personality was abandoned, to be replaced not by Descartes's opposition between mind and body but by a new dualism consisting of conscious mind (the true self) and unconscious mind (affected by forces "outside" the soul, including the body).

There is, however, a major gap in all accounts of these developments: Against whom is this strategic defense being organized? Why did it become necessary to develop theories of the unconscious—at first electrical and magnetic theories, then cortical and symbolic ones—when such ideas had not seemed essential earlier? Why does one find psychologists, throughout the 1800s and as late as the 1890s, protesting strongly that their science preserves a theologically respectable account of human nature? Modern accounts of psychology's history tend to be silent concerning the antispiritualist theories that stimulated this interesting defense, because modern historians have not understood that the "new scientific psychology" of the late 1800s was launched in defense of a spiritual view of reality; indeed, they have often mistaken the religious pro-spiritualists for materialists.

OFFICIAL VERSUS UNOFFICIAL PSYCHOLOGY

Throughout the 1800s, respectable psychologists and philosophers defended their views against atheists and materialists but rarely presented either the names or the true positions of their opponents. The revolutions of 1848 surely had something to do with this style of theorizing. These widespread democratic uprisings frightened the aristocrats, who still dominated both the churches and the states of Europe, and correspondingly emboldened the rising middle and professional classes to assert more authority. Tacit alliances were made between the old regime and these new upwardly mobile elements to stem the tide of "chaos" and "disorder" that was ostensibly rising from below by liberalizing both theological doctrine and political practice. In the decade following 1848, the so-called vulgar materialists came to the fore in Germany, and across Europe the positivist movement gathered strength, even as it became increasingly divorced from the peculiarities of its founder, Auguste Comte. Ludwig Büchner's materialist *Kraft und Stoff* (Force and matter) became a Europe-wide best-seller but was exceeded in popularity by Herbert Spencer's positivist writings. At the same time, as almost a mirror image of these developments, "spiritualism"—séances, talking with the dead, spirit rapping, and the like—enjoyed immense popularity in the 1850s. Mainstream religious thought found itself hemmed in between two kinds of sacrilege, one materialist, the other a kind of promiscuous and overzealous spiritualism.

At the time, mainstream thinkers often attacked the promoters of scientific psychology as allies of atheism, but even a superficial reading of their work reveals how false this accusation was. It was the much reviled Spencer who came up with the ultimate Victorian "truce" between science and religion: Religion is concerned with that which is unknowable in the universe; science, which traffics in knowledge, should not and cannot deal with the unknowable. Although thinkers like Spencer were labeled materialists and even atheists by their enemies, this was nothing more than name-calling. Many of the so-called materialists were in fact Berkeleians who denied the existence of matter. Thinkers who refused to rule out divine creation or even divine intervention in the course of nature or history surely posed little threat to established verities, although poor Büchner and several of his allies lost their academic positions, thanks to their own and their opponents' inflated rhetoric. It is a scandal that historians of psychology and philosophy still repeat the ancient attacks on the early psychologists. The ideas of the real atheists and radical materialists—who were hardly mild souls like Spencer—were not referred to explicitly by either the self-styled positivists and materialists of mid-century or the more mainstream philosophers who opposed them. Moreover, many of the strongest attacks on orthodoxy came not from atheists or agnostics but from spiritualists—whose self-proclaimed access to the world of souls undermined the structure of organized belief and worship.

Going back to the period before 1848, one finds a further puzzle. Between 1815 and 1848 all European countries had what amounted to an official philosophy, promulgated from university lecterns and church pulpits and reinforced by the police and often by severe censorship laws and practices. To a large degree these official philosophies consisted (in Britain, the United States, France, and parts of the Hapsburg Empire) of pastiches of Scottish "commonsense" theorizing or (in certain other German-speaking regions) a theologically inspired objective idealism with roots in Kant's writings. According to the founders of these positions, Thomas Reid in Scotland and Immanuel Kant in East Prussia, psychology could never become a scientific discipline. Indeed, as I shall show in Chapter 2, both these thinkers claimed to rescue the realm of the sacred precisely by *banishing* psychology from the sciences. It comes as something of a surprise, then, to see that after 1815 even those thinkers who acknowledged Kant or Reid as an intellectual forebear were not only offering "sciences of the mind" but using them to defend the faith! Dods, like many other phrenologists and mesmerists, was simply trying to piggyback his views on those of the official thinkers.

Here is confusion heaped upon confusion. In the second half of the nineteenth century, scientific psychologists saw themselves as proponents of the liberal Protestant image of mankind, in opposition to—what? Some sort of materialistic, scientific, atheistic theory, one would suppose, but no traces seem to be left of that dastardly theory! How is a reader to believe there was such a thing? In the early 1800s, the adherents of "official" psychology—later remodeled and modernized as a modern science—broke with its founders to defend the soul from atheistic assault. But, again, little trace is left of the bad guys.

Part of the problem here lies in how easy it is for us in the twentieth century to forget that *published* philosophy and science for the most part had to be supportive of church and state in all European countries before 1848, and in many of them afterward as well. Radical ideas, even those that might have been hotly debated and contested, could not be discussed in public by professors, whose lectures were often attended by the secret police, at least until 1848. And even after 1848, it could be very dangerous to publish material that might be misconstrued as condoning atheism or materialism. Modern readers tend to ignore these important facts of earlier intellectual life. This means that we have partial histories of ideas—histories of official ideas only, and histories in which some of the major motivations of those official ideas are often hidden from view, by prudence, censorship, or both.

Once the historian confronts the clandestine presence of important philosophical currents, some relatively straightforward solutions present themselves. The one adopted in this book is simply to widen the net. In the 1800s not all work in philosophy, psychology, or even physiology was undertaken by professionals. George Lewes stands as an excellent example: he made important contributions to the dissemination of physiological knowledge in the period between 1850 and 1880, even though he was what we would call a journalist and had no official scientific position. In addition, anyone seeking to uncover radical ideas in circulation before 1848 needs to look at *non*official literature and at writings that could not easily be censored. This means studying the work of poets and other "popular" writers.

Historians of philosophy and psychology may well balk at being told they need to integrate Coleridge or Balzac into their narratives, but I see no alternative. As of 1815 neither the discipline we call psychology nor the one we call philosophy existed. The widespread belief that psychology emerged from philosophy is historical gibberish: In what sense is there greater intellectual or historical continuity between the historian and bellettrist David Hume and a modern philosophy professor than between Hume and a modern professor of psychology? The case of Great Britain is very instructive. Although Jeremy Bentham, James Mill, and John Stuart Mill all feature prominently in any decent history of British philosophy, none of them ever held, or even aspired to hold, an academic position. They were, and considered themselves to be, writers, polemicists, and thinkers. Moreover, John Stuart Mill, like almost any literate Englishman who grew up in the first quarter of the nineteenth century, insisted on the value of the philosophical ideas of such writers and poets as Carlyle, Coleridge, and Wordsworth. Modern historians' omission of such writers from their accounts of philosophical or scientific ideas therefore seems to me a serious mistake. Worse, the assumption that scientific and even cultural trends in the nineteenth century developed largely independent of religion—as part of a secularizing trend—is patently false. As James Sheehan, a distinguished historian of Germany, noted recently: "In contrast to most historians, who view the nineteenth century as a resolutely secular age, most contemporaries regarded religion as a critically important cultural and political issue. . . . Despite the undeniable power of secularization, nineteenth-century politics and culture remained permeated by religion."

The proof of the pudding is in the eating, and the proof of a method is in its results. I intend to justify the present book's wider-than-usual scope not by methodological arguments but by results. The standard version of the story of psychology appears to me at best one-sided (because it emphasizes the "official" theories) and at worst misleading (because it is difficult for historians who limit their field of view to reconstruct the arguments and oppositions that motivated changes in the official positions). To the extent that the new story I offer is compelling and makes sense of some of the confusions already mentioned, it will have proved worthwhile to avoid the narrow focus of most historians of psychology. Any new questions and problems this version raises will also vindicate my choice of focus. We shall see in the discussion on Lewes, for example, that as late as the 1860s there were several institutional avenues that the "new" psychology might have taken: it might have become allied with medicine, physiology, or even science journalism. Instead, it became an academic and laboratory-oriented discipline with an affiliated clinical wing and in fact became one of the forces against which modern philosophy defined itself as an academic and logic-oriented discipline. The historical emergence of these fields can be studied adequately only by contrasting the career paths of thinkers who correspond to our modern image of psychologists with those of thinkers who do not fit nicely into our modern schema.

A New Story of Psychology

The story I tell in the following chapters starts with my reconstruction of the early version of the "official" European philosophies of the post-Napoleonic era and the radical theories to which the official theorists were, I argue, largely responding. The official theories descended from the work of Reid and Kant, both of whom offered clever ways of reconciling science and religion within an Enlightenment framework. This reconciliation, however, required abandoning the viability of a science of human nature. Both Kant and Reid believed that religion could be saved in the modern world only by showing how psychology could never be a real science, so that the soul could not be analyzed scientifically. Within a very few years their proposed truce between religion and science was shattered. The discovery that oxygen was the basis for respiration (which refuted the hypothesis that the brain was an organ for dephlogisticating air) and the advances in the electrical sciences of the 1790s gave a major push to neurophysiology. Thinkers started speculating about the electrical and chemical basis of life and sentience. Perhaps Reid and Kant had "proved" that no one could study human beings scientifically, but, nonetheless, many scholars seemed hell-bent on doing so—the old truce was off, and a new one had to be arranged.

Many of the doctors and natural philosophers who speculated on the nature of life and mind in the period between 1790 and 1815 found that their views were increasingly unwelcome to authorities of all sorts. Especially when they touched on the nature of the human soul, these ideas—or their proponents—tended to be suppressed. For this reason I think it appropriate to speak of an "underground psychology," although the period of aggressive censorship and repression really began after 1815 and the restoration of the ancien régime by the Congress of Vienna. The first great representative of this underground psychology was Erasmus Darwin, grandfather of Charles Darwin. Erasmus Darwin was probably the most up-to-date general scientist of his day; among other things, he coined the term *oxygen*. He was well versed in then-current electrical theory, but he expounded his scientific ideas largely through long poems with essays appended as notes to the poems. The English translator of Linnaeus and a widely respected medical doctor with an interest in "nervous" diseases, Erasmus Darwin offered a radical view of human nature in writings that were published over the two decades following the beheading of Louis XVI and Marie Antoinette by the French revolutionaries.

For Darwin all of animate nature was possessed of sensibility and feeling, even plants. He sought the material basis for this sensibility in a subtle fluid or ether in the body and nerves, basing his ideas on the influential fluid theory of electricity developed by his friend Benjamin Franklin. Although he was not the first to do so, Erasmus Darwin was the most influential scientist to reject the prevalent doctrine that all mental states derive from the motion of particles in the brain. Like Whytt before him, he favored an explanation positing a much broader distribution of feeling and sentience throughout the body. But unlike Whytt, Darwin refused to couch his theory in the religious language of the "soul," and this difference was crucial to the reception of his ideas. His works were read throughout Europe and were both promoted and caricatured by popular writers of gothic stories. The most famous of these Darwinian gothics is Mary Shelley's *Frankenstein,* which is discussed in Chapter 3.

Erasmus Darwin's radical philosophy of life and mind was abandoned by his erstwhile supporters as the European reaction against revolutionary France set in. Wordsworth and Coleridge came to criticize both his poetry and his science. Yet Darwinian ideas continued to inspire a younger generation of scientists and writers, such as Humphrey Davy and Percy Bysshe Shelley. Shelley in particular developed Darwin's ideas and his methods. Shelley's first major poem, *Queen Mab* (which was suppressed, but very popular in a variety of underground editions), far surpasses Darwin's heroic couplets in style but still adopts the format of appended notes to discuss scientific and philosophical issues at length. We shall see that Shelley's idea of eros, or love, was an attempt to epitomize Erasmus Darwin's psychology and therefore became a kind of whipping boy for the official theorists.

What the orthodox theorists were concerned about was this: If life, mind, and feeling are concomitants of the arrangement of organs and of a fluid ether in animal bodies, what role was left for either God or the soul? A God who does nothing more than organize matter to feel, think, and act is not much of a deity—for what is to guarantee *how* these creatures will feel, think, and act? Both Erasmus Darwin and Percy Shelley argued that the way we act is a function of our upbringing—of social, not divine, intervention. And both deplored the "bad influence" of religion on this upbringing. Further, if this theory of fluid materialism is correct, does it not mean that animals also have souls or, as Mary Shelley (along with E. T. A. Hoffmann, Edgar Allan Poe, and many others) later suggested, that a scientist could even organize inert matter into an animate being? Conversely, if souls and spirits are nothing more than a special kind of electromagnetic ether, might we not be able to influence them through material means (for example, Mesmer's use of magnets to induce "crises" and "magnetic sleep") or perhaps even somehow contact lost souls, as the spiritualists claimed to do? This "natural supernaturalism" (to borrow M. H. Abrams's phrase) originated with Shelley's circle and flowered in the spiritualist movement half a century later. The theorists used their new science to call into question almost every basic orthodox assumption about the nature of the soul, and official theorists responded by deploring the atheism in this underground psychology. After 1815 anyone who tried to publish anything like this early materialist psychology in a scientific form—even in so-called liberal England—risked prosecution, censorship, and worse.

But the official theorists had to do more than deplore the sacrilegious excesses of these Darwinian theorists—they had to provide some sort of alternative that was intellectually respectable. Studies of the "science of mind" flourished across Europe after 1815, frequently incorporating facts from the fields of anatomy and physiology. In many cases the goal of these theories was a kind of "master science" that would not only allow analysis of the human mind but provide both logical and moral rules for thinking. Mental and moral sciences flourished, as did all manner of logics, many of which claimed to be guides to right thinking, not just investigations of thought. All the published versions of these theories uniformly placed mental states in the cerebrum and asserted that human experience begins with the simple sensations that arise there. Complex mental states were said to derive from the association and the assimilation of those experiences—and if a mind did not follow the right associative path, the result might be deviant thoughts or actions.

Despite this philosophical emphasis on the cerebrum, certain physiologists still puzzled over whether the spinal cord might be able to sense or feel. The rapid success of the "Bell-Magendie Law" concerning the organization of the spine needs to be interpreted in this context. Charles Bell in 1811 and François Magendie in the 1820s suggested that the dorsal side of the spine was a sensory (input) side and the ventral a motor (output) side. This view led quickly to the idea that the brain received and interpreted the spinal inputs and ordered whatever outputs were needed to go back down to the spine. Hence, the mind could still be located in the brain—an argument summarized, and bolstered with copious facts, in Johannes Müller's *Elements of Physiology,* published in the 1830s and on these issues easily the most influential physiological text of the entire century.

This newer physiology thus explicitly avoided treating matter in general as having such properties as feeling or thought. Müller, for example, posited both a "vital force" and "mental energies" or forces that existed independent of matter, even if they might eventually be found to be confined spatially to parts of the brain. This kind of scientific psychology assigned mental life to a special domain and was consistent with the idea that human souls were created independently of the rest of nature. The idea that God might create a brain in humans with a special power enabling it to come in contact with the immaterial realm of the soul seemed very plausible in those days—especially when to oppose this idea was to fly in the face of powerful religious and secular authorities. This position about the mind and brain—one that clearly elevates psychology to a special status among the sciences—dominated official European thought until at least 1848 and continued to exert considerable influence up until the end of the century.

The problem with putting the soul in the brain is that doing so fails to explain all those things that seem to go on in and around our bodies or brains without our being aware of or in charge of them. For example, although the discipline of psychophysics was born directly out of Müller's physiology, it soon created problems for psychological theory. The early psychophysicists attempted to measure how changes in physical energies corresponded to or affected changes in psychological energies. They would stimulate a sense organ or part of the body very slightly and see whether that stimulus was noticed; then they would increase the stimulation and see whether that was noticed, and so forth. It became apparent that a cluster of subthreshold (that is, imperceptible) stimuli might be registered merely as a single stimulus and, worse, that various circumstances could alter the thresholds, including repeated experience of the same stimuli. It began to appear that subthreshold stimuli *were* noticed—but *by what?* Not by the conscious mind in the brain, because in that case they would not be subthreshold. So who or what was registering the subthreshold impressions? At around the same time, doctors studying sleep disorders, hypnosis, and behavior under the influence of alcohol also were beginning to wonder about states in which their patients seemed to register sensations without being conscious of them. How is it possible to call a sleeping person by name and wake her up without her being aware that her name has been called?

The opponents of Erasmus Darwin's underground psychology had essentially created a variant of Cartesian dualism. Müller, for example, considered himself a Spinozist of sorts. These theorists argued that the mind is a special thing, made up of ideas (conscious states) in the brain, and that everything else in the world is just physical matter in motion. Awareness grew after 1848 that this dualism was inadequate, in view of all the subthreshold phenomena. These posed no problem for such writers as the elder Darwin and Percy Shelley, because for them matter in general was capable of feeling, not just the special matter in the human brain. In their view, human experience could be open to many aspects of the world that are closed off according to proponents of the mind-in-the-brain doctrine—aspects of the world that the official theorists wanted to keep separate from the soul. As I shall try to show, proponents of the "new psychology" in the second half of the nineteenth century thus required a special theory of the unconscious in order to preserve a certain purity in the conscious mind. Indeed, the 1860s produced an outpouring of theories of the unconscious, almost all of which fit the bill and many of which were directed either against the materialism of the underground psychologists or against the claims of the spiritualists, or both.

The unconscious sensations and processes postulated by the new psychologists thus seemed to support the increasingly widespread "liberal" view of the human soul. Although they cannot, by definition, be studied through introspective methods, unconscious processes were found necessary to theory and so were brought into even the speculations of classical introspectionist experimental psychology. Similarly, although unconscious processes cannot be studied physiologically (perhaps their physiological manifestation is observable, but not the feelings or thoughts it clothes), classical modern physiological psychologists also made extensive reference to them. Indeed, almost all of the self-professed "new" psychologists of 1860–1890 swore allegiance to some version of positivist methodology in science, a methodology in which scientific explorations are

expected to have reference to verifiable phenomena from beginning to end. It is thus deeply ironic that these same new
psychologists rested their basic account of the human mind on
unconscious feelings and processes that are in principle impossible to observe!

Two of the most famous psychologists of the turn of the
century recognized the inconsistencies and inadequacies of this
new psychology. Both Sigmund Freud and William James realized that the new psychologists' modified Cartesian approach
limited the notion of what constituted human experience to a
small number of basic cerebral responses to stimuli. The rest
of human existence was therefore classified either as unconscious feeling or as a kind of thought (the result of interpretation of unconscious feelings by unconscious processes). The
mind, according to this new psychology, was always rational,
although irrational bodily and unconscious feelings might per-
turb it. Freud himself was willing to accept that this notion of
the mind might hold true for "normal" psychology (as he says
in *The Interpretation of Dreams*), but of course he was not willing to accept so limited a psychology as explaining all of human
motivation and mentation, much of which is not "normal" according to liberal Protestant morality.

James went even further than Freud. He always explicitly
rejected the dichotomy between conscious and unconscious,
precisely because he disagreed strongly with the basic assumptions of the cerebralists about what constituted the sensations
that they claimed lay at the heart of human experience. Instead of the momentary, atomistic, punctate nature of the sensations that featured centrally in all the theories of the new psychologists, James emphasized that even our simple sensations
are complex, fringed, flowing, and dynamic. Although James
is often described as a key founder of the new psychology in
America, he was nothing of the sort. He saw himself as the

deepest and most principled critic of this school and also, not incidentally, of the liberal Protestant conception of the soul. The book concludes with a review of James's insightful critique of the new psychology and a discussion of some of his ideas for rethinking human nature.

2

The Impossible Science

The consensus in Europe during and immediately after the French Revolution was that psychology as a science was impossible. This was not the position of a few retrograde theorists but the thoughtfully articulated opinion of the best-placed academic thinkers. Much of what we now call psychology and philosophy emerged from the reversal of this opinion under the onslaught of an ostensibly sacrilegious and materialistic psychology.

An important terminological shift took place during this time as well. In Locke's day, the English terms *natural philosophy* and *moral philosophy* were used in tandem to refer roughly to what we would now call natural science and social science. By the middle of the eighteenth century a host of other terms were being used to denote all or part of "moral philosophy," such as the Latin *psychologia* (both empirical and rational), and the pseudo-Greek *pneumatology*. In Scottish philosophy the phrases *intellectual powers* and *active powers of the mind* gained some currency, and *pneumatology* was occasionally used to refer to the science of the soul. By the turn of the century, however, the word *metaphysics* was increasingly used to denote much that we would now call psychology (although terms like *moral philosophy* were still common as well). Around 1815 Percy Shelley wrote: "Metaphysics is a word which has been so long applied to denote an inquiry into the phenomena of mind that it would justly be presumptuous to employ another, [although] etymologically considered it is very ill adapted to express the science of mind." (Shelley also referred to Kant, whom we would call a philosopher, as a "psychologist.") In the next decade the Scottish philosopher James Mackintosh spoke of *metaphysics* as a "problem word" for which no one could give a precise meaning, although it obviously had something to do with the soul. And a decade later, at the end of the 1830s, the young Charles Darwin also used *metaphysics* to label his notebook of psychological inquiries and writings. Still later, after 1848 and the rise of positivism, *metaphysics* came to have a negative connotation as the most abstract and abstruse of speculations. Readers must be careful to note the date of a discussion of "metaphysics" so as not to misinterpret the meaning.

While revolution was sweeping France, academic theorists argued that metaphysics (psychology) was not a science, or at least that it could not be an empirical science in the same way that physics or chemistry could. The two most important proponents of this broad view were situated literally at opposite ends of the continent: Immanuel Kant in East Prussia and Thomas Reid in Scotland. It is no exaggeration to say that these were the two most influential psychologists between the French Revolutions of 1789 and 1830. Their views on psychology were widely taught, analyzed, and discussed. I shall call the position that emerged under their influence traditional European metaphysics. Ironically, as I have already mentioned, traditional metaphysics is *not* a position to which either Reid or Kant would have subscribed, because it endorsed at least a form of scientific psychology; nevertheless, it is a set of views that arose in large part because of the influence of Reidian and Kantian arguments.

Reid and Kant

Neither Kant nor Reid was opposed to the study of psychology —on the contrary, both were deeply interested and acute practitioners of the discipline. Nevertheless, they both had strong reasons for attacking any pretensions of treating psychology *as a science*. Kant and Reid took Newtonian mechanics to be the model empirical science, arguing that explanations showing patterns of efficient causality and conforming to empirically determinable laws are essential to real science. Both Kant and Reid assumed that such laws would be expressed mathematically and that controlled experimentation (perhaps mixed with observation and modeling, as in astronomy) was the proper method for deriving the laws.

Kant argued that the various claims about the nature of the human mind or soul are impossible to evaluate scientifically in this manner. He attacked the "rational psychology" then popular in Germany for claiming to be able to prove such propositions as "the soul is unitary and simple." Instead, as Kant showed in the antinomies of his first *Critique*, diametrically opposing views of the soul could be sustained with equal rational force. In his "anthropology" Kant endorsed a kind of natural historical model for psychology, using observational techniques to illustrate how different people(s) and nations have developed and how they react in diverse situations. Kant's "critique" was a novel discipline, or method, intended to undercut all pretense that a science of metaphysics could extend beyond this sort of observational procedure.

Reid's attack on psychology as science had a different origin from Kant's but a similar outcome. Responding to the notion that ideas are cortical impressions of bodily states—a fundamental premise of Cartesian and Lockean psychology— Reid objected to theories that tried to account for meaningful psychological states on the basis of sensory impressions. Reid argued that psychological capacities, such as the ability to perceive external objects (which Reid saw as central to all mental powers), could not be explained as causal outcomes of physical stimuli affecting the mind or the body. All such accounts, he tried to show, violated the concept of efficient causality, provided insufficient scientific explanation, or both. The causal effects of, say, light on the retina are one thing, the sensory awareness of light (visual sensations) is another, and the visual perception of objects is yet a third. The widely believed claim (originating with Descartes and running through the work of Locke and the *philosophes,* and beyond) that the first caused the second, which caused the third, is a confusion of category, as we would now see it—because physical stimuli cannot be the efficient cause of mental states, nor can sensory (nonintentional) states be the cause of perceptual (intentional) states.

In many ways, Reid and Kant were in agreement. Both argued that Newtonian science was the model par excellence for any science. Thus, if psychology were to be scientific, psychologists would have to show that meaningful human experience was a function of matter and motion only—just as Newton had showed how the movements of planets and the colors of the rainbow were caused by different patterns of matter in motion. Not only did Reid and Kant doubt that such an account of experience could be developed, but both argued that the very idea of such a science was incoherent. Both worried very much about the model of the human being as a kind of robot, which, they believed, was implicit in this kind of science.

Reid's argument against a scientific psychology was the simpler: If you reduce any real human belief or experience to matter and motion—to the so-called impression of stimuli on the mind—you must reduce all perception of things outside the mind to internal states of the mind. But perception of external objects is not the same thing as the having of sensations. Although I *perceive* the rose as a beautiful object in my garden, I only *sense* its feel, color, and smell. The Cartesian psychologists argued that it is from the physical effects of stimuli on my brain and their associated subjective impressions that I formulate in my mind the belief in the rose as an objective thing, the belief that sensory impressions cause perceptions. Or as a later British philosopher, James Stirling, put it, "The skin knows the scratch, it knows nothing of the thorn." The study of scratches, Reid explained, can be reduced to causes and effects, to matter and motion, as in any good Newtonian science. And the study of how scratches feel is just the study of the mental effects of physical causes. But the study of thorns and our beliefs about them — or of any perceived objects — cannot be reduced to such a cause-and-effect analysis.

Reid did not argue against the *distinction* between the concepts of stimulus, sensation, and perception; on the contrary, it was Reid who sharpened these three concepts into modern form, thus setting the stage for many a nineteenth-century dispute. Reid's claim was that *explanation* of the causal interrelationships among these three kinds of events is not possible. He especially objected to theorists who glibly tried to make hypothetical causal accounts of sensations do the work of explanations of perceptual beliefs. When one senses a scratch, after all, there are many things that might be scratching, and a thorn, especially a thorn on a rosebush, is only one. Feeling the scratch is by no means equivalent to knowing the thorn. Yet, as Reid pointed out, many psychological theories give the appearance of working, solely because they surreptitiously and fallaciously substitute knowing for feeling. William James was later to suggest that a version of this error was *the* psychologist's fallacy.

For Reid the ultimate fact in psychology was teleological: God had so arranged our bodies and minds that upon receipt of a certain stimulus, our bodies feel a given sensation and our minds conceive a particular perceptual belief. In an intriguing parallel to Kant's *Critique of Judgment,* Reid argued that the relations among our various animate and conscious properties are those of parts to the whole, contrived by the Deity with the purpose of adapting us to the rest of His Creation. Like Kant, Reid argued the need for a descriptive psychology, to elucidate the modes of this adaptation of the self to world, but denied even the possibility of an experimental, causally based psychological science.

Traditional Metaphysics

If experience is essentially ideas in the mind, and if one distinguishes between sensory data and perceptual beliefs, then Reid's conclusions follow inexorably. A causal and experimental science might evolve that could be used to study the formation of *sensory impressions*—but such a discipline would not necessarily be relevant to the study of *perceptual beliefs*. And experimental results about stimuli or our physiological responses to them can be, at best, only tangential to an understanding of our perceptual beliefs. But what if experience is not restricted to the mind? What if perceptual beliefs are independent of sensory impressions (as when one is unconscious of the sources of one's beliefs or awareness)? Erasmus Darwin, the young Coleridge, and the Shelleys all considered such alternatives to Reid's framework. And it was in response to this underground current of materialism that the next generation of official philosophers after Reid and Kant felt obliged to fashion what those two theorists had said was impossible. I refer to such post-Reidian and post-Kantian theorizing as traditional metaphysics in part because it became established doctrine in pulpits and professorial chairs all across Europe between 1815 and 1848.

Traditional metaphysics is nowadays, often disparagingly, dubbed faculty psychology. The idea is that God has shaped the human mind into a number of distinct organs, or faculties, each with its own "office" or pattern of activity. In most cases—

perhaps even in all—the faculties require a material stimulus, a material process, or both, in order to be made manifest. Reid's claim that we can never know how God so arranged it that sensory impressions give rise to perceptual beliefs is transformed into the doctrine that each faculty makes manifest a God-given correlation between mental and physical processes—in this case between physical sensation and mental perception.

Franz Josef Gall (1758–1828), the founder of phrenology, worked within this theoretical framework, at least after 1810. He conceived of the mind as divided into many organs or capacities, from memory and reasoning to avarice and self-love. And he thought of the brain as a tool of the mind: the brains of people with different personalities took on different shapes and sizes because the exercise of particular mental powers altered the physical organ and its form. In turn, the differential growth in the brain caused subtle changes in the shape and conformation of the skull, which could be read off by a careful student of these phenomena. Thus, the famous "phrenological bumps" are indirect symptoms of mental activity, and the changes in brain size are direct symptoms of the mental activity (much as a bodybuilder's reduced wardrobe is an indirect symptom of his exercise regimen, while his expansive chest is a direct symptom). Further, careful self-control might enable one to alter the balance of forces among all these mental organs and thus might eventually change the shape of one's head. Gall's phrenology was Reidian in the sense that, like Reid, he doubted that one could study mental states as such. Yet Gall was obviously much more willing to speculate about possible correlations between physical (cerebral) and psychological states than Reid had been. But everyone else seemed to like to speculate about these impossibilities, too. Indeed, Kant and Reid are perhaps the only two thinkers who stayed true to the conviction that it is impossible to explain the relations between matter and mind.

Many later theorists, even among those who strongly rejected phrenology, nevertheless utilized correlational frameworks derived from traditional metaphysics. Because traditional metaphysics did not permit the study of causation, much nineteenth-century mind-brain theorizing proceeded along correlational lines. Speculations about differences in psychological constitution between males and females, or between the races, were often based on the physical traits displayed by members of those groups. The consequences of "dissolute" ways of life, such as opium eating and excessive alcohol consumption, also began to be studied within this framework.

Reid and Kant's critique of causal explanation in psychology was taken over and used largely for polemical purposes against the opponents of traditional metaphysics, and rarely for criticism of traditional metaphysics itself. Materialists could always be accused of trying to give a causal explanation for something that could not be causally explained. But the various popular faculty psychologies of the early 1800s (often dubbed moral philosophies or sometimes even moral sciences) were rarely subjected to this same criticism.

Reid had criticized versions of the doctrine of the association of ideas, which holds that perceptual beliefs are a function of the senses—that is, that beliefs result from the association of impressions drawn from different sensory states. It was thought that a kind of mechanical law establishing the linking of similar sensory data might adequately explain how perceptions arise from sensory impressions. The perception of a thorn, according to this theory, might be the association among a series of (feelings of) scratches and their antecedents and consequences. Associationism was already a major trend in psychological thinking by the 1780s, when Reid pointed out that its claims were hollow. The so-called mechanical laws of association could not account for the perceptual beliefs that guided appropriate sensations together and kept inappropriate ones apart. Imagine that you truly experience nothing but splotches of color, splashes of light, and perhaps some smears of visible motion. Mechanical principles of association—such as contiguity or succession—would be next to useless in explaining how one registered a complete visual world. Two contiguous splotches of color might come from two different objects and be involved in entirely separate events. According to what mechanical principles could you associate just the right visual data to distinguish each of the half dozen ballet dancers, and follow individual dancers' movements, as they are performing *Swan Lake* in front of you? How could you even tell which sensations "went with" which dancers? Reid argued that it is the perception that helps us properly distribute and associate the sensations, not the other way around, and his point has yet to be answered by the associationists. Despite the power of Reid's arguments, the next generation of Scottish philosophers—Thomas Brown and Dugald Stewart—essentially embraced associationism and downplayed or misconstrued Reid's objections.

VICTOR COUSIN: AN EXEMPLARY TRADITIONAL METAPHYSICIAN

Victor Cousin's (1792–1867) career illustrates many of the features of the traditional European metaphysics of the first part of the nineteenth century. A proponent of an increasingly modified Scottish commonsense philosophy, Cousin was influential across the entire continent and in America as well, especially through his writings on the history of philosophy. Alternately stymied and abetted by political events in reactionary post-Napoleonic France, Cousin eventually became minister of education under Thiers in 1840, exerting a direct and powerful influence on higher education in France for the next generation.

All during the Enlightenment, and even into the Napo-leonic era, French psychology was a bastion of Lockean think-ing—just the kind of theorizing that Reid had criticized. For example, in the mid-1700s Condillac argued that the human mind is furnished with nothing but ideas derived from the senses and faint images or memory traces of those ideas. He claimed that all complex thought, feeling, and belief had to be explained in terms of the association of ideas. Partially under the influence of Kant, the influential French thinker Maine de Biran (1766–1824) had begun to develop a traditional meta-physical theory in opposition to the views of Condillac and his later followers, who came to be known as the *idéologues* in the early 1800s. The idéologues themselves asserted that sensory data do not accumulate by themselves; rather, they are gathered through active attention to the external world. Biran went fur-ther and stressed that in addition to attention and ideas, a per-son has volition. He began to equate consciousness more with volition than with sensory inputs, an emphasis that strongly ap-pealed to subsequent French thinkers. Among the first of these followers of Maine de Biran was Paul Royer-Collard (1763–1843), who was made professor of philosophy in Paris in 1811 despite the fact that he had been a spy for the Bourbons in the 1790s. Royer-Collard promoted a "philosophy of perception" that built on the theories of Reid, Stewart, and other Scots but incorporated some elements of Maine de Biran's ideas as well. It was Royer-Collard who gave Cousin his first big career break.

Cousin had taught primarily at the Ecole Normale, where he had begun his lecturing career in 1813. But in 1815 Royer-Collard somewhat surprisingly chose the manifestly unprepared Cousin to take over his chair in philosophy at the Sorbonne, a post Cousin held until 1820. During that period, Cousin be-came interested in German idealism, especially the work of Friedrich Schelling and G. F. Hegel, and he visited Hegel and others in the German-speaking countries. Thus was born what Cousin called his eclecticism, in which he proposed to integrate the best of all previous philosophies. (It is an interesting and unresolved question why Cousin eagerly sought connections between Scottish philosophy and Hegel's ideas, whereas Dugald Stewart at the same time professed to be completely baffled by Hegel.)

In 1820 the assassination of the duc de Berry brought an intense reaction across France, and the Ecole Normale was closed. For the next eight years Cousin had to work—like an eighteenth-century scholar—as a tutor for a noble family. He also suffered the indignity of being arrested in Prussia in 1824 as a French spy (Hegel helped him to prove his innocence). In 1828 Cousin was restored to his chair at the Sorbonne; after the July Revolution of 1830 he became a state councillor and academician.

Cousin was a prolific writer and educator. His volumes on the history of philosophy, like those of his friend Hegel, exerted widespread influence on the way people thought about the evolution of philosophical ideas. Both Cousin and Hegel presented modern philosophy as a kind of dialectical struggle between British empiricists and Continental rationalists. Prior to Cousin's work, such an attempt to contrast Continental with British thinking would have been considered wrongheaded. Subsequently, most texts on the history of philosophy have followed Hegel and Cousin's view, and only recently have historians begun to reassess these supposed oppositions.

Cousin attacked the French Lockeans, from Condillac down to the idéologues, in a way reminiscent of Reid's critique. Reid had maintained that the Lockean (really Cartesian) "way of ideas" led to materialism. That is, argued Cousin, the notion that mental states are ideas that are the effects of physical causes (stimuli and the impressions they make on our bodies and brains) makes no sense except in the kind of materialist interpretation given to it by Diderot or, worse, d'Holbach. As far as Cousin was concerned, ideas had better stay locked up in the skull where they could be safely said to be nonmaterial; any hints of a broader interpretation of experience or perception ought to be squelched. Cousin thus equated Berkeleian or Humean phenomenalism with materialism, an interpretation that seems breathtakingly obtuse to modern students of philosophy. Yet this confusion was still current in the 1880s when, for example, the Berkeleian T. H. Huxley was widely attacked for his "materialism."

Cousin promoted his ideas in his lectures on eighteenth-century philosophy and also in *The Elements of Psychology,* an immensely popular chapter-by-chapter duel with Locke's *Essay on Human Understanding.* Although Cousin nominally endorsed Reid's critique of Locke, he was unable, like every other traditional metaphysician, to articulate a complete and coherent version of Reid's alternative to Lockean epistemology. In particular, Cousin botched his account of Reid's theory about why perception is distinct from and independent of sensation. Reid had argued against confusing the physical impressions that cause sensations with mental impressions; this argument, though, because it looked dangerously like a critique of the notion that ideas exist solely in the cerebrum, could open an avenue for some form of materialism. The prospect seems to have unnerved Cousin and distorted his interpretation of Reid.

Cousin (followed by Hamilton, Mansel, and others who will be discussed later) transformed Reid's everyday concept of perception into an almost mystical idea of intuitions of Realities. For Reid, perception is possible because God has fashioned our bodies and minds to be able to perceive the things around us so that we can use them for good or ill. For Cousin, perception is made possible by a God-given mental power of intelligence or reason, which directly grasps universals. Responding to Locke's attack on enthusiasm (*Essay,* book 4, sec. 19), Cousin endorsed the philosophy of the Scottish school (or rather what he took it to be) as the "spontaneous intuition of truth by reason, as independent as possible of the personality and of the senses, of induction and demonstration." Thus, the common sense of the Scottish Enlightenment was transformed into the enthusiastic intuition of nineteenth-century orthodoxy. Perception of the external world, which for Reid had been tied to the senses, based on experience and not on reason, Cousin twisted into a quasi-mystical access to Truth, with an eye toward religious and moral orthodoxy. It was to be his greatest contribution, one that was reflected after 1848 in the worldwide spread of spiritualism.

THE RISE OF TRADITIONAL METAPHYSICS

The success of traditional metaphysics—which Kant and Reid saw as an impossible science—was quite impressive. Fichte and many others in German-speaking countries developed post-Kantian taxonomies of the powers of the soul and began to speculate about the mechanics of the soul as well. In France, Reid's influence on Royer-Collard and Kant's on Maine de Biran defeated Lockean psychology even before Napoleon had met his Waterloo. The French version of commonsense philosophy was one of the few doctrines that survived the defeat of Napoleon and the reaccession of the monarchy. Dugald Stewart's influence in Scotland (and on the Continent as well) at this time was immense. This traditional metaphysics or faculty psychology was featured in philosophy curricula all over Europe—in Paris, Naples, Vienna—and at faraway Harvard College; it figured prominently in the *Encyclopaedia Britannica* of the 1820s. The concert of opinion in Europe about the workings of the mind was every bit as broad based and strong as the concert among the reactionary powers that ruled the European nations with such an iron hand from 1815 to 1830.

Everywhere, students were taught that the human mind has powers of intuition as well as of perception, and that these powers of intuition give us access to the great moral truths of religion. This science of the mind (called either moral philosophy or mental philosophy) was strongly allied with orthodoxy and the maintenance of the cultural influence of the ancien régime all across Europe. In America it was allied with Unitarianism and republicanism as well as with orthodox Protestantism and Federalism. Although its adherents used a vocabulary and concepts derived from Reid and Kant, the new science of the mind—which I am calling traditional metaphysics—was vastly different from the psychologies devised by those two great thinkers.

After 1830 the unity of support for traditional metaphysics began to erode under the influence of new philosophical positions, and especially with developments in physiological and experimental analyses of neural and mental phenomena. Nevertheless, thanks to Cousin's eclecticism and the strength of a new generation of Scottish thinkers in Great Britain, traditional metaphysics was still very much alive up through 1848. Although disagreeing about much else, the French-, German-, and English-speaking proponents of traditional metaphysics increasingly endorsed psychological theories that made room for Cousin's intuitionism, a sanctimonious transcendentalism that would have disturbed Kant and Reid. Nevertheless, this kind of intuitive psychology found a home with a broad array of writers: the right Hegelians, Cousin and his French followers, William Whewell in England, and William Hamilton and his many followers throughout Britain and the United States. Indeed, it is almost impossible to find a textbook on moral philosophy or metaphysics from this period that does not promulgate something akin to Cousin's intuitionism.

A representative text is John Abercrombie's *Inquiries Concerning the Intellectual Powers and the Investigation of Truth*. First published in 1830, this book on psychology by a medical doctor went through several editions, including at least two pirated American ones. It was used, particularly in America, as a college textbook. Especially interesting is the way Abercrombie attempts in his book to be faithful to Reid but fails because of his eagerness to critique the materialism of certain (unspecified) thinkers.

Unlike many other traditional metaphysicians, Abercrombie presents a competent version of Reid's attack on psychology as a science: "The mind can be compared to nothing in nature; it has been endowed by its Creator with a power of perceiving external things; but the manner in which it does so is entirely beyond our comprehension" (p. 25). Although Abercrombie *says* that a naturalistic account of the mind would be beyond our comprehension, he nevertheless proceeds to give an account not very different from what one finds in Cousin or Dugald Stewart. He begins with the mainstream Cartesian doctrine that matter is a certain combination of properties — solidity, extension, and divisibility — and that these properties can be known by the senses. Mind, on the other hand, is characterized by the properties of thinking and willing, which are known through inner sense (which Abercrombie equates with consciousness). He then reviews Dugald Stewart's use of a theory from physics to undermine materialism in psychology. Abercrombie, like Stewart, alludes to the work of the eighteenth-century Ragusan scientist and priest Rudiger Boscovic. Boscovic, a founder of what later came to be called field theory in physics, showed that Newtonian theory could be reconstructed on the assumption that no matter exists at all and that the smallest "elements" in the world are infinitely small points of repulsive force.

Stewart used this theory of Boscovic's as a stick with which to beat the materialists, and Abercrombie—though he denies the relevance of natural science to psychology—eagerly follows him down this path, quoting Stewart as saying, "Of all the Truths we know, the existence of minds is the most certain. Even the system of Berkeley concerning the nonexistence of matter is far more conceivable than that nothing but matter exists in the universe" (p. 30). Thus, although Reid is right to say that we cannot know about the physical nature of the mind, one thing we can know about it is that the materialists are wrong—even that they are much wronger than the idealists! The trick here is to accept uncritically Abercrombie's deliverances of consciousness or inner sense while being critical about the deliverances of the other senses. When Abercrombie insists we can know *that* there is a "remarkable connection" between the brain and the mind but can know nothing about the nature of this connection, we had better take it with a grain of salt. Like all traditional metaphysicians, and despite his careful attempt to get Reid right, Abercrombie ends up supporting some kind of idealistic scientific psychology, to overcome the "inconceivable" theory that "nothing but matter exists in the universe," a theory whose proponents neither Abercrombie nor most other traditional metaphysicians can bring themselves to name.

Traditional metaphysics was inconsistent and illogically defended—as Kant and Reid could have warned—but it served well enough in its function of propping up orthodox religious views, at least in Europe. Ironically, this special treatment of inner sense, and the puzzles to which it leads, still plague philosophy late in the twentieth century.

3

Frankenstein's Science

Try as they might, Metternich and his allies in reaction could not completely eradicate progressive thinking about the nature of society and individual psychology. Although the set curriculum of most academic institutions and texts followed the kind of popularized Reidian or Kantian psychology I have dubbed traditional metaphysics, there was at the same time a widespread if nonacademically based alternative psychology, which might be broadly characterized as fluid materialism. It had its roots in Franklin's two-fluid theory of electricity, with branches in Mesmer's animal magnetism and Galvani's and Volta's competing theories about electrical phenomena in animal tissues. Increasingly, some thinkers were led to speculate that an understanding of electricity—or perhaps of some other, subtler, fluid within the nerves—would unlock the secrets of life and the mind.

Joseph Priestley was perhaps the earliest proponent of this materialist psychology, and he was roundly attacked, first by Kant and then by a mob organized by the British authorities to drive him out of the country. It was Priestley above all who placed associationism (derived from the work of David Hartley) at the center of materialist psychology and launched a tradition in the fields of psychology and physiology of looking for associations among neural processes and pathways. But there is associationism and there is associationism. Priestley's associationism postulated that the association of *ideas* was a major force in mental life, a concept highly consistent with mainstream thought in the tradition descending from Locke. In some ways, Priestley did mainstream psychology a service by emphasizing Hartley's doctrine of the association of ideas and de-emphasizing his doctrine of neural vibrations as the basis for association. (In Priestley's edition of Hartley's book, almost the entire discussion of vibrations in the nerves is left out.) Despite their many other disagreements, traditional metaphysicians universally praised this emphasis of Priestley's on association of ideas at the expense of studying neural mechanisms. The association of ideas might prove useful to psychology, but if the convergence of ideas was in fact determined by physical mechanisms within the nervous system, it must be a form of the dreaded materialism. It was Erasmus Darwin, a friend and colleague but no follower of Priestley's, who attempted to update Hartley's physiological psychology, using the latest scientific information available in the 1790s.

ERASMUS DARWIN'S ALTERNATIVE PSYCHOLOGY

Erasmus Darwin's *Zoonomia* (the first edition appeared in 1792–94, but many subsequent editions were published all over Europe) launched a true alternative psychology, later popularized in his poem *The Temple of Nature* (1803). In *Zoonomia*, Darwin defined ideas as the motions of fibers in our organs of sense, and the pattern of these motions. In an addendum to the text he went so far as to say that the theory that ideas are uniquely mental events and not part of everyday nature is nothing but a ghost story. Darwin was a medical doctor by training and a member of the rising bourgeoisie. A kind of no-nonsense attitude characterized his science, even when it was expressed in heroic couplets.

A second key innovation by Darwin was related to his novel definition of ideas. He claimed that the immediate objects of thought are the movements of the relevant neural fibers. The mind does not first make contact with a feeling or sensation and then formulate ideas; rather, the mind simply *is* the body and all its feelings. If ideas are any and all embodied feelings (not merely cerebral impressions of bodily feelings), then at any one time we may have a large number of different ideas. Erasmus Darwin's concept of the mind, unlike the traditional theory of the soul, allowed that the mind could be multiple, even divided against itself, just as the body can be. Darwin was happy to accept laws of association (among other psychological principles), but he saw associations as determined by the bodily mechanisms, not by the ideas themselves, and certainly not by the transcendent soul. Darwin debunked all such "ghost stories" and set out to show how diseases could be classified according to their disruptive effects on our bodily machinery, including our neural associations. Most diseases were psychosomatic, he thought, and could be cured by diet, exercise, and healthy living —which included adequate access to noncoercive sexual intercourse, especially for women. This was progressive medical advice for his day. It is notable that sin does not enter the picture. Defenders of orthodoxy certainly noted this, and duly attacked Darwin as much for what he did not say as for what he did.

It was largely fear of the implications of Erasmus Darwin's theory that gave rise to the insistence that the causes of our ideas (mental states) could not be known. The young Thomas Brown (whose mature work will be discussed in the next chapter) lambasted fluid materialism in his popular *Observations on the* Zoonomia *of Erasmus Darwin* (1798, p. xx). "The systems of materialism," Brown wrote, "chiefly owe their rise to the groundless belief, that we are acquainted with the nature of causation." Whereas the materialists and mentalist opponents can agree that sentience exists, "the mentalist acknowledges, that he is ignorant of the nature of that which causes his ideas; . . . the materialist, on the contrary, maintains that he is conscious, not merely of ideas, but of the nature of that which causes his ideas." Again, to use Reid's terms, we sense pricks but perceive thorns—supposedly, we are directly aware of the feeling of being pricked but only infer the existence of thorns. Of course, if we cannot know what causes our ideas, then the story of psychology as a science will be a very short one—yet paradoxically, much of the "new" and ostensibly scientific psychology of the nineteenth century arose in defense of the theory of indirect perception. Reid, who had insisted that we could directly perceive the causes of our ideas, had flatly stated that no scientific analysis of that capacity was possible. The nineteenth-century scientific psychologists insisted that we cannot directly perceive the causes of our ideas but proposed to make a science analyzing those causes, anyway.

If the association of ideas in Priestley's sense could be accepted into psychology, Darwin's kind of materialist association, with its emphasis on bodies and energy, most certainly could not. In *The Marriage of Heaven and Hell* (1793), William Blake has the devil say a number of Darwinian things, such as:

1. Man has no Body distinct from his Soul for that calld Body is a portion of Soul discernd by the five Senses, the chief inlets of Soul in this age;

2. Energy is the only life and is from the Body and Reason is the bound or outward circumference of Energy;

3. Energy is eternal delight.

Blake, the great antinomian, endorsed these ideas and loathed the orthodox thought that "God will torment Man in Eternity for following his Energies." But few others in those days would go along with such heretical thinking.

Four major implications of the elder Darwin's fluid materialism threatened to undermine established truths. To the extent that one could talk of a soul within the context of Darwin's theory, it was to be found throughout the body, as Blake and some later Romantics often emphasized. This supposition meant first that the soul lacked mental unity, although it may have had physical coherence; and second that even the visceral feelings would have to be treated as equal in importance to rational thought. As far as orthodox thinkers were concerned, physical lust and ideal love were by no means adequately distinguished in Darwin's theory, which upset the entire established ranking of mental states and thus, third, threatened to obliterate the distinction between animals and human beings. Indeed, like his more famous grandson, Erasmus Darwin tended to emphasize the continuity between animals and men (especially in his last work, *The Temple of Nature*). Fourth, this theory left no separate and distinct sphere for mental activity. All thought is embodied in our feelings and reactions; hence, there seems to be no place for an immortal soul. It was not even possible to fall back on the old position that the brain is merely a physical vehicle for thoughts and feelings within the soul, because that could only be the case if the sole object of thought were mental events, not states of the nerves, as in Darwin's theory.

It is difficult to ascertain how widely disseminated Erasmus Darwin's views were in Europe. In the periodical literature of the Napoleonic era his name is often mentioned, even in French, Italian, and German sources. His biographer, Desmond King-Hele, perhaps goes too far in making Darwin out to be the greatest scientific intellectual in Europe as the nineteenth century dawned—but then again, perhaps not. Who would have been Darwin's rival? It is difficult to think of a serious competitor even among the French. His relative obscurity nowadays should not lead us to ignore the impact of Darwin's fluid materialism, which was, at the very least, one of the major physiological and psychological theories propounded between 1789 and 1815.

I believe that Darwin's influence on subsequent psychology has been overlooked because of the peculiar form it took. After 1815, opponents of Darwin's ideas took precautions not to mention his name or his writings. And, because no mainstream thinkers adopted his views, he was for decades merely the subject of anonymous abuse, at least as far as "official thinking" went. By the middle of the century, however, the ultimate pattern in the reception of Darwin's ideas was already becoming clear: all Darwin's concepts were taken up as true . . . of the *unconscious* mind, not the conscious mind. Both his assertions of fact and his speculations could thus be domesticated: if they did not apply to the conscious mind, they did not affect the human soul.

But although I speak here of reception or assimilation of Darwin's alternative psychology, my terminology may be misleading. In general, and especially after 1815, the officialdom of church and state attacked his theory with full force throughout Europe. The battle was hardly one of ideas alone. No one could hold a professorship anywhere in Europe or the United States and defend Erasmus Darwin's psychology. After 1815 the publication of such views became punishable in most European countries by imprisonment. Thus, before I can describe how the very few who promoted Darwin's ideas managed to do so, it is necessary to describe the difficult circumstances in which they operated.

The Suppression of Psychology as a Natural Science

After the final defeat of Napoleon, state and religious authorities (often the same people, in almost always interlocking bureaucracies) exerted enormous efforts to prevent the dissemination of ideas such as those of the elder Darwin. Censorship, the use of informers, and highly active secret police forces were the norm in all European countries between 1815 and 1830. The authorities were out to crush pantheism, atheism, and materialism—all assumed to be enemies of the status quo—and fluid materialism along with them. A number of historians have argued that the emerging sciences of phrenology and mesmerism specifically were under attack. I would maintain that those ideas were suspect only insofar as they were seen as overlapping with fluid materialism. Once the second generation of mesmerists gave up Mesmer's claims that a physical (magnetic) force was at the root of mesmeric phenomena and once the second generation of phrenologists began promoting their moderate nativism, together with the traditional metaphysical doctrine of instinct and intuition, these theorists and their ideas were widely accepted, if not admitted into the strongholds of the elite. Such was not the case for Erasmus Darwin's intellectual heirs.

In contrast to mesmerists or phrenologists, those who advocated studying life and the mind within the framework of natural science were prosecuted, even in the most liberal of the European states at the time, Great Britain. One of the most important cases of such repression is that of William Lawrence (1783-1867), a distinguished but radical surgeon (soon to be editor of the insurgent medical periodical the *Lancet*, and when he eventually recanted, Princess Victoria's surgeon). Lawrence was a follower of F. X. J. Bichat, who believed that research on electricity and other physical forces would ultimately reveal the connection between neural structure and mental function, yielding a kind of natural science of the soul. Doctors should rejoice in this, Lawrence believed, because it meant that insanity is not a disease of the soul (treatable, if at all, only by moral suasion) but a physiological disorder, perhaps curable by medicine, as Darwin had suggested. In 1819 Lawrence prepared a work explaining these ideas, his *Lectures on Physiology, Zoology, and the Natural History of Man.* After a brief time, the book was pronounced blasphemous and an orchestrated campaign was launched against it. Leading figures in the medical establishment asked the Royal College of Surgeons to force Lawrence to expunge the alleged blasphemies and to desist from lecturing. Lawrence withdrew the book and lost his lectureship.

A few years later, pirated editions of the *Lectures* began to appear. In 1822 Lawrence sought to block their publication. In a remarkable judgment, Lord Eldon found that Lawrence had forfeited his rights in the matter because British law did not protect those who impugned Scripture. In the end, at least nine pirated editions were produced. (Blasphemous medical books sold much better at the time than ordinary ones.)

One of William Lawrence's patients, who was to marry the author of *Frankenstein*, suffered even worse problems owing to state suppression of his work. In 1813 Percy Shelley had 250 copies printed of the first of his great dramatic poems, *Queen Mab*. Directly influenced by Erasmus Darwin's poetry as well as his theories, this poem included extensive prose notes, amounting to a series of essays on such forbidden topics as republicanism, atheism, and materialist psychology. "Every atom is sentient in unity and in part," wrote this young poet. Percy Shelley argued explicitly for treating humans as part of nature and for seeing psychology, morals, and politics as sciences in quest of causal laws: "Were the doctrine of necessity false, the human mind would no longer be a legitimate object of science; from like causes it would be vain that we should expect like effects." Whereas Reid and Kant had used this argument to attack scientific psychology and defend human freedom, Shelley turned it around. A true psychology would recognize motives as nothing more than complex causes, and laws of cause and effect would become discernible. Where actions seem to be without causes, he said, "these are the effects of causes with which we are unacquainted." He suggested that a scientific psychology would "introduce a great change into established notions of morality . . . there is neither good nor evil in the universe, otherwise than as the events to which we apply these epithets have relation to our own mode of being."

Shelley was always acute at seeing the implications of his philosophical ideas. In particular, he took pleasure in emphasizing that this new moral psychology would desanctify marriage and legitimate divorce—an implication made explicit in order to annoy his orthodox readers as well as to justify his own behavior. Marriage, far from being made in heaven, is a natural relationship, "the worthiness [of which should be] estimated by the quantity of pleasurable sensation it is calculated to produce. . . . the connection of the sexes is so long sacred [only] as it contributes to the comfort of the parties, and is naturally dissolved when its evils are greater than its benefits."

These ideas were an affront to both the intellectual and the religious status quo. To see marriage as a voluntary union of two individuals as opposed to a divinely ordained state and sacrament was bad enough. But throughout his work Shelley championed the even more radical idea that this voluntary union was holier than the official sacrament of marriage. In the early 1830s, Heinrich Heine spelled this heretical idea out in the seventh part of his *Seraphine:*

> Upon this rock we'll build a church,
> All suffering transcended—
> The church of the third New Testament;
> The days of pain are ended.
>
> Annulled the great Antithesis
> That held us long deluded;
> The stupid torments of the flesh
> Are over now, concluded.

Do you hear God on his dark sea?
He speaks with a thousand voices.
And do you see how his sky overhead
With a thousand candles rejoices?

God dwells both in the heaven's light
And ocean's dark abysses;
God's spirit dwells in all that is—
He dwells in our kisses.

Shelley, much more so than the subsequent image of Romantic poets would suggest, was interested in all the everyday activities of human beings, not just love or sex. He was a deep student of science and medicine and, following Darwin's lead, believed there was a fundamental connection between diet and health. For this reason, many of Shelley's more serious discussions of the implications of his psychology revolved around his vegetarianism, expounded at great length in the notes to *Queen Mab*. Like Feuerbach and the German materialists of forty years later, Shelley argued that the intake of food was a key ingredient in a person's constitution and that proper diet was a basis not only for good physical and mental health but for the formation of progressive characters, capable of educating and reforming the world. Historians of philosophy have often noted, usually with scorn, Feuerbach's extreme materialist phase, illustrated in his claim that "man ist was man ißt" (we are what we eat)—but they would be better advised to try to explain the widespread appeal of the doctrine throughout the middle of the nineteenth century than to make fun of it.

Shelley was accused of seditious and blasphemous libel, and *Queen Mab* was banned. The English government set spies to follow him and his friends and to read his correspondence, so that Shelley at last chose self-imposed exile from what he saw as a ruthless and tyrannical state. He tried in various ways to have parts of *Queen Mab* published, to promote some of his ideas, but with little success. As with Lawrence's book, pirated editions began appearing, including one from Richard Carlile, an important working-class publisher and fighter for a free press. More bans and trials ensued, but the text was out of the bag. *Queen Mab* quickly became known as the Chartist's bible. Many a cobbler and cordwainer cut his philosophical teeth on Shelley's works and his quotations from d'Holbach, Voltaire, Drummond, Erasmus Darwin, and Spinoza. Meanwhile Shelley was refining and developing his ideas.

The battle between traditional metaphysicians and the proponents of psychology as a natural science was thus not an equal one. The former had access to publication, pulpits, and professorships; the latter risked prosecution, imprisonment, loss of position, and banishment. The rapid success and proliferation of materialist ideas across Europe after 1848 suggest that ideas such as those of the elder Darwin and Shelley were much more widely known of and discussed than the printed record indicates — especially the published philosophical works, which tended to conform to academic and ecclesiastical standards of what was respectable. Historians of philosophy need to know much more about what radical surgeons and poets were thinking, not to mention cobblers. It will hardly be easy, however, to find out what those thinkers were saying, because the widespread use of police spies and informants inhibited the expression of unorthodox views even in private correspondence, much less in print.

Here is one example of the mischief severe censorship has done to the history of ideas. It is widely believed that the nineteenth-century resurgence of Spinozist thinking — especially as it related to pantheism and the unity of the mind and body — arose from theological discussions sparked by such "left Hegelians" as Feuerbach and David Strauss in the 1830s and

1840s. Supposedly G. H. Lewes in the early 1840s was the first in nineteenth-century England to write seriously on Spinoza; Marian Evans followed, with an unpublished translation of *The Ethics*. (Evans later lived with Lewes, after which she published as George Eliot.) But, as will be discussed in Chapter 8, Lewes heard of Spinoza in discussions with a group of artisans he met through Leigh Hunt in the 1830s. Leigh Hunt was one of the exiled Shelley's key literary contacts back in England and knew of Shelley's translation of Spinoza's *Tractatus*. Spinoza's ideas, perhaps viewed through the lens of Erasmus Darwin's psychology, may have influenced philosophical opinion in London well before reaching the broad reading public or the conservatives at Oxford and Cambridge.

The Psychology in *Frankenstein*

One way in which modern readers can trace the underground history of psychology is through works of fiction. Historians of science and philosophy ordinarily do not use stories and novels as texts to chart the spread of ideas. But surely when all other resources are inadequate, this method is worth a try.

During that era, writers of fiction were able to publish much bolder discussions of certain psychological or philosophical topics than were professors, doctors, or other official theorists. For example, E. T. A. Hoffmann's novella *Master Flea* was published in Berlin in 1822, even though it contained ideas taken straight from Erasmus Darwin. In the story, Master Flea (who comes, not incidentally, from a *republic* of fleas) has built an amazing microscope that enables the hero, Peregrinus Tyss, to see so minutely into other people's brains that he can read their thoughts directly from the movements of their nerves. Hoffmann spoofs this Darwinian notion to create many amusing twists and turns of the plot. Under the microscope, Peregrinus "saw the strange network of veins and nerves, but noticed also that when the people talked with exceptional eloquence about art and learning . . . their veins and nerves did not penetrate into the recesses of their brains, but curved back, so that it was impossible to discern their thoughts with any clarity. He communicated this observation to Master Flea, who . . . remarked that what Peregrinus had mistaken for thoughts were nothing more than words, vainly endeavoring to become thoughts."

Because Hoffmann had dared to make fun of a Berlin magistrate in the draft of this delightful story, the Prussian police confiscated the manuscript. Before it could be published, Hoffmann died, but his widow was granted permission to have it printed in 1822—minus the jabs at the magistrate but with the science fiction version of the Darwinian psychology intact. Had these ideas been expressed in nonfictional form, they surely would not have seen publication—as William Lawrence and Percy Shelley could attest.

Shelley's wife Mary Godwin Shelley used her novel *Frankenstein* to discuss ideas about the relation between the mind and the body, and also about the nature of moral development, that could not have been published in nonfictional form at the time. For this reason, as is now widely recognized by students of her writings, *Frankenstein* offers us an important glimpse into the thinking of followers of Erasmus Darwin in the decades after his death and the suppression of his ideas. First published in 1818, *Frankenstein* emerged in large part from Mary Shelley's attempts to think through the implications of Darwin's psychology. In his preface to the first edition, Percy Shelley mentions that Erasmus Darwin had in fact envisaged the possibility of creating something like the Frankenstein android; and in her preface to the third edition of the book (1831) Mary Shelley describes the origin of her famous novel, a story-telling contest with her husband and Byron, and again mentions Erasmus

Darwin's work as having in part provided the inspiration for the basic idea of reanimating dead tissue to form a living android.

Victor Frankenstein is following as a scientist in the footsteps of the elder Darwin: "I was led to examine," the character says, "the cause and progress of this decay" (that is, the decay of living tissue), and such studies helped him succeed "in discovering the cause of generation and life." But not only is life science capable of being studied causally; so is psychology. Mary Shelley follows Hartley and Darwin carefully in her description of how Frankenstein's android, abandoned by his creator, develops psychologically. In the creature's original state, "no distinct ideas occupied my mind; all was confused." What confused the creature was a bewildering array of sensations. But some of the sensations were more pleasurable than others, and these captivated the creature's mind. The most powerful feelings were elicited by the creature's witnessing scenes of social intercourse among the family members upon whom he is spying: seeing the aging father playing music for his daughter, the creature "felt sensations of a peculiar and overpowering nature: they were a mixture of pain and pleasure, such as I had never before experienced." Mary Shelley had thus picked out what was deemed most objectionable in this underground psychology: that the feelings associated with ideas were or are more important than the provenance or meaning of the ideas. If mental life is organized, even in part, by such hedonistic associationism, what then of our immortal souls?

Shelley uses the fluid materialist psychology of her day to show how both language and morals emerge from the association of weaker feelings with these powerfully strong sensations of social origin. "I perceived," says the android, "that the words they spoke sometimes produced pleasure or pain, smiles or sadness, in the minds and countenances of the hearers. This was indeed a godlike science, and I ardently desired to become acquainted with it." Such acquaintance is made by the creature's straining to associate the names of familiar objects and people with their referents. Like her mentors Hartley and Darwin, Mary Shelley did not try to explain how a creature whose experience was limited to sensations could come to perceive the significance of such a thing as a pained countenance. She understood that even simple objects or people can have multiple names (like the boy in the family, who is called alternately Felix, brother, or son) but was able to convince herself that the bewildering associations of sound and sense could nevertheless be worked out. Mary Shelley also recognized, however, that in principle some associations are not readily made under any circumstances: the android discovers that he can hear the sounds of some words, even though he does not grasp their reference, words "such as good, dearest, unhappy." Later associationists would wring their hands at both these problems.

To understand such words, the materialist psychologists argued, required experience with people and their ways. Here is the beginning of the great nineteenth-century conflict between experiential, or empiricist, psychology and nativist psychology. According to the standard metaphysics, knowledge of good and evil, right and wrong, was not based on experience, and certainly not on the sensations of pain and pleasure; on the contrary, writers like Cousin, Maine de Biran, and Stewart held that each of us has a direct intuitive apprehension of right and wrong. These later thinkers ignored Reid's warning that the concept of "moral sense" was incoherent—that apprehension of good and evil could never be by the senses alone but requires an additional form of judgment. Reid's own response to this was to argue that morals were empirical (he spoke of moral judgments and moral perceptions based on experience combined with intuitive—that is, God-given—standards of conduct). Although this view influenced American thinkers, especially Thomas

Jefferson, it appears to have been abandoned in nineteenth-century Europe, even by followers of the Scottish school. They substituted for it the traditional metaphysicians' assertion that apprehension of right and wrong was innate and intuitive.

Mainstream metaphysicians shied away from Reid's empirical ethics, for reasons well understood by the materialists and illustrated in the narrative of *Frankenstein*. If moral evaluation derives from experience, then certain repeated patterns of association might generate moral monsters—people who get pleasure from acts that the rest of us judge to be evil. At first, when his experience derives primarily from reading history, the android feels "the greatest ardour for virtue arising within me, and abhorrence for vice," but these terms, as the android explains, should be understood as "relative . . . to pleasure and pain alone." Hence, when it emerges that human beings cannot stand to look at him, and that even his creator finds him horrific, the android develops inverted morals: what destroys humans will destroy his greatest pain and therefore represents the greatest good.

Contemporary critics detested this point of Mary Shelley's book and attacked her for promulgating false morals or an amoral position. "Our taste and our judgment alike revolt at this kind of writing," said a writer in the *Quarterly Review,* "and the greater the ability with which it may be executed the worse it is—it inculcates no lesson of conduct, manners or morality." A psychology that treated humans as natural objects, that did not assume them to have a transcendent soul—as did the traditional metaphysics—would offer a picture of mental and moral development frighteningly like the one in Shelley's novel. Materialist psychology threatened the moral fiber of society.

Natural Supernaturalism and Erotic Experience

The android in Frankenstein nicely exemplifies M. H. Abrams's doctrine of natural supernaturalism. Both Erasmus Darwin and Mary Shelley believed in the soul as a constellation of forces and properties — properties that ran the gamut from basic life forces (such as respiration) to psychological propensities (feelings and thoughts). I believe that the application of this natural supernaturalism to psychology is just what Kant was warning against in his *Critique of Pure Reason*. There, in one of the few passages where he deigns to name his opponents, Kant lambastes Priestley for promoting the doctrine of the body as equivalent to the soul.

Priestley's doctrine of the material soul, however, was only marginally naturalistic. Much of his argument (that our bodies are our souls) was designed to fit into his own unique brand of Unitarian Christianity. Priestley's interpretation of original Christianity (before it was "corrupted" by the Nicene creed) was that it was Unitarian, not Trinitarian, and that Jesus' promise of resurrection meant resurrection of the body. God has the power, Priestley asserted, to reassemble humans from their constituent particles, even after the corruption of the grave.

Although Victor Frankenstein's procedure may have been modeled on Priestley's heterodox notions, neither Mary Shelley nor Erasmus Darwin before her intervened in the theological debate over resurrection. They were not interested in the arguments in the Christian "ghost story" about the immaterial soul. Unlike Priestley's theological theorizing, Mary Shelley's concerns were decidedly natural, in precisely the sense of a modern psychology: What are the *natural* processes by which a newborn organism comes to acquire a soul — feelings, thoughts, and the knowledge of right and wrong?

One thing that Frankenstein's android conspicuously misses is another of his own kind. The android, once he gains the power of thought and expression, demands that Frankenstein create a mate for him. Again, the plot development echoes a key theme of Erasmus Darwin, that sexual love is not merely the basis for the creation of the race but also the focal point for all psychological feelings of unity and harmony with others and with the world.

Desmond King-Hele, the most acute commentator on Erasmus Darwin, speaks of "organic happiness" in this context. This happiness is organic because, at least for Darwin—and for the Shelleys as well—any organic system divided into sexes should have a suite of feelings appropriate to both competition and cooperation, disharmony and harmony. Erasmus Darwin was notorious for "anthropomorphizing" the sexual lives of plants in his poems, providing a mixture of titillation and education. On careful inspection, however, much of Darwin's apparent anthropomorphizing merely reflects his idea that erotic feelings are of primary evolutionary significance in the psychology of all creatures.

From these Darwinian sources, Percy Shelley seems to have developed a concept of the material soul whose *every* experience is erotic, in the original, Greek sense of the term. The Greek distinction between two kinds of love, *eros* and *agape,* became more pronounced after the advent of Christianity. Agape became associated with grace, the calm love of God for all of us, whether or not we are deserving. Eros is the love that fires the soul to reach outward and complete itself with external things. Eros motivates the self to search for virtues in objects which, because they are lacking in the self, can then be combined harmoniously with the self (hence, God is not in need of eros). For the natural supernaturalists—by contrast with the neo-

Platonists—this seeking and combining is *physical;* effected, like electricity or magnetism, through the ether.

One of Shelley's first mature poems, *Alastor,* is a meditation on the nature of experience, and it is shot through with Erasmus Darwin's conception of organic happiness, or what might be called an erotic view of the world. The young Shelley sees all things in the world as possible objects of love and hence as fit objects for experience and imagination. Like Darwin, he sees human sympathy for others as the "gravity" that makes our social world revolve in its course. Like Darwin, he sees sexual love (not merely the act of intercourse, but the panoply of associated feelings and thoughts) as the quintessence of this eroticized experience. *Alastor* thus begins (ll. 1–4):

> Earth, ocean, air, beloved brotherhood!
> If our great Mother has inbred my soul
> With aught of natural piety to feel
> Your love, and recompense the boon with mine.

Later (ll. 651–53) Shelley speaks of "the Poet's blood / That ever beat in mystic sympathy / With nature's ebb and flow."

The classic Greek theory of eros is set forth in Plato's *Symposium,* a dialogue that Shelley translated for his own use in 1818, the same year *Frankenstein* was published. After this, one begins to find in his poetry a mixture of Platonic and Darwinian ideas, as in these lines from "The Sensitive Plant" (ll. 74–78):

> For the sensitive plant has no bright flower;
> Radiance and odour are not its dower—
> It loves—even like Love—its deep heart is full—
> It desires what it has not—the beautiful!

In his psychology, Percy Shelley has thus contrived to link experience and knowledge to love. Love is the motive force that pushes us to complete our incomplete selves, including our incomplete minds as well as our incomplete bodies and lusts. Erasmus Darwin and Percy Shelley offer not a clockwork Newtonian universe set in motion by an act of God but a material world animated by eros, from which comes the craving for knowledge as well as for reproduction.

The fourth book of *Prometheus Unbound*, which stands in many ways as Shelley's utopia, summarizes this psychological doctrine in a metaphor combining Darwin's fluid materialism and Shelley's erotic view of experience (ll. 400–411):

> Man, one harmonious Soul of many a soul
> Whose nature is its own divine controul
> Where all things flow to all, as rivers to the sea;
> Familiar acts are beautiful through love;
> Labour and Pain and Grief in life's green grove
> Sport like tame beasts—none knew how gentle they could be!
>
> His Will, with all mean passions, bad delights,
> And selfish cares, its trembling satellites,
> A spirit ill to guide, but mighty to obey,
> Is as a tempest-wingèd ship, whose helm
> Love rules, through waves which dare not overwhelm,
> Forcing life's wildest shores to own its sovereign sway.

Today we find it difficult to read a poem like *Prometheus Unbound* and find a *theory* of experience in it. Poetry seems to us an unlikely place to find a theory of life or experience worked out. We would sooner believe that all that love of nature is purely metaphorical, or just camouflage.

I am arguing, on the contrary, that writers like the Shelleys were not only serious about their psychological theories but serious about them as *scientific* theories. The care with which the ideas are spelled out in narrative or poetic form gives the lie to the assumption that they are just casual metaphors. It seems plausible that the example of Erasmus Darwin, who developed his scientific ideas in verse, inspired Percy Shelley to do the same. And although Mary Shelley used the form of the gothic novel to work out her ideas, her intention of making a serious philosophical and scientific statement is manifest.

The poetic, erotic, and materialist psychology—*Frankenstein*'s psychology, we might say—had little chance to thrive, however, because such doctrines could not be promulgated safely. Mary Shelley cleverly gave this psychology the form of a gothic tale (and thus invented the science fiction novel). Her analysis of a being who was admittedly depraved was hugely successful, despite hostile reviews. But to a large degree the scientific psychology she used to set up her moral situation was overlooked, as readers—and even critics—tended to react to the situations in the story without analyzing their psychological underpinnings.

Percy Shelley's work and his ideas about erotic experience met a much worse fate. Mary Shelley, for a variety of reasons, heavily edited much of Percy's poetry when it was finally published at the end of the 1830s. By then poetry was no longer used as a vehicle for disseminating scientific ideas. Fluid materialist ideas can be found in Balzac and even Stendhal, but they never again appeared in a strictly scientific format.

In his great poem on the soul, *Epipsychidion* (ll. 169–73) Shelley wrote:

> Narrow
> The heart that loves, the brain that contemplates,
> The life that wears, the spirit that creates
> One object, and one form, and builds thereby
> A sepulchre for its eternity

In his unfinished "Treatise on Morals," Shelley echoes this thought: "The only distinction between the selfish man and the virtuous man is that the imagination of the former is confined within a narrow limit, while that of the latter embraces a comprehending circumference. In this sense wisdom and virtue may be said to be inseparable and entire of each other." The science of the mind that was to replace Shelley's science of the soul and that was to dominate the nineteenth century fell within the narrow limit described by Shelley and bore little resemblance to the comprehensive science he had envisaged.

4

The Breakdown in the Concert
of European Ideas

Traditional metaphysics was an unstable theory for psychology, despite the support it received from the authorities. Its instability arose out of the understandable desire of its proponents to say something meaningful about the way the mind works — even though their official theory required them to claim that no one can really analyze the soul because the soul is not a natural entity. Thinkers like Stewart and Abercrombie were adamant in claiming that any analysis of the mind's relation to nature is "beyond the reach of human faculties" (Abercrombie, p. 25). Yet at the same time, these writers insisted that materialistic accounts of the mind were wrong and could be shown to be wrong. In making this assertion, they ignored their own statement of the limits to critical faculties.

EMERGENT NATURALISM

The rise of associationist psychological theories after 1820 should be seen in the context of attempts to naturalize aspects of traditional metaphysics. In particular, the associationists were dissatisfied with what they saw as overly general statements about "laws" and "dispositions" of the human mind. They wanted what we would now call psychological mechanisms to replace them. This conflict is well illustrated in the different estimations of the state of psychology offered by Dugald Stewart and his erstwhile student James Mill. In his *Dis-*

sertation Exhibiting a General View of the Progress of Metaphysical, Ethical, and Political Philosophy Since the Revival of Letters in Europe (which was prefixed to the fourth edition of the *Encyclopaedia Britannica* in 1819), Stewart offered a strong defense of traditional metaphysics. For example, in writing about John Gregory's essay of advice to physicians, Stewart explained that Gregory correctly emphasized "the laws of the union of the mind and the body and the mutual influence they have upon one another." Stewart went on to caution, however, that "it is only the *laws* which regulate the union between mind and body . . . which are here pointed out as proper objects of philosophical curiosity; for as to any *hypothesis* concerning the *manner* in which the union is carried on, this most sagacious writer" (p. 425) was well aware that they were not susceptible of scientific analysis. Did Stewart really think that students would accept general statements of laws or regularities without trying to discover the causal sequences underlying those laws?

The great Scottish Enlightenment doctor Robert Whytt (1710–66)—whose theories seem to haunt much of the nineteenth century—had argued at length in his works on neurophysiology for Stewart's methodological conclusion: that hypotheses about how the nerves support mental life are bootless and unscientific but that it is nevertheless possible to articulate laws concerning patterns governing the relation of mind to body. Whytt discussed an instance of such relations—that the mere idea or memory of an object can produce the same physical reaction as the object itself: for example, a person may start to salivate at the thought of a toothsome meal just as surely as if food were being eaten. Whytt attacked the self-styled Newtonian physiologists (he had in mind George Cheyne, Steven Hales, William Porterfield, and David Hartley) who at that time were offering hypotheses about the manner in which mental processes were subserved by neurophysiological ones. Later,

Reid was to attack Locke, Berkeley, and Hume on just the same point: their assumption that the impressions caused by stimuli are causes and sensory states the effect.

Whytt's and Reid's arguments were simply dismissed by the materialists of the early nineteenth century, who drew an assumption they took to be obvious about the relation of mind and matter: that material changes caused mental changes. But because materialist ideas could not be safely promulgated anywhere in Europe until the late 1840s, it is perhaps not surprising that several nonmaterialist critiques of traditional metaphysics, most of them consciously representing orthodox religious or ethical views, tended to dominate the psychology of the period.

The Scandal of Philosophy

One of the specific ways in which traditional metaphysics responded to the Kantian and Reidian arguments against scientific psychology was to invent a new sense. Kant spoke of the "scandal of philosophy" (and it is important to remember that by *philosophy* he meant something closer to what we call science than to modern philosophy), which was the inability to prove the existence of the external world. Reid was content to avoid proof in this matter and merely to assert that science should be based on the plausible assumption of the existence of objects. Kant went well beyond Reid by investigating how a proof of the existence of external objects might be developed, ultimately offering his transcendental arguments as a kind of substitute for such a proof. The empirical world of causal interactions, of space and time, Kant asserted, could be proved to exist only if one assumed that the transcendental human soul participated in the construction of these phenomena. (That is, the soul itself as an entity outside space and time—and hence beyond all knowledge and experience—participated in the creation of space and time.) Thus Kant called himself a transcendental idealist but an empirical realist. The phenomenal world, the world of experience, the only world we can experience, could be proved real, but only by hypothesizing a transcendentally active soul.

Kant embraced transcendental idealism in response to the problem of proving the existence of the external world. Although few followed him in this response, many followed his statement of the problem. Across Europe, Kant's "scandal of philosophy" was understood in the following way during the Napoleonic years. To be scientific about psychology, one had to be a "sensationalist," that is, to begin with an analysis of the "impressions made on the senses" (to use the language of the times). In the early 1800s it was widely accepted that a scientific psychology had to do this. Although Kant had shown how misguided this approach was — as had Reid, even more clearly — their critique had little impact. The "scandal" was that no one could show how knowledge of the external world — of real objects — derived from sensory impressions alone. As no one has as yet solved this problem, we can be confident that it is a formidable one.

Repeated attempts have been made to resolve this scandal, and some lessons have even been learned. Perhaps the most important lesson derives from George Berkeley's acute *Essay on Vision*. In 1709 the young Irishman made a name for himself in the intellectual world with this essay, in which he repeatedly emphasized that visual sensations (which he called ideas, or sometimes minimum sensibles) were all of things like spots of light and color. Hence, vision alone could not furnish our awareness of solid objects (the eye knows the patch of color but not the rose, as it were). In this text he asserted that "touch teaches vision" — in other words, that it is only by associating visual sensations with tactile sensations that we gain knowledge of external objects.

This theory quickly became popular and is still widely taught and accepted. A single question, however, easily reveals its incoherence: What are the sensations of touch? Because vision supposedly delivers only sensations of light, vision cannot inform us about the external world. But what are the sensations of touch that supposedly can so inform us? In fact, as Berkeley himself knew—and proceeded in 1710 to publish to the world, in *The Principles of Human Knowledge*—tactile sensations give us no more information about solid, extended external objects than do visual sensations. Tactile sensations enable us to determine what is hot or cold, smooth or rough. Even when combined with light and color, they are not enough to constitute a real, external object. When Samuel Johnson "refuted" Berkeley by kicking a stone, he knew quite well that he could not kick a colored, rough-textured association of sensations—and so did Berkeley. In the end, Berkeley used his formula "touch teaches vision" as a stepping stone toward the doctrine that *no* external objects exist. It was the staying power of both Berkeley's immaterialism and Johnson's commonsense refutation of immaterialism—and the lack of a meeting ground between the two—that gave rise to Kant's "scandal of philosophy."

One solution was to *invent* a new sense, a sense that would, perhaps coincidentally, receive impressions of solidity and externality. Several thinkers broached this idea, in a variety of ways. Perhaps the earliest and most influential was Thomas Brown.

Thomas Brown Invents the Muscle Sense

In 1812 Thomas Brown (1778–1820) succeeded Dugald Stewart in the chair of moral philosophy at the University of Edinburgh. Brown had made his name as a young scholar by attacking unpopular theories. At a time when Hume was still anathema to the elite in Scotland, he defended Hume's theory of causation by modifying its language and arguing (rightly) that Hume, properly construed, provided a bulwark against Erasmus Darwin's materialist psychology and materialist interpretations of phrenology. At age nineteen, Brown attained notoriety for his slashing *Observations on the* Zoonomia *of Erasmus Darwin* (1798), which argued that our perceptual experience informs us only of patterns of change, not of cause and effect, just as Hume had insisted. "The systems of materialism," Brown wrote in his preface, "chiefly owe their rise to the groundless belief, that we are acquainted with the nature of causation . . . the materialists [and Erasmus Darwin in particular, falsely] maintain, that he is conscious, not merely of ideas, but of the nature of that which causes ideas."

Brown's philosophy is summarized in his lectures, *Philosophy of the Human Mind* (1820), which were exactly that, his lecture notes, published posthumously and widely disseminated in Great Britain, France, and the United States. (Brown preferred to spend his energies composing bad poetry.) Although typically categorized by historians as a follower of Reid, Brown was no such thing; he explicitly acknowledged his deviations from Reid's philosophical positions. Brown did not think, as did Reid, that we perceive external objects themselves. On the contrary, he assumed that such a doctrine of external perception was tantamount to the dreaded materialism. "It is evident, that . . . the real object of sense is not the distant object, but that which acts immediately upon the organs, — the light itself, not the sun which beams it on us. . . . The reference to the distant sun . . . is the effect of another principle of our intellectual nature [than perception], — the principle of association, or suggestion. . . . without which, indeed, our mere transient sensations would be comparatively of little value." For Reid the object of a sense is always the distant object, and our sensations are

different entirely from our perceptions; no amount of suggestion or association could turn them into perceptions. As far as
Brown was concerned, this lumped Reid with the materialists.
Brown took as the starting point for his account of the mind the
very factor that Reid believed led to confusion and incoherence
in psychology—that is, the assumption that the impressions of
the senses are basic to our perception of the external world.

One implication of Brown's sensationalism is that the young
child will have to learn to distinguish self from nonself on the
basis of sensations alone. A Reidian might acknowledge that
learning is involved, but the learning would be based on the
Reidian assumption that even babies perceive external objects.
In Brown's view, babies could not perceive objects but only have
sense impressions. It was thus Brown, above all others, who be-
queathed to nineteenth-century psychology one of its central
problems, a naturalized version of Kant's scandal of philosophy:
How can an infant come to perceive objects as external from
and independent of itself, and how can it do so on the basis of
sensations alone? "There will be, in the first momentary state,"
Brown explains, "no separation of self and the sensation,—no
little proposition formed in the mind, I feel, or I am conscious
of a feeling; but the feeling and the sentient I, will, for the moment, be the same." As Brown understood, once one accepts
sensationalism, it is clear that in a childhood state "we know as
little of our bodily frame, as of th[e] material universe." Luckily,
"our muscular frame, is not merely a part of the living machinery of motion, but is also truly an organ of sense. When I move
my arm, without resistance, I am conscious of a certain feeling;
when the motion is impeded, by the presence of an external
body, I am conscious of a different feeling" that arises only in
part from touch. The other component of this difference in feeling is muscular, and from it we get sensations of solidity—without muscle sense, touch would comprise nothing more than

painful or pleasant feelings. Touch could not teach vision about external reality (even Berkeley knew that!) but perhaps muscle sense could be the teacher. Brown argues that muscular feelings have three physical causes: alacrity or, conversely, lassitude; different degrees of motion; and greater or lesser amounts of contraction. How can these help us to learn about the external world? The key for Brown—and for almost every theorist for the next hundred years and more—lies in the subjective feelings of *resistance* and *extension* associated with some of these physical states. (It is tempting to speculate about why a doctrine of knowledge based on feelings of resistance and extension should emerge in Britain and come to dominate much of European thought at the beginning of the era of imperial domination, but I will allow readers to ponder this conjunction for themselves.)

Those thinkers who were persuaded by Berkeley's "touch teaches vision"—and there were and are many, despite Berkeley's subversion of his own thesis—are mistaken, Brown argued. Carefully analyzing the sensations of touch, Brown argued that they provide no information about the external world. Indeed, Brown approvingly cited Berkeley to suggest that we are so used to associating ideas of "outness" with tactile impressions (this is what Berkeley said we did with visual impressions) that it takes great analytic power to separate the actual tactile sensations from the associations.

It is just such a separation between true impressions and accreted associations that Brown claims to effect, and he takes this separation to mean that all our impressions of resistance and extension derive not from our skin but from our muscles. The first part of Brown's argument is that it is only because we have a muscle sense that our minds can be informed about the whereabouts of our bodies: "These muscular feelings, tho' they may be almost unnoticed by us during the influence of stronger sensations, are yet sufficiently powerful, when we attend to them, to render us, independently of sight and touch, in a great measure sensible of the position of our body in general, and of its various parts." Brown maintains that feelings often attributed to touch, such as those of smoothness or roughness, are really due to the differential resistance of a surface to our efforts in handling it.

Brown's second point is that the very idea that touch gives us information about extension or shape (which he calls figure) is incoherent. "If, indeed, the mind could know, that a part of its external corporeal organ is compressed into the form of a square, or that another square surface is compressing that organ, the difficulty would be at an end; for it would then most undoubtedly, have that very knowledge of extension, the origin of which we seek." But of course the underlying question is how we would ever know that anything was in fact a square (or any other shape). In answer to this question of how we can come to know shapes, Brown developed a line of reasoning that was copied in one form or another by almost every major nineteenth-century psychologist:

> The infant stretches out his arm for the first time, by that volition without a known object, which is either a mere instinct or very near akin to one,— this motion is accompanied with a certain feeling,—he repeats the volition which moves his arm fifty or one thousand times, and the same progress of feeling takes place during the muscular action. In this repeated progress, he feels the truth of that intuitive proposition, which, in the whole course of the life that awaits him, is to be the source of all his expectations, and the guide of all his actions,—the simple proposition, that what has been as an antecedent, will be followed by what has been as a con-

sequent. At length he stretches out his arm again, and instead of the accustomed progression, there arises, in the resistance of some object opposed to him, a feeling of a very different kind which, if he persevere in his voluntary effort, increases gradually to severe pain, before he has half completed the usual progress. There is a difference, therefore, which we may, without any absurdity, suppose to astonish the little reasoner; for the expectation of similar consequents, from similar antecedents, is observable even in his earliest actions. . . . To any being, who is thus impressed with belief of similarities of sequence, a different consequent necessarily implies a difference of the antecedent . . . however, the infant, who as yet knows nothing but himself, is conscious of no previous difference; and the feeling of resistance seems to him, therefore, something unknown, which has its cause in something that is not himself.

Those who are familiar with the details of Kant's theory of knowledge will notice that Brown has here naturalized one of Kant's fundamental ideas: that spatial knowledge may be based on the temporal succession of impressions. Whereas Kant could appeal to transcendental structures of the understanding to explain this transformation of time into space, Brown cannot. And he thus becomes the first in a long line of theorists forced to attribute sophisticated logical powers to the minds of infants (who have increasingly been viewed as little reasoners from Brown's day forward). Brown continues this discussion, for example, by emphasizing that the infant is a kind of logician. He urges us to remember that although the infant may not have the capacity to articulate the terms of its reasoning, this should not be assumed to debar the infant from accomplishing serious rational operations. He then quotes from the elder Darwin's poem *The Botanic Garden,* canto 3, stanza 5:

> So—when the mother, bending o'er his charms,
> Clasps her fair nursling in delighted arms;—
> With sparkling eyes the blameless plunderer owns
> Her soft embraces and endearing tones,
> Seeks the salubrious fount with opening lips,
> Spreads his inquiring hands, and smiles and sips.

Brown comments that even in this case "many a process of ratiocination is going on, which might have served as an example of strict logic to Aristotle himself." What Darwin regarded as perceptual experience Brown attributes to a combination of logic and sense impressions; he is the first in a long line of nineteenth-century psychologists to treat perception as if it were ratiocination by way of the muscles.

IMPLICATIONS OF THE MUSCLE SENSE

The hypothesis of a muscle sense thus served as an attempt to solve a naturalistic variant of the scandal of philosophy. But in addition to offering some intriguing new explanations for our knowledge of the external world, the muscle sense strategy had a number of dangerous implications, implications that were noticed only gradually.

The most dangerous implication is that seemingly anyone can invent a sense. There is no way to determine whether resistance is a muscle sensation or a skin sensation. Brown's arguments, suggestive as they are, cannot be reconciled with his adherence to instrospective method in psychology. We simply do not have introspectable feelings from our muscles. Brown himself admits that we feel resistance as a tactile sensation—

he argues that this is a misattribution resulting from a process of unnoticed association. Clearly, one could ask how it is that he noticed what ordinarily goes unnoticed, and why he is confident that it is not his introspectively unsupported assertion that is the misattribution! The answer could be that it seems more plausible from the analysis of the *physical* causes of different sensations that resistance derives from muscles rather than from the skin. Maybe so, but this admission, if followed through consistently, would leave sensory physiology an objective science that makes limited use of introspective evidence—that is, just the opposite of what Brown wanted. (This path was indeed followed by some in the nineteenth century. A result of this way of thinking was the discovery that there are in fact sensory receptors in muscles—but that we appear to have no conscious awareness of their signals.)

Scoring a goal for the objectivists is bad enough for a committed introspectionist like Brown, but there is worse to come. Brown is claiming that impressions from the muscle sense are never really felt as such, not even in the newborn; but he is also claiming that these impressions count as the premises (antecedents) in logical arguments. If important sensory data never come to awareness in pure form but nevertheless must be thought about "with strict logic," then a powerful unconscious mind must be registering these data and ratiocinating about them; indeed, such a powerful unconscious mind must exist even in infants. Whereas Berkeley and other sensationalists had developed a fairly simple, even elegant, account of knowledge based on two factors—impressions and the associations among them—Brown and later thinkers had to add to this at least one layer of unconscious impressions (an impossibility for Berkeley or any strict introspectionist) and also a layer of unconscious reasoning or thinking.

This would seem to be a high price to pay for the new sense.

Was it worth completely undermining what we had thought was meant by a *sense* and adding confusion to what impression and thought had meant? Moreover, these problems might have been anticipated by anyone who had given careful thought to Reid's injunction that grounding psychology on the concept of sensory impressions was an intellectual disaster. Perhaps surprisingly, even in the wake of Brown's work, few psychologists went back to Reid (or to Kant); instead, many forged full speed ahead, into these unknown and perilous waters.

Motor Theories of Mind

Brown's combination of associationism, sensationalism, and a modified empiricism was so influential that it came to characterize much of English (and, to a lesser degree, German) psychology up until the 1880s. Several of Brown's questionable innovations became unquestioned dogmas within a relatively short span of time. That sense impressions must be the basis of perception and knowledge; that given a certain innate (and unconscious) mental competence, learning was the basis of much of our perception and knowledge; and that learning typically involved associating complexes of impressions—these innovations of Brown's dominated much of nineteenth-century psychological thinking.

In addition, what one might call Brown's motor theory of perception (to use twentieth-century terminology) was the basis for later thinking about spatial perception and cognition. Reid had argued that perception (of external objects) was a fundamentally different psychological process from sensation (awareness of states of feeling).

Brown is explicit about his rejection of Reid's distinction and his belief that sensations of muscular movement are the basis of all our knowledge of the external world. Following Brown, most nineteenth-century thinkers made a very different use of Reid's distinction between sensation and perception: sensations were said to be transformed into perceptions, via processes of association, memory, and something like logical judgment. Indeed, Brown asserted that "Perception . . . is only another name . . . for the result of certain associations and inferences that flow from more general principles of the mind." Essentially he wanted to eliminate *perception* in reference to either a special class of mental states or a specifiable psychological process, beyond that of association among sensations. John Stuart Mill was to adopt this position of Brown's without acknowledgment, with important consequences for later psychology. Brown had to deny that perception is a truly distinct psychological process because, at least as Reid had used the term, perception as a primary source of information about the world was *not* based on sensations, associations, or inferences. For Brown, this meaning of *perception* was intrinsically materialistic and therefore must be rejected. The majority of students of perception in the next century followed Brown in holding that the psychological process Reid called perception did not, strictly speaking, exist.

> Certain feelings are referred by us to an external material cause. The feelings themselves, as primarily excited, are termed sensations, and when followed by the reference to an external cause, receive the name perceptions, which marks nothing more in addition to the primary sensations than this very reference. But what is the reference itself, in consequence of which the new name is given? It is the suggestion of some extended resisting object, the presence of which had before been found to be attended with that particular sensation, which is now again referred to it.

Brown goes on to make it clear that this "suggestion" involves the association of any sensation (visual, tactile, auditory, and so on) with a muscular sensation—the feeling of resistance to our action—so that perception as such (knowledge of external objects) would be impossible without the muscle sense. "In all but one class of our sensations [muscle sense], then, it is evident that what Dr Reid calls perception, as the operation of a peculiar mental faculty, is nothing more than a suggestion of memory or association." Furthermore, Brown argues that even feelings of resistance are not so much perceptions in Reid's sense as a kind of intuitive belief in the externality of the causes of muscular motion.

James Mill codified, organized, and extended Brown's theory. (In explaining Brown's theory, I have doubtless given the impression that it was clear and organized, but in fact it is buried in scores of pages of Brown's awkward purple prose.) The elder Mill enunciated several principles of association and introduced the important concept of a *fused* sensation, by which he meant an association of two or more sensations that, through repetition or intensity, come to be felt as a single sensation. This concept of a fused sensation he applied to many cases of perception of external objects, arguing that the apparent visual awareness of external things, for example, is based on a fusion of visual with muscular and tactile sensations.

What is of course most striking about these muscular sensations is, as I have stressed, that we never seem to be conscious of them. Unlike smells and sights, we never appear to have the kind of feelings Brown and Mill tell us we have. James Mill suggests that feelings of rest, discomfort, and stretching might be instances of muscular sensations, but he is aware that "there are some muscles of the body in constant and vehement action, as the heart, of the feelings attendant upon the action of which we seem to have no cognisance at all." Still, "this is no argument" against their existence, because the lack of consciousness can be explained by habitual inattention. As late as 1869, when he was editing his father's book for republication, John Stuart Mill spoke of "the paradox . . . of . . . feelings which are not felt," noticing this important inconsistency on which all later associationist psychology rested. Supposedly all our knowledge derives from sensations, and supposedly sensations are the simplest modes of feeling, and supposedly feelings are simple mental (conscious) states. But associationist accounts of how sensations become perceptions all require that many of our sensations go unnoticed. This applies to vision and other sense modalities as well as to muscular sense; for example, we are rarely conscious (if ever) of the changing hues of visible objects as we change position with respect to them and the light source, although these sensations are supposedly the basis of our seeing the color of the objects in the first place.

If one is going to hypothesize that we have feelings of which we are unaware, why not go whole hog? Could we not have feelings that give us direct information about something other than pushes, pulls, or points of light and touch? Two theorists of Brown's generation developed ideas along these lines: Maine de Biran (1766-1824) in France and Arthur Schopenhauer (1788-1860) in Germany. Both these thinkers claimed, although for different reasons, that we have a direct awareness of our own efforts of will. That is, Schopenhauer and Maine de Biran argued that we have feelings of striving and trying, independent of any muscular impressions. Such feelings were supposedly a direct apprehension within the soul of its own strivings. At the same time, a widespread and popular school of "illuminism" (descended in part from Emanuel Swedenborg's teachings) held that individuals have direct consciousness of their souls, and perhaps even of the godhead within the soul. Some of Maine de Biran's and Schopenhauer's writings seem to hint at a similar illuminism, and perhaps for that reason they exerted little influence until after 1848, when, with the increased interest in spiritualism, both thinkers achieved their greatest fame. Despite the apparent lack of interest in the first part of the century in the theorists of feelings of effort, by the 1850s muscle sense was often overshadowed by one or another form of the sense of effort, even in theories identified with the Mills' associationism.

Alexander Bain (1818–1903) is typically treated as an associationist follower of the Mills who developed a more empirically based account of perception and volition than that found in either James or John Stuart Mill's work. Bain, however, emphasized the sense of effort as much as or more than muscle sense and thereby modified Brown's and the Mills' theory into something much closer to a modern motor theory of perception. Bain was impressed by the spontaneous activity of animals and infants, not their receptivity to impressions, muscular or otherwise. He was perhaps the first scientist after Whytt to emphasize the importance of overall muscle tone and the closure of sphincter muscles during normal activity as evidence of a psychologically important fact—that continual, multilevel motor activity is a basic part of animal life.

Bain's is the first true motor theory of perception, emphasizing that perception itself is dependent on prior motor *activities,* not just on prior muscle *sensing.* It is only as a consequence of our activity that muscular feelings arise, and it is only because of these muscular feelings that we perceive external objects. To use another anachronistic term, muscular sensations are, for Bain, response-produced sensations. In addition to the muscle sense that according to Brown gives us information about resistance, Bain claimed two other kinds of information are feelings associated with movement: feelings of effort (as in the mental effort of attention), and feelings of the rate of muscular contraction (a kind of effort of bodily attention). From his motor theory of perception, Bain derived his conception of a belief. For Bain, a belief is not only a mental state but also a state of preparedness to act. In fact, a belief *is* that upon which one is prepared to act. Bain's psychology thus set the stage for pragmatism.

Another important motor theorist of the mind was William B. Carpenter (1813–85). A distinguished comparative anatomist and student of the "philosophical anatomist" Robert Grant, Carpenter was turned down for the chair of medicine at Edinburgh in 1842 because of his Unitarian beliefs. In 1844 he was so widely suspected of having penned *The Vestiges of Creation*—the infamous evolutionist tract—that he had to issue a denial. (Later he befriended the true author of that work, Robert Chambers, a Scottish polymath.) Carpenter explicitly saw his work in neuropsychology as modernizing and improving on Gall's conception of brain and mental science. Like most serious phrenologists, Carpenter was a strong moral crusader (he was especially associated with the crusade against drinking alcohol), but unlike the phrenologists, Carpenter followed Hartley (the Unitarian hero) and not the Scottish philosophers (the Presbyterian heroes). Whereas earlier writers (such as Erasmus Darwin and James Mill) had emphasized the need to bring Hartley's associationism up to date, Carpenter attempted to bring other aspects of Hartley's theory, especially his approach to volition and moral judgment, into mid-nineteenth-century science. His most important writing on the mind is his *Mental Physiology* (1874). That book grew out of long chapters on the subject in his earlier (and very popular) *Principles of Human Physiology,* which went through several editions in the 1840s and 1850s. In many ways, Carpenter was a transitional figure. Carpenter even called his work physiological metaphysics on occasion, and his emphasis on "character" and its formation as central to psychology echoes the writings of Gall, Spurzheim, and Combe as well as the ideas of Hartley.

Whereas Bain applied the motor theory of mind epistemologically, Carpenter tended to apply it ontologically. He regarded "all the physical forces of the universe as the direct manifestation of the Mental force of the Deity." Lotze drew an analogy between God's creation of the cosmos and our soul's ordering of the mental "microcosmos." Similarly, Carpenter found an interesting parallel to his speculations on the "correlation of natural forces" in the idea that our experience of activity is the source of all our ideas about power or form. "It is to me very interesting," he wrote, "to find the two lines of argument—the one starting from the correlation of the Physical, Vital, and Mental forces . . . the other from our own subjective consciousness" running together (*Mental Physiology*, pp. 693-96; see also pp. 10-14).

Carpenter found one important parallel between the Deity and our souls in his concept of volition. Although God receives information from the entire universe, and must act (if truly omniscient) on the basis of all the relevant information, God's acts are not *determined* by the information. The same is true of our souls or wills, which receive all relevant information but may act independently of incoming impressions. Like Bain, Carpenter saw that any activity would in itself produce new sense impressions, but unlike Bain, Carpenter distinguished between impressions that simply activated nerve channels in the spine or brain, reflexlike, and impressions that necessitated conscious deliberation prior to action. These latter were cases of free action, Carpenter insisted. Although he emphasized free action, Carpenter also noted that a great deal of habitual action did not require such deliberation and could be handled "automatically" (phrasing Carpenter introduced to replace Hartley's "secondary involuntary acts"). Just as God designed the universe to act on its own most of the time, so our minds allow our bodies to act automatically in many instances, Carpenter maintained, on the basis of "unconscious cerebration." Some of our habitual actions are apparently carried out by reflexlike mechanisms that are both cerebral and unconscious. Carpenter explicitly called these cerebral reflexes, although he credited Thomas Laycock with originating the idea.

CEREBRAL REFLEXES AND THE END OF TRADITIONAL METAPHYSICS

Carpenter's application of the concept of cerebral reflex was unusual and important: he used it to explain Braid's results with hypnosis, and other examples of what are now called dissociated states. If hypnotists can divert a person's conscious attention, or cause a relaxation in it, then they may be able to engage habitual cerebral reflexes that would not otherwise be activated. The hypnotic state, according to this view, is one in which automatisms and unconscious cerebration dominate conscious deliberation and action. A hypnotist might arrange for a person to believe that the solid object in front of her was an apple, for example, when in reality it was an onion. And, if the correct automatism were truly activated, the hypnotist's victim might well bite into the "apple," even though she would never do so when normally conscious. Carpenter thus distinguished between two forms of what he called ideomotor action. In the first, an idea is conscious and freely deliberated—this is ordinary voluntary behavior; in the second, the idea results from something other than deliberation, nevertheless setting off the cerebral reflexes so that an action follows. Carpenter suggested that this second kind of ideomotor activity might be invoked to explain many of the "spiritualist" phenomena then in vogue, such as people in trances giving voice to messages from departed souls. Thus Brown's "suggestion" was transmogrified into Carpenter's concept of "suggestibility": that some people are especially susceptible to this second kind of ideomotor action and that they themselves can act out their unconscious ideas, or be made by a hypnotist to act out such ideas. The theory of suggestibility was used to create the mysterious event at the heart of the first English detective novel, Wilkie Collins's *The Moonstone,* and was also to have a great impact on the classical era of psychoanalysis, from Charcot and Binet through Breuer and Freud.

By the 1840s traditional metaphysics was dead. Even many who professed support for introspectionism no longer believed that a science of the soul could be constructed on the method of introspection. Indeed, many professed introspectionists betrayed its ideals in their own work. Moreover, it was widely believed that some more naturalistic method and theory must be developed to understand the soul. This was not to be a materialist theory—no respectable theorists proposed that!—but a naturalistic theory of the soul. It could include the old introspectionist methods, but it must also go beyond them. Muscle sense and the sense of effort were not going to be understood fully without extensive knowledge of anatomy and physiology. And the significance of volition required, at the least, a natural history of will power, such as that found in Bain's work, or an account of the dissolution of volition, as described in Carpenter's and others' studies of inebriation, dreaming, and hypnosis.

5

The Brief Life of Natural Metaphysics

The traditional metaphysics that held sway throughout the Western world from 1815 to 1830 did not give way suddenly to one or even a few different theories. Instead, thinkers chipped away at exposed places in the edifice of the traditional theory. If theorists were right to advocate recognition of a new sense, whether a muscular sense or a sense of effort, then many of the traditional claims about the impossibility of knowing the external world could be proved wrong, for they would be based on an inadequate inventory of our sensory experience. Many of the traditionalist critiques of associationism could be shown to miss their mark because associationist theories now included associations linked with sensations of muscular effort. The assaults on traditional metaphysics thus challenged both its epistemological and its psychological assumptions.

Alternatively, some thinkers challenged the traditional views on ontological grounds. This course was decidedly riskier, because the challenger could always be accused of materialism or atheism. As a matter of fact, several challengers were attacked in this way, and many were also criticized for being "Spinozists" (a label that still connoted materialist atheism to the orthodox, and usually warranted the attentions of the secret police). Nevertheless, the traditional view was highly susceptible at just this point: once it became possible to map out systematic relations between psychological and physical states, hypotheses about the physical basis of mental life seemed appropriate, despite the orthodox ban on them.

The inadequacies of the traditional metaphysics being preached from pulpit and lectern stemmed from traditional thinkers' resistance to treating psychology as a natural science. Most traditional metaphysicians did not, like Reid and Kant, deny that psychology (as we now call it) could ever be scientific, but neither did they actively pursue the goal of making it scientific. On the contrary, most of the major theorists in the early 1800s argued that mental and moral philosophy (Britain), *psychologie* (France), pneumatology (Scotland), or metaphysics (as this discipline was still often called throughout Europe) was different from natural philosophy (which came to be called natural science or physics only in the 1830s).

This very slight relaxation of orthodoxy—it was not *necessarily* false that psychology could be a natural science, it was simply false *in fact*—opened the door to a generation of thinkers who are little known and poorly understood today. Although later on in the nineteenth century psychology came to be seen as a science of mind (or even of behavior), the first moves in this direction were made by thinkers who wanted to create a natural science of the *soul*. This phrase even sounds a bit nonsensical to our post-positivist ears, but many of the most important theorists who came of intellectual age between 1815 and 1848 were striving in this way to naturalize metaphysics, to study the soul scientifically.

Naturalizing Metaphysics

The fundamental idea animating most of these theorists was that the soul exists as some kind of force within nature (contrary to the assertions of Kant or Reid). Often this force was identified with certain physical or psychological manifestations. The best-known example is Mesmer's "animal magnetism," which he identified with an unusual variety of magnetism, and also with certain psychological manifestations (termed magnetic sleep and magnetic crisis). As early as 1815 however, his student A. M. J. Puységur's claim that animal magnetism was primarily a psychological force (which we would call suggestibility) had come to rival Mesmer's physicalist explanation of magnetic sleep.

The confused state of physical theory between the time of Franklin's two-fluid theory of electricity and the work of Ampère and Faraday in the 1820s contributed to the ease with which assertions could be made about "natural" forces affecting our thoughts, feelings, and behavior. Electricity, magnetism, heat, and gravity were understood to be natural forces and also to be somehow related to one another, but the relationships were dimly understood at best. In this context of intellectual uncertainty it became possible to speculate that the activity of the soul might be based on some relation among these forces. Although the interchangeability of forces was neither proved nor understood until midcentury, many theorists—Ørsted, Schelling, and Erasmus Darwin among others—speculated on the possibility that electricity, magnetism, heat, light, and other forces were really variants of one or two basic forces. Experimentation and argument took years to catch up with imagination.

In this context two conclusions seemed highly plausible: first, that states of the soul might well be related to an as-yet-undiscovered physical force or form of force; second, that contemporary theorizing about such forces was inadequate to solve many of the important issues that would be raised. Erasmus Darwin's verdict that events like the creation of an android were "not impossible" was well understood by thinkers all over Europe, not just the young Mary Shelley. But many of these thinkers believed that in emphasizing existing physical forces, Darwin overlooked the very real possibility that some sort of *mental* or *spiritual* force would prove a better explanation of life and mind, and perhaps even contribute to a new theory of nature as well.

From this emerging perspective, traditional metaphysics was missing an adequate conception of mental life in relation to force—modeled on but by no means identical to a Newtonian dynamics. The most likely candidate for a mental force was the will. At least three important thinkers—Maine de Biran and Schopenhauer, as mentioned in Chapter 4, as well as Johann Friedrich Herbart (1776-1841)—claimed that will gives us direct, introspective evidence of our own powers. Another strong possibility was some sort of vital force, either of a general sort inherent in all living tissue or of a more specific sort to be found only in the nervous system. This neural energy or force might or might not be identified with will. Johannes Müller (1801-58), whose immensely influential textbook on neurophysiology was published in the 1830s, supported the idea of neural forces, identifying some with will and others with sensory powers. Müller spoke of "specific *nerve* energies" (my emphasis) to refer to the different kinds of *mental* forces associated with different nerve tracts. Ironically, Müller's student Herman von Helmholtz was among the first to propose the theory of the conservation of energy and quickly applied his discovery to arguing that these mental forces, his teacher's pet notion, could not be real. Yet, while Helmholtz and others abandoned Müller's *ontology* of mental forces, they nevertheless maintained the *explanation* that our different psychological states are based on different mental forces! Thus, even late in the nineteenth century, the differences between different sensory states (that is, between seeing colors and hearing tones) were routinely explained—even by Helmholtz—as the result of different specific nerve energies, even though that no longer meant what Müller had intended it to mean, and almost no one actually believed that such neural energies existed as autonomous mental forces.

Although these natural scientists of the soul by no means formed a single school of thought, I find it convenient to unite them under the label *natural metaphysicians,* because all of them, even the most influential, ended up as *transitional* figures between traditional metaphysics and psychology conceived of as a natural science. The idea of a natural science of the soul was barely a decade or two old when the discovery of the conservation of energy, along with the rise of positivism (not unrelated events) made natural metaphysics untenable. In its short life, however, it promoted several ideas that have been very influential both directly and indirectly—that is, as a result of the attacks on them. These ideas include:

- That there exists some sort of internal force or power in minds (a will?)
- That ideas themselves may have some of this power (Herbart)
- That mental forces help to organize the phenomenal (or even the noumenal) world
- That introspection reveals the results of a "play of forces" and is thus both indispensable and inadequate: indispensable, because the mental forces can nowhere else be observed; inadequate, because it is introspection that makes us wonder what gives rise to the play of forces in the first place.

This last idea of the natural metaphysicians was the one that most strongly influenced the first generation of self-described physiological or experimental psychologists.

Three Natural Metaphysicians

To provide a brief overview of these ideas, I have chosen three of the more notable scientists of the soul. The first, Schopenhauer, is generally classified as a philosopher; the second, Johannes Müller, as a physiologist; and the third, Gustav Fechner, as a psychologist. Each of these thinkers, in his own way, challenged the traditional metaphysical consensus and offered an alternative ontology. Following my brief overview of three traditional metaphysicians, I take a slightly more in-depth look at the work of perhaps the most influential natural metaphysician, R. H. Lotze.

Arthur Schopenhauer (1788–1860) was the heir of a well-to-do merchant family of Gdansk and the son of a well-known woman novelist with whom he was unable to get along. All his life an ardent Anglophile (he read the London *Times* daily), Schopenhauer was almost certainly better informed about English-language philosophical trends than any of his German contemporaries. Although he was aware of Brown's attempts to rectify Kant's epistemology "by dint of muscle," Schopenhauer chose to improve on Kant (perhaps the only modern philosopher for whom he showed real respect) in a completely different way. In one sense, Schopenhauer can be read as inverting Brown's theory of perception. Whereas Brown's muscle sense supposedly gives us data from which we can infer that there is an external world resisting our efforts, Schopenhauer says we are directly aware of our efforts (our will, not its results, nor resistance to its results) and that this knowledge helps us to interpret what is going on around us.

Unlike Kant, Schopenhauer resolutely refused to supernaturalize noumena. He treated our consciousness of self as direct access to the real, noumenal self. What writers such as Erasmus Darwin and Brown (and, later, Bain and Wilhelm Wundt) referred to as a sense of effort, Schopenhauer saw not as a form of sensory experience but as a direct knowledge of our noumenal being. Although direct and personal, this knowledge is limited primarily to the fact that the noumenon exists. This self or noumenal existence Schopenhauer labeled will, although he acknowledged that it bears only a metaphorical resemblance to the will as experienced. Indeed, in his major work, *The World as Will and Representation*, first published in 1819 and added to substantially throughout his career, Schopenhauer was quite explicit that it is impossible to be certain whether your will and mine are two things or one, or whether there is more than one will in the entire universe.

Although our direct experience of the will is limited, our experience of the phenomenal world that reflects the will is not, and it offers Schopenhauer many insights into the distribution and nature of will. In his *The Will in Nature* (1836) Schopenhauer noted that evidence of will can be seen in both the anatomy and behavior of plants and animals. When we see the behavior of another person or animal, we can infer—thanks to our internal awareness of our own will—the power or force that lies behind the action. Moreover, because Schopenhauer considered biological development a form of action, even the anatomy of other creatures is evidence for these hidden forces. He considered the emphasis of Linnaean botany on the sexual organs of flowers to be consistent with the idea that the noumenal will of beings like plants can manifest itself in specifically different anatomies. Schopenhauer explained how many forms of behavior, especially aggressive and sexual behavior, should be understood as phenomenal representations of a noumenal will. Schopenhauer also developed an aesthetic theory quite novel for the West, although well known to India. His aesthetic is based on the notion that much art is driven by an urge to become will-less, to abandon all the idiosyncrasies of our individual and particular existence and strive to find a kind of universal, Platonic idea: great works of art help us to lose even the appearance of having separate wills and enable us to enter into the will of the world.

In this world where what is real is will and all aspects of behavior and mind are mere representations thereof, there can be no free will, because these mere phenomena cannot take on causal powers. We may represent to ourselves that we spontaneously choose a certain course of action, but this is an illusion. Schopenhauer is a sort of exaggerated Humean, arguing that reason is always a slave to the passions, and that the brain itself is an organ formed largely to subserve those functions of the will needed for procreation. Schopenhauer also argued that his ontology "explained" why personalities seem to be inborn and innate. For Schopenhauer, personality is the phenomenal representation of a particular will (or particular aspect of the world will) and as such it must consistently reflect that noumenal being.

Instead of being attacked for his unorthodox ideas, Schopenhauer was simply ignored for most of his life, despite the great vigor and clarity with which he wrote. It was only in 1852 that C. Fortlage devoted a chapter to Schopenhauer in his history of German philosophy, which led to a discussion of Schopenhauer in the an issue of the *Westminster Review,* at that time edited by Marian Evans. By all accounts, that British publication of 1853 put Schopenhauer on the European intellectual map, and his uniquely pessimistic ontology became as important in the 1850s and 1860s as Hegel's objective idealism had been in the preceding two decades.

Despite the suddenness and intensity of the new-found interest in Schopenhauer, his philosophy was attacked by all but a very few. Not even the thoughtful reviewer of the *Westminster* could resist attacking Schopenhauer's beliefs. The same reviewer who understood and was willing to state that "according to the consistent Kantis[t], physical theology, with its high priests Durham and Paley, is but an amiable absurdity, based on an illegitimate extension of the law of cause and effect to an object which lies beyond its jurisdiction"—this same reviewer was by no means willing to consider Schopenhauer's main ideas with equanimity. The review ends with a strong caveat: "Those who construe any of our remarks into an acceptance of such a system of ultra-pessimism have totally misapprehended our meaning." Schopenhauer is "genial, eccentric, audacious, and, let us add, terrible." The reviewer adds, "We only wish we could see among the philosophers of modern Germany a writer of equal power, comprehensiveness, ingenuity, and erudition, ranged on a side more in harmony with our own feelings and conviction than that adopted by this misanthropic sage of Frankfort." Many writers were to attempt to fulfill this wish, most especially those associated with the rise of modern psychology, such as Helmholtz and Wundt.

Not all critics of traditional metaphysics were as outspoken as Schopenhauer. One of the most effective and influential critics of early nineteenth-century thought, Johannes Müller has long been seen as a conservative. This view of Müller is an inheritance from his students' time. Müller has perhaps had the oddest misfortune of any scientist: to be so eclipsed by his students (especially Helmholtz and Emil du Bois Reymond) that his views are rarely evaluated on their own terms.

Müller's physiology was a unique combination of the best of German *Naturphilosophie* with Müller's own interpretation of Spinoza. Although he explicitly renounced Spinoza's metaphysics, it is unclear whether he genuinely meant to distance himself from Spinoza or merely from the troubles associated with being a Spinozist. In any event, much of Müller's philosophy in his tremendously influential *Handbuch der Physiologie des Menschen* (1834–40) reflects a careful assimilation of specific doctrines of Spinoza's *Ethics* into nineteenth-century life science. (Historians of psychology often label Müller a Kantian, but this claim does not survive careful reading of his text.)

Müller's most important contribution to psychology was his doctrine of specific nerve energies: that each sensory nerve produces its own unique sensory (subjective) quality. Müller considered this doctrine an updating of Spinoza's notion that our perceptual ideas are, literally, mental reflections of states of our bodies. It is only because our nerves are material, and set into motion by other material causes, that the specific ideas we get from them can constitute experience of the world: "The immediate objects of the perception of our senses are merely particular states induced in the nerves and felt as sensations. . . . but inasmuch as the nerves . . . are material bodies . . . they make known to the sensorium, by virtue of changes produced in them by external causes, not merely their own condition, but also properties and changes of condition of external bodies. The information thus obtained by the senses concerning external nature, varies in each sense, having a relation to the qualities or energies of the nerve." Müller, like Shelley (whom he never read) and Spinoza (whom both he and Shelley read), believed that every natural occurrence exists as an effect of a series of causes, and that one can work backward from effect to cause, given enough knowledge. Our nervous systems, Müller claimed, are endowed by the Creator with such knowledge that when they feel their own states, they also learn something of the external world. The former (internally oriented) aspect of feeling is sensation (in Reid's sense) and embodies Müller's hypothesis of specific energies; the latter (externally oriented) aspect of feeling is perception, which Müller saw as based on sensation.

Unlike Reid and Kant, Müller argued that it is possible to

explain how perception emerges from sensation so long as one understands the forces involved. Once we know what kinds of psychological changes occur in each sensory nerve, we can offer hypotheses about how these changes can be interpreted as the effects of specific causes and thus how knowledge of the changes constitutes knowledge of the causes. This is strikingly like the theory found in Schopenhauer's *Fourfold Root* (1817) and even, albeit more distantly, like that in Descartes's *Optics* (1637), but it is unclear whether Müller was directly influenced by those works. Unfortunately, following Helmholtz, most commentators on Müller have simply misread him and assumed that the specific nerve energies are purely physical states of the nerves. Regarding this, Müller (like Spinoza) was quite clear: the goal of his theory was to explain how the physical differences are equivalent to and manifested in *psychological* differences. Müller intended his doctrine of specific nerve energies to be understood as referring to specific differences in *both* mental feeling and physical force.

Where Müller thus differed from both Schopenhauer and Descartes was in his insistence that the nervous system—and all animate matter—embodied a nonphysical force, a vital principle. This vital principle, Müller believed, acted differently from ordinary physical matter and could in fact cause ordinary physical matter to behave in ways inexplicable by the laws of physics or chemistry. Müller was such a confirmed vitalist that he denied that Friedrich Woehler's production of urea (an experiment often held up as one of the death knells of vitalism) proved one could make an organic compound out of ordinary inorganic material. "Urea, however, can be scarcely considered as organic matter, being rather an excretion than a component of the animal body . . . it has not perhaps the characteristic properties of organic elements."

Oddly, Müller's attitude toward his vital principle was not

unlike Kant's attitude toward the hypothesis of noumena. Little, if anything, can be known about the action of this vital principle, although one can describe which phenomena are correlated with it:

> Whether the vital and mental principles be transmitted from the brain through the medium of the nerves to the semen or germ; whether the mind in a latent state be contained in the blood; whether in such a condition it exist in every part of the body, though . . . active only in the brain, which is organised as its instrument . . . are all questions which it is impossible to answer. . . . [Nevertheless,] for consciousness, imagination, thought, volition, will, and passion, the brain is absolutely necessary, and although the principle for the production of ideas, thoughts, & cet. is present in a latent state in the impregnated germ, yet the whole organisation of the brain must be created in this germ before mental principles can become free, and the ideas, thoughts, and will, be manifested.

In hindsight, we can see that Müller's vital principle in physiology—just like Kant's schematism in psychology—became a constraint, not an aid to scientific thought. Müller's hypothesis of vital principles and mental forces did not lead to discoveries of new facts, and it tended to reduce all theoretical exploration to the simple pattern of associating nerve tracts with specific mental states. Yet Müller's influence was so great that even after his concept of mental forces was abandoned, his explanatory schema remained widely used.

It is instructive to note that traditional metaphysics would have had considerable grounds on which to criticize Müller. Take, for example, his well-known account of voluntary action:

"The primitive fibres of all the voluntary nerves being at their central extremity spread out in the brain to receive the influence of the will, we may compare them, as they lay [*sic*] side by side in the organ of the mind, to the keys of a pianoforte on which our thoughts play or strike." Not only Kant and Reid but even Thomas Brown would have blanched at the calm with which Müller proposed not only to spatialize the mind but to locate it within a particular region of space. If the immaterial will can navigate its way through space well enough to locate different regions of the neural keyboard, why couldn't it "play" on the spine or even on the muscles directly?

Müller argued that once the thought strikes the brain "key," it gives rise to "currents or vibrations" in outgoing nerves, which then cause muscular motions. And, Müller claimed, repetition of thoughts causes repetitions of paths of vibration, thus leading to the kind of automaticity associated with habit. This idea (expressed more crudely in Hartley and Erasmus Darwin) became a fundamental tenet of psychology after it was incorporated by Bain. Yet it is utterly dependent on something like the absurd spatiality of the piano keyboard metaphor and flies in the face of everyday experience. Müller, Bain, and others in fact used the example of learning to play the piano, claiming that repetition of a musical idea or phrase would produce a habit, not only in behavior, but also in the relevant nerve tracts. To quote Müller, "the more frequently the same fibres are thrown into action, the easier does their action become." But this is just plain wrong: the practiced pianist makes very different movements than the unpracticed one does, and uses a wholly different posture and attack, making movements of greater fluidity, usually with very different dynamics, and obviously with far fewer missed notes. Similarly, the skilled musician learning a new piece often *reduces* the number of movements, *eliminating* gestures that occurred when the piece was first attempted. Hence, if repetition of musical ideas and performance rendered the original muscular motions easier to achieve, then the novice's hesitant, inadequate playing would become *more* hesitant and inadequate, and the expert's perfunctory or tentative run-through would become more, not less, tentative.

Müller's theory rests on a confounding of *habit* in the sense of skilled behavior with habitual action along a neural pathway. These are two very different things, however. The first time we perform an action—whether we are skilled in that kind of activity, like a professional musician sight-reading a piece, or are naive, like a student musician—there is always a great deal of wasted movement, hesistancy, and incorrect timing. How could repetition of such infelicitous movements produce the smooth, skilled movement that we ultimately see? Müller assumes that when we practice an action, our neural pathways somehow record and register only the smooth essence of the act, so that repetition produces skilled performance. In this conviction he has been followed by the majority of nineteenth- and even twentieth-century psychologists, from Alexander Bain and William James through B. F. Skinner and Jean Piaget. Yet the theory is untenable. Unless the nervous system can know, in advance of attaining skill, which pathways relate to coordinated and which to awkward movements, practice—mere repetition—cannot yield smoothness or the neural paths that allow it. If we want to understand how coordinated action emerges from repetition of often awkward movements, we need to understand how habitual actions (and their underlying neural control) *change* with practice.

In Johannes Müller we have a scientist whose particular conceptual innovations—the hypothesis of specific nerve energies and the motor keyboard—dominated later thinking long after his ontological views were in disrepute. He can be contrasted with Schopenhauer, whose own knowledge of botany and zoology is now obviously woefully out of date, but whose metaphysical views keep resurfacing, especially in metaphysical theories propounded by natural scientists. Gustav Fechner (1801–87) offers a third case: someone whose main work is almost totally unknown and who is nowadays revered for an innovation he himself considered a rather minor incident in a busy career.

Fechner, like Müller, offered a kind of Spinozist metaphysics. But, whereas Müller emphasized Spinoza's quasi pantheism, Fechner emphasized Spinoza's views on substance, in particular his "dual aspect" theory of mind and body. Fechner combined this dual aspect metaphysics with a kind of generalized atomism, through which he claimed to be able to show in particular how both electricity and mental force were constituted atomically. Fechner argued that the modern physical worldview showed only one side of the universe, the mechanistic side, the interplay of the atoms according to physical laws. But another side of the universe existed, the subjective, living side, the mental atoms. Fechner went so far as to speak of a "day view" (which acknowledged life and mind) and a "night view" (which did not).

According to Fechner's day view of reality, reductionist science is, literally, topsy-turvy. Science should begin with the phenomena of the most organized parts of reality and work backward to the simplest and least simple parts. Influenced by the global and fieldlike phenomenon associated with magnetism, Fechner developed a kind of forerunner of the Gaia hypothesis in which he argued that "cosmorganic" organization (the earth—or even the universe—conceived of as a monad) is primary, organic matter is secondary, and inorganic matter tertiary. Like Müller and Schopenhauer, he saw organization as held together by forces—although he tended to see such forces as internal to each monad, or at least to a given level of reality.

On the basis of his energeticism and organicism, Fechner developed a novel concept now known as the sensory threshold. He based both his theorizing and his experimental work in this area on that of E. H. Weber, a mentor at Leipzig. Weber had studied what we now call the just noticeable difference, which he conceived of as a fraction. If you are holding a ten-kilogram weight and I add to it a one-kilogram weight, chances are you may not even notice any change. But if you are holding a ten-kilogram weight and I add to it a ten-kilogram weight, it is very likely that you will notice the change. Hence, a just-noticeable difference in a sensory impression is not an absolute value but a fraction. Weber had found experimentally that the just-noticeable difference (jnd) was a constant, expressible as the ratio of the old stimulus value to the new stimulus value. More generally, Fechner referred to Equation 1 as the Weber Fraction, where Σ represents the change in the stimulus and Δ is the original stimulus value:

1. $\Delta\Sigma / \Sigma = V$ (where V is a constant value)

Fechner argued that the sensory change should follow the physical change in some coherent way. Thus, if S represents the magnitude of a sensation (itself caused presumably by stimuli of the value Σ) and ΔS the change in that magnitude, then ΔS should be a function of C as well. Fechner assumed that the changes—ΔS and $\Delta \Sigma$—were both differentiable, and so he rewrote the relationship between sensory values and the Weber fraction by integrating:

2. $S = C \log_e \Sigma + k$ (where k is a constant of integration and C is a constant)

Not being able to ascertain k empirically, Fechner rewrote this equation for the case of Σ at threshold (that is, where its sensory value would be 0 by definition). Hence, k = -C log$_e$ Σ threshold

Then, by substituting for k in Equation 2, Fechner wrote:

3. S = C log$_e$ (Σj / Σ threshold)

In words, this says that sensation acts as a scale representing the "distance" in jnd's that a stimulus (Σj) is above zero (in other words, above threshold). And this scale, being logarithmic, is nonlinear. That is, at low absolute values of stimuli, small changes in stimulus value will be noticed, whereas at high absolute stimulus values, the same small changes will not be noticed. A stimulus thus has a different psychological significance, depending on factors independent of itself. If I whisper to you in a quiet library, you will hear me, but you will not if I whisper to you in the midst of a howling storm.

An especially important aspect of these ideas was Fechner's interpretation of the jnd. Fechner asked, What happens to the sensory registration of the one kilogram when it is added to the ten-kilogram weight that one is already holding? We know that under many circumstances the one kilogram can and will be noticed, but we also know that the one kilogram will fall beneath the jnd—Fechner says "below threshold"—when Δ exceeds a certain value (in other words, when a significant weight is already being held). Perhaps influenced by Herbart (who believed that all mental elements were forces) Fechner argued that such impressions of below-threshold stimuli existed as part of a *world mind,* and that individuals became aware of them only when they exceeded the required value.

Fechner's psychophysics is often said to be a theory for relating the natural and the mental world by means of a mathematical function (the nonlinear function expressed here as Equation 3), but this assertion simply ignores Fechner's ontology. He was trying not only to relate the physical and the psychological but also the daytime and nighttime view of the world. He thought he had *evidence* supporting the existence of his world soul, and evidence supporting his idea that individual units are secondary to larger, more encompassing entities. Just as individual stimuli draw meaning from the context of other stimuli, so, Fechner argued, individual sensations draw their meaning from the context in which they occur.

Fechner had come to these inverted atomistic views as a professor of physics in Leipzig. The atomism and invocation of hypothetical forces found throughout the works of such figures as Müller, Fechner, and Lotze was very much of a piece with current trends in the physical sciences. When the new generation of physical theorists emerged—with Helmholtz, Hertz, and du Bois Reymond at their head, much of what counted as scientific positivism was aimed at eliminating these hypothetical atomistic and dynamic concepts (theories of forces), in psychology as well as in physics. Wundt and other early self-styled experimental psychologists did not abandon Fechner's dual aspect theory—on the contrary, they built on it. The first generation of self-styled experimental psychologists, however, wanted nothing to do with the *ontological* theories of their predecessors. They strongly opposed the dynamic and atomistic theories of Hartley, Erasmus Darwin, Herbart, Fechner, and Lotze. Thus, two opposite trends began to emerge: psychological theorists increasingly began to postulate unconscious processes, and yet these same theorists claimed to want a psychological science that clung as close as possible to the phenomena, and criticized earlier psychologists for their unfounded ontological assertions. In effect, *physical* positivism dominated, and it forced psychologists to *abandon* a *psychological* positivism, which would have militated against adopting the hypothesis of unconscious mental states and processes. The irony of theorists' proclaiming that they were sticking to the phenomena, while postulating unconscious (and unobservable) processes, was not lost on some thinkers (notably Brentano), but as we shall see, this inconsistency proved no barrier to transforming naturalistic metaphysics into a positive science.

R. H. LOTZE:
LAST OF THE NATURAL METAPHYSICIANS?

Traditional metaphysics died out for two reasons. First, in institutional terms, it was ill adapted for the increasingly professionalized and specialized academia that emerged all over Europe, at first slowly after 1848, and then more rapidly after 1871 (as will be discussed in the next chapter). Second, as professionalization increased, so did secularization, and appeals to either authority or intuition, which had both tacitly and explicitly guided the work of Cousin, Stewart, and others, could no longer succeed. Ultimately, agnosticism replaced transcendentalism among the professional elites, and traditional metaphysics was replaced by scientific positivism. This scientific positivism in its purest forms always maintained that the true nature of matter, the soul, or the deity was unknowable. In this regard scientific positivism should be distinguished from Comtean positivism, and even from Spencerian positivism, for both those thinkers imagined that they had more knowledge of the transcendental—of what Spencer incongruously chose to call the unknowable— than was considered possible by the agnostics.

Scientific positivism attained success in the latter part of the nineteenth century by allowing for the expansion of scientific activity without provoking direct conflict with religious doctrine. Thus, the ideology was well suited to a Europe still dominated by church-based institutions but increasingly reliant on scientific advances. Scientific positivism was however far better suited to maintaining rapprochement between *physical* science and religious orthodoxy than between biological or especially psychological science and mainstream religious beliefs.

Positivist physicists like Ernst Mach and Heinrich Hertz denied that science could give an account of the nature of any physical force. Instead, they argued, physics should be understood as providing a mathematical picture of nature only, but as making no claims about the true nature of force or matter. This view certainly made for a rapprochement between science and religion, but the same view has a different effect when psychophysics is interpreted positivistically. Psychophysics yields correlations between physical and mental states—such as the Weber Fraction—which can be expressed mathematically. In the positivistic interpretation, even though psychophysics can reveal nothing about the true nature of either mental or physical states, psychophysicists do search for laws constraining the relation between mental and physical states—for example, Fechner generalized the Weber Fraction into a psychophysical function describing sensory sensitivity—and many people regarded the claims about the discovery of laws in psychophysics as encroaching on the domain of religion.

The parallel with Charles Darwin is here quite striking. The scientific positivists (including Darwin's "bulldog," Huxley) argued that Darwin's results spoke neither for nor against belief in God. Positivists interpreted Darwin in the light of their agnosticism. How can one know, they asked, that the causes and effects lumped into the term *natural selection* do not have a deity as their hidden or transcendent cause? Darwin repeatedly resisted this line of argument, and for good reason. One of the key rationales for his theory was a critique of teleological biology, especially the argument from design. Darwin took seriously the claim that God had created the world. Unlike the positivists, he did not treat this claim as being untestable because beyond the bounds of our knowledge. On the contrary, he tried to determine what natural phenomena would be consistent with the hypothesis of creation, as opposed to what phenomena would be predicted by his own theory of natural selection. Time and again, Darwin found that the theory of creation was undermined by evidence, whereas the theory of natural selection was strongly supported by available evidence.

The best discussion of Darwin's argument against design can be found in the conclusion to his *Variation of Animals and Plants Under Domestication,* in which Darwin was responding to the well-developed version of the design hypothesis advanced by the noted botanist (and Darwin's good friend) Asa Gray. Gray postulated that even though evolution proceeded by natural selection, divine design might play a role by biasing or channeling genetic variation. Instead of chance, a deity might guide variation in certain directions, to preadapt animals and species to the rigors of new environments. Neither Darwin nor Gray argued, as scientific positivists then and now would have it, that such a hypothesis was unacceptable because it touched on the actions of the unknowable Deity. On the contrary, they examined the implications of this hypothesis of guided variation, and Darwin was able to show that none of the predictions that followed from the hypothesis were borne out. In this sense, both the younger Darwin and Asa Gray were natural metaphysicians, willing to test naturalized versions of even Deistic hypotheses, and unwilling to let themselves be hampered by positivist strictures about what counted as an acceptable scientific hypothesis.

Like Darwin, whose ideas are discussed further in Chapter 9, the natural metaphysicians of this era were inclined to try to specify how brain states caused mental states, or the reverse. Johannes Müller's hypothesis about specific nerve energies is an example of the former, and his idea that the soul plays on the motor cortex as if it were a piano keyboard is an example of the latter. Darwin was able to show that God does not design animals as people design clocks. Could a psychologist show that the soul does not move the body the way people move objects? An attempt was made by R. H. Lotze (1817–81), one of Müller's most cogent critics. Although Lotze criticized Müller, he could not bring himself to abandon teleological thinking in psychology, nor even belief in a deity acting in the world. In many ways Lotze is a transitional figure, developing a natural science of the soul that was never to be completed.

Lotze is transitional in a second sense as well. He was not a specialist, although he did become a professional academic. Trained originally in medicine, he studied with both the founders of psychophysics, Weber and Fechner, in Leipzig. Indeed, while he was teaching medicine and philosophy at Leipzig in the early 1840s, he also acted as Fechner's physician, helping the older theorist through a case of hysterical blindness. In 1844 Lotze was called to take Herbart's chair of philosophy at Göttingen, and in 1881 he was called to Berlin, but he died soon thereafter. He made his name in the 1840s with physiological works attacking Müllerian vitalism and proceeded in the 1850s to attack the emerging materialism from a position strikingly at variance with that of the ultimately more successful experimental psychologists.

Lotze's attack on vitalism was straightforward. Reliance on the notion of special powers or forces would prevent inquiry and encourage sloppy thinking. Lotze here relied on Weber and Fechner's concept of a science (based on physics): a science establishes quantitative laws relating phenomena. There is no "life force" but there are special and interesting phenomena of life, which can be analyzed and reduced to arrangements that obey the laws of nature.

Up to this point Lotze's arguments were in no way unique, although he was among the earliest to make them against Müller and against what Lotze saw as Schellingian or Romantic biology. Lotze's views did set him apart in the next stage of his thinking, summarized in his *Medicinische Psychologie* of 1852. Lotze now argued that the mind-body problem was resolvable. Both mind and matter could be treated as phenomena emanating from a single set of *forces,* not substances. Lotze pointed out that it is changes in forces acting upon us (for example, resistance) that make us believe in matter, and, he claimed, it is changes in a certain kind of force that make us believe in mental states as well. Later, in his *Metaphysics,* Lotze went so far as to claim, "We might . . . speak of the soul as a definite mass at every moment [and only at those moments] when it produces an effect measurable by the movement of a corporeal mass. And in doing so we should be taking none of its immateriality from it; for with bodies also it is not the case that they are first masses and then . . . produce effects; but according to the degree of their effects they are called masses of a certain magnitude." Here is an inversion of typical nineteenth-century positivism: because things are known only through their effects on us (phenomena) these things must be *forces* that give rise to phenomena.

Although Lotze's theory of a soul possessing mass at some times but not at others did not catch on, one of the implications he drew from the theory did indeed gain currency and continues to influence psychological theorizing. This was Lotze's concept of "local signs." On the basis of his theory of the soul, Lotze argued that the soul cannot be influenced by the spatial layout of the nervous system, but only by its intensity of activity at any given point. Building on Müller's earlier claim about localization, Lotze argued that cerebral activity in different locations did, as Müller suggested, produce different mental states (for example, activity in one region of the cortex generates visual sensations, in another region auditory sensations). But all the soul could know of this activity was its intensity, the locus of that intensity, and changes in intensity at that locus. The soul could not directly intuit spatial patterns of neural activity of varied intensity, as Müller had suggested. (If it could directly intuit such patterns, then the soul must perforce occupy space, but this was a contradiction in terms, for only matter is extended.) Knowledge of the locus of activity was the "local sign" of a mental state, which would coexist with knowledge of the intensity of that state, and of all changes in intensity of that state. As we have seen, associationists like Thomas Brown in Scotland had made similar arguments, claiming that the soul's activation of muscles would provide it with information about bodily loci that could be correlated with sensory input, but Lotze's theory was not associationist (except in the sense that it invoked an innate association), and it focused on cerebral activity, not a cycle of response–produces–sensory activity as in the theories of Brown or Bain. Also, whereas the associationists appealed to a *series* of sensations to yield information about space, Lotze claimed the local sign could be inherent in a single sensation. Lotze also emphasized that the mental processes involved here are unconscious, thus blocking introspective analyses of these ideas.

Various forms of the local sign theory (some much more associationist and empiricist than his) have exerted considerable influence in sensory physiology ever since Lotze's development of the notion. Interestingly, Lotze's other critique of Müller, also based on his theory of the soul, has been rather influential but much less widely acknowledged. In his magnum opus, *Microcosmos,* Lotze attempted to refute the teleological view of the soul as a kind of God within the body (vol. 1, p. 285), although he did not completely vanquish it.

> We deceive ourselves when with a favourite simile
> we compare the body to a ship—the soul to its

steersman. For the latter knows, or at least may know, the construction of that which he directs. . . . Far from possessing this comparatively perfect insight into the working of the machine, the soul, on the contrary, is like a subordinate workman, who knows indeed how to turn one end of a winch . . . but understands nothing whatever of the internal transference of movements by means of which a completed product is turned out.

Explicitly attacking Müller's analogy between the motor cortex and a piano keyboard, Lotze added that the soul (or mind) simply would not know what the notes were, nor where the keys for the different notes were placed. The soul "is ignorant of the relative situation of these notes, it knows not that this and not another note corresponds to the particular movement which it intends to make" (p. 203). Astonishingly, this important argument remained essentially unheard for nearly a century, although it has recently been taken up in discussions of motor control.

Lotze followed this argument up by asking what sort of information the soul might have about movement, and in doing so he anticipated James's theory that the willing of movements derives from memories of movements. "We bend our arm, not by giving a particular impetus to each of its several nerves, but by renewing in ourselves the image of the feeling which we experienced in a similar position" (*Microcosmos*, vol. 1, p. 305). Thus, for Lotze the soul can act within itself, calling up a memory or noticing a local sign, but it cannot act on the body. Instead, the soul's internal actions simply give rise to correlated bodily movements. He alludes here to something halfway between Leibniz's pre-established harmony and James's doctrine of ideomotor action. Somehow the soul's own actions lead to appropriate bodily actions; an idea of action causes the bodily effects. The soul "does not itself carry out the operation, but in a manner unknown to it the vital mechanism executes its commands" (*Microcosmos,* vol. 1, p. 303). Thanks to the doctrine of local signs, the soul can also learn about the body's pattern of responses to stimuli: even when the body is acting on its own, the soul can keep apprised of changes in activity at different loci and register the feelings associated with particular movements.

Lotze thus stands as the source of two very different developments in psychological science. On the one hand, students of motor and sensory physiology began their quest at this time to locate the neural pathways associated with local bodily activity. They were unconcerned with whether the soul was willing or perceiving while the body was engaged in those activities because they were intent on studying these purely bodily facts. Studies of how localized electrical stimulation of the cortex generates specific movement patterns are good examples of the attempts to examine how the "vital mechanism" translates mental cause into bodily effect. The *assumption* that the cerebral activity is tantamount to a "command" of the soul was still made, following Lotze, even though there could now be no question of mental content in that command, because the cerebral event was nothing more than the result of an experimenter's stimulus. What would be the mental content of an efferent pattern exciting contraction in a muscle unbeknownst to the subject? On the other hand, students of ideomotor behavior could analyze patterns of mental activity, asking questions about cause and effect among ideas (for instance, What causes an idée fixe or its accompanying obsessive behavior?) without concern for the neurophysiological substrate of this activity. Lotze's influence among practicing psychologists and neurophysiologists, although not acknowledged, seems to have been considerable.

Natural Metaphysics and
Experimental Psychology

Although the great mid-nineteenth-century attempts to create a science of the soul all failed, and although they are nowadays viewed as metaphysical, not naturalistic or scientific systems, they nevertheless exerted tremendous influence on the later so-called founders of scientific psychology. In fact, many members of the first generation of self-styled experimental psychologists in Germany incorporated elements of natural metaphysics into their work.

Even in their experimental activities, the later scientific psychologists were beholden to natural metaphysics. Fechner's extension of Weber's measurement techniques launched psychophysics as a key subdivision within psychology. Where Fechner used these methods to try to develop a theory of the nature of the soul and of the ontology of sensations, later psychologists focused on experimental design, measurement, and accuracy in mapping the correlations between stimulus and sensation.

Lotze's summary of earlier work on reflex action, including his controversy with Eduard Pflüger over whether the spinal cord was sentient, was also a major inspiration to later empirical workers. Yet, with the exception of Lewes, the later physiological psychologists contented themselves with analyzing the stimulus-response patterns of the reflexes and downplayed earlier interest in using these data to fashion a theory of sensation or of the soul. Shelley's science of wide circumference was being shrunk down to a positively narrow dimension.

One of the most important innovations in experimental psychology in fact came about when a student of one of the natural metaphysicians tried to test his teacher's theory. As was mentioned above, Helmholtz was extremely skeptical about Müller's theory that a special force exists in the nerves, with such properties as the instantaneous transmission of mental states. He thus undertook to measure the rate of transmission of nerve signals. Once this was established, other psychologists—especially Wundt and his students in Leipzig and Franciscus Donders in the Netherlands—invented methods for measuring the time course of some of the component processes of thought. To oversimplify slightly: once Helmholtz had ascertained the rate of action in nerves, the psychologists measured the total duration of a cognitive task (such as choosing a correct answer) and "subtracted out" the nerve transmission time, inferring that the remaining duration was ascribable to psychological, not neural, processes. Here again, the new generation of experimental psychologists was interested primarily in measurement, not in testing the nature of thought or developing a theory of the soul or mind. Later, positivistically oriented commentators have not been able to see that it was only because of the questions framed by the natural metaphysicians—which would not have been raised at all, had it not been for their metaphysical significance—that this form of experimental psychology emerged in the first place.

Natural metaphysics, thus shorn of its main theoretical concerns, was transformed into experimental psychology, in large part by a positivist impulse. The concepts and even some of the experimental procedures of earlier thinkers were retained, even though their primary concerns were ignored. But whereas the natural metaphysicians admitted—had to admit—that their concepts of mind, soul, sensation, and will were based on theory, the later, positivist-inspired experimentalists often pretended that their concepts were descriptive and owed nothing to theories about the nature of mind or the soul.

6

1848 and All That

The intellectual transformations of the 1840s were rapid and significant, but they pale in comparison with the socioeconomic and technological changes of that decade. The unprecedented developments in transportation and communication in those years were a major factor in the shaping of modern Europe. Railroads, transoceanic steamers, telegraphs, post offices, and modern roads all began to be built and used extensively during this period. The industrial revolution already had altered the landscape in Britain and Belgium and was beginning to do so in other places. Many cities experienced major growth in population. Modern social legislation (sanitary reforms, for example) began to be discussed and even implemented. Such reform movements made possible the expansion, over the next three decades, in the tier of professional workers in national bureaucracies, including teachers and educators at the secondary and tertiary level.

None of the revolutions that erupted across Europe from the Atlantic Ocean to the Ural Mountains in 1848–49 succeeded in its stated aim. "Democracy," as historian Jerome Blum puts it, "was held in equal contempt with socialism and communism by conservatives and liberals alike" (*In the Beginning*, p. 41). Yet none of these mass movements could be ignored. Everywhere the revolution was defeated, but in many places political and social reforms began to be implemented.

Although no new democracies emerged anywhere in Europe, the revolutions by no means failed to change the social scene.

The failure of the democratic populist uprisings of 1848–49 finally relieved many rulers' fears of being overthrown. Across Europe, ruling classes had handily resisted the revolutionists, and rather quickly, at that. Furthermore, the practical effect of 1848 was an increasing alliance between the old ruling classes and the new middle classes—and this alliance had an immediate and significant effect on intellectual activity. To put it baldly, the importance of theology as an ideological enterprise to keep academic opinion in line was discredited in favor of a view of the world, and even of the intellectual scene, based primarily on economics. To run post-Chartist Britain or the emerging Prussia or the France of the Second Empire required merchants, bankers, scientists, technologists, and educators in unprecedented numbers. As Eric Hobsbawm has pointed out, the decades after 1848 were a time in which evolutionary, not revolutionary, thought flourished in the increasingly industrial and bourgeois cities of Europe. The new middle class was much less fettered by traditional religious orthodoxies and was indeed developing an ideology in which European Man [*sic*] was to be seen as the pinnacle of evolutionary development.

This modernist, and positivist, and historically "progressivist" view took several decades to evolve. Nor did the revolutions bring in a period of general cultural liberalization; on the contrary, even in supposedly liberal countries the conservative reaction only gradually—very gradually—thawed. In Britain, which of course had had no revolution, the government nevertheless declared it a felony to advocate the formation of a republic. Hippolyte Taine's (1828–93) experience shows both that the Second Empire was no place for intellectual freedom and that times were changing. Taine studied at the Ecole Normale Supérieure from 1848 to 1851, and although he was first in his class, he failed his aggrégation because of a thesis defending Spinoza's ideas on the relation of the mind to the body. Nevertheless, by the 1880s Taine was a venerated thinker and Spinoza's views on the dual aspect of the mind-body problem were among the most widely accepted in Europe.

To understand how scientific psychology emerged in the second half of the nineteenth century, we must be careful not to lose track of more general cultural transformations. Intellectual changes by no means always parallel social or institutional changes, but the two nevertheless need to be seen together. Part of what transformed both psychology and philosophy into the disciplines we now know was major changes in the nature of the universities and the intellectual professions. These changes made possible both an increasingly "professional" perspective on many intellectual problems and an overtly positivist approach to previously sensitive metaphysical issues.

OFFICIAL VERSUS UNOFFICIAL PSYCHOLOGY AFTER 1848

As we saw in Chapter 4, the official psychology of the traditional metaphysicians was already moribund by 1848. This can be demonstrated merely by listing the most distinguished defenders of traditional metaphysics circa 1840 across the European continent: Frederic Bouterwek, Victor Cousin, Immanuel Fichte, William Hamilton, Theodore Jouffroy, and William Whewell. Who but a specialist has heard these names, or knows what they stood for? Herbert Schnädelbach, in his *Philosophy in Germany, 1831–1933* (p. 3), writes: "The same cholera to which Hegel succumbed drove Arthur Schopenhauer from Berlin, putting an end to his academic career: thus, the year 1831 also symbolizes the departure from the university of those elements in the philosophical thought of the time which still have a direct influence in our day. Ludwig Feuerbach, Marx, Engels, Kierkegaard, Nietzsche—not one of them was any longer a professor of philosophy in the way that Kant, Fichte, Schelling, and Hegel had been."

Thus, even in the German-speaking cities and states (for nothing like the modern German state existed in 1848), where there were far more universities than anywhere else, official thought was no longer as dynamic as unofficial thought. At the same time, the general cultural transformations—increases in numbers of professionals, new intellectual societies and periodicals, better communications and transportation—helped intellectuals everywhere in Europe glimpse just how besieged official thought was.

It is only toward the end of the century, with the rise of British Idealism, German neo-Kantianism, and Pragmatism, that the official thought disseminated by the universities and churches begins to regain something of its leadership role. Hence, if it is true that scientific psychology was born during the 1860s and 1870s, modern philosophy as we know it had not then emerged from the confusions of midcentury. Modern scientific psychology got off to a successful start at a time of considerable intellectual and institutional turmoil and was often, as we shall see, a step ahead of modern philosophy in establishing an institutional structure.

THE ORIGIN OF HYPNOTISM

As we have seen, although the official schools of philosophy exerted little influence outside academia and the church in the 1840s, unofficial thought was thriving. In politics, this was the period of great ferment in socialist thought. It was also a period of considerable controversy in the study of mesmerism and phrenology. Many thinkers, like Dods, were trying to unite the two approaches. And moves were afoot to have mesmerism, phrenology, or both replace the traditional metaphysics of the schools. Like the revolutions of 1848, these gambits fell short of their most important goal, but they nevertheless had a significant effect on the intellectual world.

What made the greatest impact was the proof that animal magnetism and mesmerism were not physical processes but were in fact based on psychological processes. Already in 1834 Johann Jung-Stilling's *Theory of Pneumatology* proclaimed that animal magnetism proved the existence of the soul as a force in nature (hence the title). Jung-Stilling's views were a variant of natural metaphysics, because he held that the soul was literally an immortal spirit, a "divine spark," and not made of baser stuff.

In response to Jung-Stilling, John Elliotson (1791–1868) defended a materialist view of mesmerism in his popular textbook, *Human Physiology* (1835). Elliotson, a proponent of phrenology as well as animal magnetism, was one of the innovators who used animal magnetism as a form of analgesia and anesthesia in the 1830s and 1840s. Elliotson held the chair of medicine at University College, London, in the 1830s but was forced to stop mesmerizing patients in 1838 because of a scandal conerning his involvement with two sisters who had become his star demonstrators of magnetism. In protest, Elliotson resigned his chair. Despite his fall from official grace, Elliotson enjoyed considerable popularity and maintained a very successful private practice (treating, as well as befriending, such luminaries as Dickens, whom he trained to be a competent magnetizer). The possibilities inherent in a professional career were now such that a determined individual would not be squelched by official disapproval. Elliotson went on to launch a periodical, the *Zoist: A Journal of Cerebral Physiology and Mesmerism and Their Application to Human Welfare* (1843–56), which was, among other things, a literary rallying place for social reformers.

Interestingly, despite Elliotson's general successes, he had some difficulties with the phrenologists. His attempt to found a phrenomagnetic society was scuttled by the majority of London phrenologists—many of whom, such as the very influential George Combe (1788-1858), were adherents of traditional metaphysics. The phrenologists looked down on mesmerism precisely to the extent that it was touted as being based on material forces, such as animal magnetism. Elliotson's belief that mesmerism was a medical practice based in a material, scientific reality undermined any serious rapprochement between the two groups, mesmerists and phrenologists.

Elliotson believed that the fact that a patient in magnetic sleep appeared to feel no pain, even from a surgical procedure, was proof positive of the physical reality of animal magnetic force. It was also in the 1840s, however, that James Braid (1795-1860) and others introduced controlled experiments into the study of mesmerism and discovered that no physical agency was involved in the process. Even when used as an anesthetic, then, mesmeric trances were psychological processes, not the result of an unknown physical force. Braid coined the term *neurypnotism,* later modified to *hypnotism,* to refer to these psychological processes. Braid analyzed the psychological forces, calling attention to phenomena we would now label suggestibility and obsessive thinking. He argued that hypnotism would prove to be an important medical tool for all cases of illness in which the symptoms had no physical causes.

Although Braid himself was something of a natural metaphysician, who tried to undergird his psychological analysis with a neurophysiological theory, the success of his critique of the physical basis of animal magnetism heralded a great spiritualist revival in the mid-1800s. Braid had shown that a supposedly physical process was in fact psychological. He had not denied the phenomenon of mesmeric trance, but he had shown that even a powerful phenomenon such as anesthesia could be produced as a psychological effect. What other phenomena supposedly based on physical forces might prove to have a psychological basis? Could dream states, trances, and even inebriation be seen as evidence for the effects of spirit on matter and not the other way around? The rapid spread of séances, spirit rapping, and related practices after the 1850s may not be tied directly to Braid's work, but it was definitely interpreted in this spiritualist, antimaterialist context. Unfortunately, the story of spiritualism is so convoluted that in this book I shall only allude to it, primarily to remind the reader of its importance as a social force and significant intellectual trend. Spiritualism as a scientific worldview—and however odd this sounds to us now, this is surely what spiritualism represented for such people as A. R. Wallace and Arthur Conan Doyle—is a subject whose proper analysis would require a whole book.

WILL, MATTER, AND PSYCHOLOGY

The successes of the psychological interpretation of animal magnetism caused a major shift in psychological theorizing in midcentury. Whereas traditional metaphysics tended to place issues of cognition at the center of the study of the mind, the psychological theorists of midcentury placed *volition* front and center. For many thinkers, hypnotism had replaced animal magnetism; that is, the belief that one person could control another's mental state had replaced belief that some physical agency created a physiological state of magnetic sleep. To some it appeared not only that the mind was stronger than the body but that, properly directed, the force of a hypnotizer's mind could impose itself on the subject's mind.

One of the major intellectual effects of these novel ideas was a revival of earlier theories of the will. The work of Arthur Schopenhauer, which had been largely ignored, began in the early 1850s to be debated all across Europe. Similarly, the theories of Maine de Biran, which had been known only to a small coterie, became very influential, at least in France, in the 1850s and 1860s. Both Schopenhauer and Maine de Biran had emphasized that volition precedes knowledge, and both—but Schopenhauer especially—had also emphasized that much of what happens when we exercise our will is hidden from our conscious mind.

Theorists like Thomas Brown or James Mill considered volition to be little more than the *connection of an idea with an action*. It was assumed that it was always possible to observe our own volitions and that these volitions had a causal power on our actions. For example, the *idea* of reaching to grab something, when considered as a volition, was supposed to be the cause of reaching and grabbing. These ideas as volitions were supposedly acquired through experience, just as all other ideas were: through association of clusters of sensory ideas.

In the 1850s this theory was turned around in a subtle but significant way. Herbert Spencer (1820–1903) and Alexander Bain both argued that will is primary, action secondary, and knowledge tertiary. Following one strand in Thomas Brown's thinking, these theorists argued that our ideas of the external world —regarded by earlier thinkers as sensory ideas—derive from whatever *resists* our attempts at action. If we try to reach and grab but something resists our arm movement, then this something must be an external object, not a part of ourselves. It was a cross-fertilization of these will-based theories with the methodological developments of natural metaphysics that gave birth to the first generation of German experimental psychologists.

Wilhelm Wundt (1832–1920) in particular was very influenced by this voluntarist version of English associationist psychology. Like the British theorists, Wundt made the autonomous action of the mind a centerpiece in his psychology. He took from Lotze the interpretation of reflexes and animal behavior as basic psychological elements (that is, psychological atoms requiring unification via will or psychological effort of some sort). From Fechner he took the idea of controlled psychophysical experimentation and measurement. Wundtian experimental psychology was thus both experimental and introspective. Further, Wundt's interpretation of introspective states was always made with one eye toward his theory of psychological atoms and one eye toward his theory of volition as an integrative force.

Thus, the self-proclaimed new experimental psychologists could and did argue that they needed not resolve the metaphysical problems of previous theorists, such as the mind-body problem. The new experimental psychology rested in part on the "phenomena" made available through the controlled introspection of early experimental psychology and in part on the phenomena revealed in the physiological laboratory. This strategy is nicely illustrated in the acknowledged masterpieces of the genre, both by the great German scientist Herman von Helmholtz (1821-94), with whom the young Wundt had studied.

In the 1850s and 1860s Helmholtz experimented extensively on both sight and hearing, and collected his research into two books that would forever change the study of perception: *The Sensations of Tone* (1864) and *Handbook of Physiological Optics* (1867). Both books followed the same pattern: first a careful physical analysis of the stimuli for hearing (acoustic energy) or sight (optical energy), then an atomistic physiological analysis to get at the supposed *sensory elements* of those senses (for instance, our sensations of tone or light), and finally, introspectively interpreted experiments on perception considered as an integration of those elements—an integration often said to be accomplished by unconscious mental processes. Helmholtz's reliance on will or mental acts is more attenuated than Wundt's, but still crucial to his endeavor. Introspection rarely reveals the hypothetical sensory elements Helmholtz derived from his physiological analysis, so Helmholtz suggested that the mind acts unconsciously to integrate or modify those elements. This is his famous doctrine of unconscious conclusions, or as it is more popularly known, *unconscious inference.* Certain areas are especially problematic, such as trying to account for how we see a three-dimensional world even though the retinal image is flat. In analyzing these problems, Helmholtz also appeals directly to the processes of resistance to volition championed by Spencer and Bain.

Dualism or Trialism?

In effect, the new psychology developed a new dualism. In Cartesian dualism, mental states are always and necessarily conscious. There can be no unconscious inferences, because an inference, by definition, is a mental act, and by definition, we are always aware of our mental acts. Helmholtz, Wundt, and the other new psychologists *redefined mental life* to include its unobservable aspects. They needed to do this because their various hypotheses about mental life were easily refuted by careful introspection, so they either had to explain why such refutations were not a problem, abandon introspection entirely, or admit they were wrong. In addition to an increasing emphasis on volition as a basic psychological force, the new psychologists thus also launched a period of broad speculation about the unconscious mind—a new dualism between conscious and unconscious mental life.

But the widespread acceptance of the existence of unconscious states ultimately led to a kind of *three-way* division of the psychological world, a trialism, not a dualism. There were now the conscious mind, the unconscious mind, and the body. In many ways, the widely held distinction between the conscious mind and the body simply echoed orthodox Cartesianism: the conscious mind is always active and thinking; the body is simply a physiological machine. But what could the unconscious mind be? It certainly had connections to the body, but it did not act like a machine; in some ways, it seemed as if it could think or will, but if it were thinking or willing, then even its "owner" was ignorant of what was going on.

One of the most popular interpretations of the unconscious mind in the late 1800s was that it was neither pure (conscious) mind not pure (mechanical) body but was, in fact, the soul. To the modern ear this sounds strained and suspiciously like special pleading, but that is largely owing to the benefit of hindsight.

Consider some of the basic features of the unconscious mind: dreaming, hypnotic suggestibility, unintended actions or slips; then consider also the surge in popularity of séances, trances, and other spiritualist activity, also associated with the unconscious mind. In this context, the notion of an intimate connection between the unconscious and the soul has a certain plausibility. The romantic idea that our souls are somehow bigger than we are, that they contain thoughts and capacities not evident in ordinary life, provided a powerful motivation for believing in the possibility that precognition, telepathy, and other unusual powers occurred during trances and other states of altered consciousness.

Wundt and the other "new psychologists" wanted merely to prove the existence of the mind and to develop a science for the study of mental activity. Because of this, they were very wary of the concept of the unconscious. In contrast, spiritualists, and later, psychic researchers like Fredric Myers (1843–1901) and William James (1842–1910), wanted to prove the existence of the soul, and to develop a science for studying its activity. They saw in unconscious states one possible avenue for that study. In effect, the "mind" psychologists wanted to banish as much of

Shelley's erotic experience from the mind as possible, placing it in the body. They tended to limit the functions of the unconscious to those of habit and memory, and to interpret those as correlated with bodily changes. In contrast, the soul psychologists saw the unconscious as an integral part of the self, including much of what Freud was later to call the nighttime psychological states—not just the daylight states studied by the emerging mainstream psychologists.

From Metaphysics to Positivism

The proponents of soul psychology at midcentury tended to be allied not with the heterodoxies later propounded by a James or a Freud, but with orthodox Protestantism. Bolstered by the success of hypnotism over animal magnetism and intrigued by the spiritualist revival, many Christian thinkers tried to revitalize Cousin's theory of a spiritual intuition as the foundation of mind. Maybe science based on external perception would reveal a mechanical world—as it seemed to be doing—but a thoughtful psychological science, one that attended to such odd phenomena as intuition, unconscious states, trances, and so on, might uncover some different truths.

A good example of this tendency was the London Metaphysical Society (1869–80)—which was originally to be called the Metaphysical and Psychological Society. Founded by James Knowles (editor of the *Nineteenth Century*), Alfred, Lord Tennyson, and others, including both theologians (Archbishop Manning) and scientists (Thomas H. Huxley, William B. Carpenter, William K. Clifford), the society was intended as a debating club focusing on a set of topics very much up in the air in those days. Among the topics mentioned in the club's bylaws were: the immateriality of the soul, the nature of miracles, the efficacy of prayer, the personality of God, and the nature of conscience. Perhaps this was the last time when serious scientists were engaged in analysis not of Christian faith or dogma, but of the supposed *phenomena* on which Christianity is based: resurrection, miracles, immortality, and efficacious prayer.

Many of the Christians in this group espoused a form of natural metaphysics. For example, Archbishop Manning believed that the existence of conscience was evidence of our soul's contact with God. William Carpenter (a devout Unitarian and, as we have seen, an important physiologist) argued that the interchangeability of natural forces was evidence that mind created the universe. While the liberal Christians spoke of evidence for these mysteries, however, the liberal scientists spoke of the lack of sufficient evidence to decide the question. Thomas Huxley held that as physiology progressed, it would give decisive answers even to such questions as what the source of intuition and conscience was—and these answers would take the mystery out of the phenomena.

Huxley, like all the other scientists in the group—and like almost all scientists in Europe or America at that time—was not a materialist, despite his belief in the progress of mechanistic physiology. He argued in two directions: one from the external phenomena of science (say, the data of physiology) and the other from introspective phenomena (for example, our belief in our own free will). He was inclined to believe that most (or all) introspectively revealed phenomena would prove to be caused by externally revealed ones. But in any event he was a phenomenalist, arguing that what is real is phenomena. If the soul (or the unconscious) is not real, it is because it is not part of the phenomenal world.

This panphenomenalism was widely labeled positivism when it was propounded by scientists. In the loosely defined meaning of the term, positivism dominated the European intellectual scene from approximately 1870 to 1890. Yet that type of positivism is inherently *unstable* when applied to psychology. The externalist (physiological) analysis of behavior and mind attributes all psychological states to antecedent causes. Introspective analysis reveals both intuitions of freedom and the appearance of autonomous psychological states. The two seem irreconcilable.

Irreconcilable or not, experimental psychologists like Wundt and many others were beginning to develop ways to *measure* the conflict between external and introspective phenomena. Studies of reaction time, for example, purported to measure exactly how much time it took a person to make a mental decision. Here was yet another kind of positivism — a way of studying, and even of measuring, the phenomena of the mind without concern for what the mind is. The analysis of the phenomena of the human mind no longer meant description of conscious mental contents, and it certainly no longer meant an account of the mind as a natural entity; it meant instead the analysis of the hypothetical and inferred states and processes of the unconscious mind, as the basis of available introspective data.

It is striking that almost all of the innovations associated with the new psychology preceded, by approximately one academic generation, what is typically thought of as the new psychology. In addition, even the experimental innovations of the new psychologists — clearly their strongest claim to originality — seem to have come about in the preceding generation. And, I would argue, most of these innovations can be attributed to that group of thinkers I have dubbed the natural metaphysicians.

Perhaps the three key areas of experimental work on which the new psychology rested were: 1) studies of reflex function; 2) reaction-time experiments, often based on inferences drawn from the study of reflexes and their timing; and 3) psychophysical studies. The basic experimental work on reflex function was carried out by natural metaphysicians such as Müller in the German-speaking world and Marshall Hall in Britain. Reaction time as a subject of study emerged from attempts by Müller's students to refute his concept of a nerve force, leading primarily to careful measurements of the speed of neural transmission and secondarily to experiments designed to "factor out" the duration of mental events (attention, decision) in excess of the neural transmission time. As we have seen, psychophysics was invented by Fechner as part of his attempt to bolster natural metaphysics.

Wundt, the nominal founder of the new psychology, aggressively pursued all three of these experimental paradigms. But he did so in a spirit quite removed from Müller's or even Lotze's. He avoided the ontological questions that natural metaphysicians placed at the heart of their enterprise. Experiment for Wundt was an aid to description, in which precision and measurement played the key role, not the testing of general hypotheses about the nature of mind. Wundt did not reject those general questions, but he tended to relegate them to fields other than experimental psychology.

Yet, despite his best methodological intentions, Wundt never quite purified his psychology of its origins in natural metaphysics. Throughout his career he appealed to the will as a kind of unobservable organizing force. (One can observe what the will effects, but not the will itself in action.) Apperception—the process through which an observer actively attends to and thereby organizes sensory feelings—was both central to Wundt's theorizing and notoriously difficult to pin down. It is for this reason that thinkers of the next generation tended to group Wundt with Fechner and Lotze. For example, Ralph Barton Perry in *Philosophy of the Recent Past* (1926) called Wundt a spiritual realist—largely on the basis of Wundt's ideas about the will—and identified Wundt with Lotze, Fechner, and even Eduard von Hartmann. Later, as psychologists increasingly avoided the ontological questions about mind, soul, and nature, they came interpret Wundt's theory more positivistically, by focusing on his experimental projects, ignoring many of his theoretical statements, and attending too seriously to the special pleading of his student Edward B. Titchener, who himself attempted to launch a school of explicitly positivist experimental psychologists. It is only in the past two decades that the complex nature of Wundt's project has been properly appreciated by psychologists and historians of psychology.

Psychology, Logic, and the Science of Science

With all the uncertainty over the status of both physical and psychological entities, it became increasingly common for intellectuals to reflect on the nature of science itself. These reflections were also spurred on by the rapid pace of technological change at the time.

Already in the 1830s and 1840s, William Whewell and John Stuart Mill were debating what constituted a science. Mill's *Logic* (1843) is as much an essay on the nature of science—including social science—as it is a study of inference. In part as a response to Mill's influence, a German neo-Kantian revival began in the 1850s and picked up steam over the next two decades. The neo-Kantians admired Mill for taking on the problem of science, although they tended to disagree with him over methodology.

Thus Kant's method of "critique" was interpreted by some mid-nineteenth-century writers as calling for a science of science, which could show us how to separate true knowledge and truth-preserving methods from falsehoods and confusion. This *Erkenntnislehre*, as it came to be known, usurped and transformed much of the popular positivist impulse and guided it toward technical philosophy. The proponents of technical philosophy increasingly allied themselves with scientists, and many of them doubtless had hopes of turning philosophy itself into a kind of science of science. Friedrich A. Lange (1828–75) wrote, in 1858: "My logic is calculus of probabilities, my ethics are moral states, my psychology rests on physiology; in a word, I try to operate only within the exact sciences. A critique of psychology in which the greater part of this 'science' is demonstrated to be idle chatter and self-deception, and [which would] form a sequel to Kant's *Critique of Pure Reason* is the book I would most like to write."

The book Lange did write, his *History of Materialism* (1865–66) was in many ways precisely such a sequel to Kant. From a twentieth-century perspective it is therefore surprising to find out that the brunt of Lange's attack is against the *materialists:* it is the materialists, not the spiritualists or the traditional metaphysicians, whom Lange accuses of confusion and idle chatter. Lange deploys a neo-Kantian dialectic but ends up echoing Dugald Stewart! Lange uses a neo-Kantian Erkenntnislehre to try to show that the theses of the so-called vulgar materialists of the 1850s simply could not be proved.

Yet, as we saw in the earlier discussion of John Abercrombie and Dugald Stewart, such materialist claims cannot be *disproved* either, as Lange should have known. Indeed, this is one of Kant's points in the section on the antinomies of reason in his *First Critique.* In this analysis, Kant shows that where our concepts produce real contradictions—such as unconscious mental states—it is always possible to prove *both* that an assertion is true *and* that it is false. The problem is not a matter of evidence, but of muddled thinking. Kant himself never claimed that he had anything like a scientific procedure for ferreting out such antinomies, and he would have scorned the idea that his method of critique could be turned into some kind of scientific procedure, a science for finding sciences, as it were. The neo-

Kantians, like Lange, were much less restrained and came close to asserting that, properly construed, (neo-Kantian) philosophy is in fact a science of science.

By the 1890s and later, the movement toward professionalizing philosophy and the insurgent *Erkenntnistheorie* was gaining strength. Philosophers who wanted to create a nonexperimental science—a kind of critique that relied on analysis and conception, not on experience or facts—began to use not only the neo-Kantian rationale but also the emerging tools of symbolic logic. Gottlob Frege and Charles Peirce, whose work created little stir in the 1870s and 1880s, now were seen as major figures in the emergence of a new philosophy. In the following chapters I trace the outlines of the battle between the positivists and the natural metaphysicians, a battle that led to the foundation of two new disciplines, psychology and philosophy.

7

The Three Unconsciousnesses
and How They Grew

The idea of unconscious mental processes, or even of *the* unconscious as an entity, was by no means original with Freud. Many thinkers throughout the nineteenth century pondered the nature of the unconscious. The unconscious of the Romantics, however—especially that of Schelling and *Naturphilosophie,* which so influenced German literature—was as much ontological as psychological. In a theory that defies easy description, many Romantics equated the physical forces (fluids?) of electricity and magnetism with irrational urges and vague feelings, feelings such as those of unity with nature or longings for oneness and sexual satisfaction. Despite his loathing for Schelling and Fichte, Schopenhauer clearly proposed his theory of a carnal will as an ontological response to the irrationalism these writers were parading as a successor to Kant's philosophy.

With philosophers, speculative physicists, doctors, mesmerists, and animal magnetizers all claiming to offer an analysis of the unconscious and its role in human life, is it any wonder that the church-vetted professors of philosophy blanched at the idea of a scientific psychology? Anything that looked even remotely like a scientific study of human nature—especially any such science that focused on our physical embodiment and carnal reality—seemed to emphasize sensuality and our animal nature too much for comfort. The repeated emphasis of traditional metaphysics on introspection as the sole safe method of proceeding in the philosophy of mind or moral philosophy in effect created a boundary between sober science and unsafe speculation. The use of physiological methodologies, which we now see as forerunners of a true, progressive psychology, was equated with worrisome, unsafe ideas about the irrational nature of the human soul.

From the Study of Mind to the Analysis of the Unconscious

Mainstream psychological theory from 1815 to 1830 had been committed to the existence of a conscious individual soul, from which all mental phenomena could be derived. Evidence of the existence and nature of mental and moral phenomena was to be based on introspection. Nevertheless, even introspection raised some questions about how wisely and well God had made our souls. The phenomena of dreams and drunkenness showed obvious ways in which the mind could be made to wander down dark pathways. Increased social awareness about the insane and increasing concern with the boundaries of sanity raised further issues. And if *physical* agencies were not involved in mesmerism, then did that mean that some *psychological* force like suggestion was more powerful than our souls? If God gave each of us a soul, how could a hypnotist apparently dominate another person's thought, will, and action?

At least three separate strands emerged in midcentury for the understanding of what we would now call unconscious mental states. These strands were: 1) supernaturalism; 2) naturalistic theories; and 3) theories of the unconscious mind. In the supernaturalist line of thought, the unconscious continued to be treated ontologically and was often associated with Kant's noumenal world — a sort of hyper-real world that lurked behind the everyday world of appearances. I call this the supernatural unconscious. According to this theory, actions that people take without consciously willing them, or even make in opposition to their conscious thoughts, are treated as being caused by forces that cannot be observed. In this view, the unconscious is not part of the world explained by science—not part of Kant's phenomenal realm—but is instead noumenal. A different group of theorists refused, however, to treat the unconscious as qualitatively different from other natural psychological phenomena, although some thinkers were willing to invent hypothetical natural forces to explain the unconscious, such as animal magnetism and the theory that a mysterious "Odilic" force explained all forms of trance.

There were two strands in theorizing about what I shall call the natural unconscious. The first kind of theory about the natural unconscious focused on unconscious ideas or mental states: it was inferred through introspection that a particular mental state had to have occurred, even though introspection did not reveal the idea. When someone calls our name and wakes us up, for example, we may have no recollection of hearing our name spoken and yet may have unconsciously registered the voice. In the second form of this theory about the natural unconscious, the existence of an entire unconscious mind, separated off from the conscious mind, was inferred. The contrast is important. Herbart, for example, hypothesized that we have many unconscious ideas and to a large degree invented the modern concept of threshold, taken over to such good effect by Weber and Fechner to explain what happened when unconscious ideas come into consciousness. But Herbart envisaged conscious ideas only; he did not believe in the existence of an entire unconscious mind, or part of the mind. Herbart would have been scandalized at Fechner's claim that the "world soul" was aware of all subthreshold sensations, or at later psychologists' promiscuous references to unconscious mental states.

The third kind of theory of the unconscious, which I shall

call the theory of the unconscious mind, was the most radically different from its predecessors. Whereas something like the notion of unconscious ideas can be found as early as the late seventeenth century in the work of Leibniz, and whereas many thinkers had been willing to postulate the existence of parts of the soul not easily accessible to rational consciousness, all prior theories had treated the unconscious as existing *in opposition* to the conscious soul. In particular, these theorists tended to treat the conscious soul as the rational soul of Christian dogma, and the unconscious as irrational and certainly incapable of rational thought. Indeed, where theorists had been inclined to see rational activity of an unconscious sort, they had unanimously attributed it to *God's mind,* not to the minds of individuals.

In the 1750s, as we have seen, Whytt had argued that the "sensitive soul" in the spinal cord was capable of feeling noxious stimuli and acting in whatever way necessary to remove the potential danger to the organism (he had in mind the capacity of a pithed frog, with no brain but with an intact spinal cord, to wipe away the irritation of an acid-soaked tissue placed on its skin). But Whytt emphasized the great difference between this and the rational soul we know through consciousness, which can feel and think many different things. All Whytt's sensitive soul can do is whatever God has arranged for it to do in order to preserve our bodies and maintain a harmony among the parts of our organism. More than half a century before Whytt, Malebranche had argued that unconscious phenomena are in fact instances of *God's* thinking, not of an individual's thinking. What Whytt had seen as a God-given ability of the spinal cord to relate stimuli to responses via a kind of unconscious feeling Malebranche saw as an instance of God's feeling and acting through our bodies to enable us to preserve those bodies.

As of 1830, the unconscious was considered to be either a supernatural or a natural source of irrational forces; when rational but nonconscious acts occurred, they were attributed not to the individual, but to his or her Maker. John Stuart Mill changed all this by hypothesizing that there must exist an unconscious mind *in individuals* that acts, at least in part, rationally. He had to make such an unusual hypothesis to salvage the associationist psychology that his father had championed and that he himself hoped to use as the foundation of all social theory. The younger Mill, in one of those delicious ironies of history, was thus simultaneously the great champion of introspectionism and empiricism in psychology and also the theorist who paved the way for the more radical theories of the unconscious mind that began to emerge in the 1860s and 1870s.

A Logical Unconscious

Mill's immensely influential version of the theory of the unconscious mind derived from his novel notion that the unconscious mind might work on the same psychological principles as the conscious mind. In honor of Mill's *Logic,* let us call this the doctrine of the logical unconscious. Starting with his discussion of mental powers in the *Logic* (1843) Mill argued that some nonconscious mental processes are identical with, or at least resemble, the process of drawing inferences and making judgments. Whereas Leibniz, Whytt, and others suggested that we might have unconscious *feelings* or *perceptions*—and of course Mill himself recognized that we can have feelings or perceptions to which we do not attend—Mill went much further and claimed that there are also rational intellectual processes within our unconscious minds. (The only previous theorist to have considered the possibility of such unconscious logical activity—

Malebranche—had, as was mentioned earlier, taken any signs of unconscious rationality as evidence for God's activity, not the activity of individual minds.)

The logical unconscious emerged in the writings of John Stuart Mill because he was fighting the battle for associationist psychology on two separate fronts. He was engaged in defending and improving his father's associationism while also developing a general logical theory consistent with that associationist psychology. Although historians have tended to identify the doctrine of "unconscious inference" in the 1850s and 1860s with Germany (especially in the work of Helmholtz and Wundt), Mill's *Logic* is almost certainly the source of that doctrine, and we know that it was read by Helmholtz and Wundt and other prominent German psychologists. (It is also probable that Mill's defense of associationism against Samuel Bailey, originally published at the same time as his *Logic* and reprinted in 1859, were also known to the German psychologists.)

The proponents of the logical unconscious often harked back to earlier ideas, especially Leibniz's notion of *petites perceptions*, as the inspiration for their thinking. But the resemblance is superficial, for it does not take into account the difference between unconscious feelings and unconscious ratiocination— between the well-known (if not always accepted) notion of an irrational unconscious, and the radical idea of a rational unconscious.

In working on what was to become his book on logic, John Stuart Mill faced a set of problems that had yet to be addressed within associationist psychology. In particular, the epistemological context of the younger Mill's work made it imperative for him to identify the supposed sources of our knowledge of truths. One of the passages of the *Logic* known to have been written near the outset of the work and which remained essentially unchanged through eight editions is the following comment from the fourth section of the introduction: "Truths are known to us in two ways: some are known directly, and of themselves; some through the medium of other truths. The former are the subject of Intuition or Consciousness; the latter, of Inference." By focusing on how truths are known, Mill changed the status of sensations within associationist epistemology. For Hartley, Condillac, James Mill, and others, what we call sensations formed the basis of all knowledge, including knowledge of truths, and no sharp line was drawn between sensations as a truth of consciousness and other truths, called inferences by the younger Mill. After Mill's work, associationists had to offer an account of these truths of inference that differed from their account of truths of intuition (sensation).

The consequences of Mill's distinction here are of profound importance for psychology. If Mill's distinction is taken as a basis for theorizing, then the first step in any account of a psychological process is to discover what intuitions are available to subjects. Once a complete list of intuitions is made, then other putative knowledge must be inferentially based on these intuitions—either false or true inferences. Mill thus turned sensations into something not unlike the premises in logical arguments. Foreshadowings of Mill's distinction appear in Berkeley's concept of minimum sensibles, and in his notion that these sensibles are a language of sorts—but neither for Berkeley nor for later writers was the issue one of truth and inference, as Mill was to see it. Logic, for Mill, is the study of the inferences we make from truths that are already known. This is the source of Mill's psychologism, his belief that logic cannot be distinguished as a special science independent of the results of the psychology of sensation and perception.

Before Mill, associationists postulated the existence of sensations and their combination into various ideas, both true and false. In the earlier associationist writings there was no necessary relationship between "sensations" and "intuitions" of truth. Some theorists seemed to believe in a more or less fixed repertoire of innate sensations, but these innate elements of consciousness took on their logical and metaphysical significance only after Mill's distinction between intuition and inference became commonplace.

Mill's careful attempt to distinguish between sensation and inference was in large part a response to the Scottish commonsense psychologists and their emphasis on intuition, or what many of them preferred to call consciousness. (John Stuart Mill used the term, grudgingly, in a similar way.) But there is an important inversion here: in Thomas Reid's epistemology, the truths of intuition are *not* identical with sensations. On the contrary, Reid invented the distinction between sensation and perception largely so that he might attribute truth to *perceptions,* not to sensations (or, in Mill's jargon, intuitions). To put it simply, Reid was less interested in whether my sensation of the color red is true than in whether my perception of this rose as an existing object (which happens to look red) is true. Reid argued that what is true in consciousness includes my perception of the rose as well as any sensation of the color or scent that I might also have. This distinction between two aspects of consciousness, sensation and perception, was considerably muddled by the 1830s, when Mill was working on his logic. William Hamilton, the last great proponent of the Scottish philosophy, never understood Reid on this point, and obfuscated the matter greatly with a number of secondary and subsidiary definitions and distinctions (see the blizzard of notes in his edition of Reid's *Works*). John Stuart Mill displayed some confusion over what should count as a truth of consciousness. That was understandable, because he saw his task in large part as drawing a clear contrast between Hamilton's and Thomas Brown's think-

amination of William Hamilton's Philosophy (1865), Mill adopted W. B. Carpenter's term *unconscious cerebration* and also made explicit his reliance on physiological "facts" in order to specify what are the basic sensations of vision and the other sensory modalities.

It is amusing to see Mill criticizing Bailey for carelessness in distinguishing between "what the eye tells us directly, and what it teaches by way of inference." If Mill were right, then the eye could tell us nothing directly, because it is only through inference that we can know even our basic visual intuitions. The rest of Mill's attack on Bailey consisted in trying to show that Bailey had begged the question by using a word like *perception* when he should have said *judgment* or *inference*. But of course it was Mill who begged the question here, refusing to allow Bailey the very distinction on which Bailey had built his theory. Bailey repeatedly looked for evidence in consciousness—as Mill, among others, had told him he should—of the visual and tactile sensations out of which Berkeley, Brown, and the Mills claimed depth perception was built. Finding no such evidence, Bailey not unreasonably concluded that their theory was wrong.

Mill's account of sensation versus perception contains an important asymmetry, one that is still found in theories of perception that incorporate the concept of unconscious inference. According to these theories, perceptions are the result of conclusions drawn on the evidence of sensations, and sensations are the basic building blocks of all consciousness. Yet neither ordinary observers nor scientists can be directly aware of these basic building blocks. These theorists would claim that in our experience of the world we automatically and unconsciously make associations and inferences in such a way that we are aware not of the sensory intuition or premise but of the perceptual conclusion. Thus the scientist studying sensations must make a series of inferences on the basis of physiological data to discover what the "basic" sensations are, and ordinary observers cannot discover their basic sensations at all.

Following this rather unusual logic, Mill responded to Bailey that the evidence of consciousness is irrelevant when it comes to the study of perception! After all, the original intuitions of both touch and vision can be, and typically are, unavailable to consciousness, at least by Mill's definitions. This is where Bailey's second argument comes into play. Bailey repeatedly asked how the association of a tactile sensation with a visual sensation can yield information about outness if neither of the sensations conveys such information. Mill actually agreed with this point but hastened to add that the process involved is more like that of inference or judgment than that of mere association. Mill used his chemical analogy to good effect here, arguing that the association of several chemicals often yields a distinctly new entity, as when the two gases hydrogen and oxygen are combined to form a liquid, water. Perhaps the combination of visual and tactile sensa—neither of which contain information about distance, according to Mill—somehow yield a perception of outness.

The slipperiness of Mill's thinking did not escape his opponent Bailey—nor, in all likelihood, Mill's supporter, Helmholtz. Mill was now claiming to explain perceptual knowledge, such as our knowledge of a three-dimensional world, through combinations of properties within sensations and even through invoking emergent properties of those combinations. Yet Mill had only the most tenuous means of backing up his assertions; moreover, and contrary to his stated plan, he rejected introspective evidence as a way of determining the properties of these supposedly basic subjective intuitions and relied on evidence from physics, geometry, and physiology!

Interestingly, although Bailey's attack was a strong one, it played a minor historical role, as little more than a rearguard action of the Scottish commonsense school against the onslaught of associationism, phenomenalism, and positivism. The Scottish school's unwillingness to countenance almost any form of unconscious psychological processes, combined with its preference for the narrowest methods of introspection, probably doomed it to extinction, even though the proponents of the logical unconscious had the less tenable argument. By the 1860s *everyone* wanted a theory of the unconscious, or so it seemed. It was widely understood that to formulate a coherent associationist account of perception without enlisting the notion of unconscious inferences was impossible. Thus, in a matter of two short decades, the idea of a logical unconscious went from being a radical innovation to being a bulwark of mainstream theorizing—a concept found useful by several different schools within the new psychology. The opponents of this theory of a logical unconscious were the natural metaphysicians, with their theory of an ontological unconscious, and the spiritualists, with their belief in a supernatural unconscious. The widespread revival of interest in Schopenhauer, the wildfire success of von Hartmann's *Philosophy of the Unconscious* (the best-selling German philosophy book of the second half of the century), and the great vogue of spiritualism in Britain and the United States made both these views strong competitors of the drier, more technical neoassociationism.

Mill's logical unconscious has explanatory value only for those who insist on basing their psychology on sensationalist and associationist premises. The logical unconscious serves to patch up the inconsistencies between the associationists' claims that all knowledge derives from either intuition or inference (to use Mill's language) and their embarrassment at being unable to point to the intuitions from which all the inferences are supposedly drawn. The concept of the unconscious that most appealed to the new psychologists of the 1860s and 1870s was thus the one that did the least explanatory work.

The opponents of the logical unconscious were not welcomed by the new psychologists—they could not be, because they doubted the fundamental explanatory trick used in the new discipline. Neither the supernatural nor the ontological unconsciousness had a place in the new psychology. Wundt and Helmholtz—and even James—abhorred Schopenhauer and von Hartmann, and made sure to say so in no uncertain terms. It is interesting that these more robust concepts of the unconscious were also incompatible with the emerging liberal Protestant theology. The idea of a natural soul that gives us direct access to the Godhead, an idea repeatedly adverted to by Schopenhauer and von Hartmann, has always been treated with derision as "enthusiasm" by mainstream Christian thinkers. And the idea of a supernatural soul, promoted by some of the medical practitioners, spiritualists, and mesmerists of midcentury, which implies that coherent unconscious (and potentially wicked) selves exist within many of us, was also anathema to mainstream European thought. It is only after the turn of the twentieth century, with Freud's work and James's studies of religious conversion, that these darker versions of the unconscious began to have a significant impact within psychology.

Mill's awkward thinking was thus revised in two ways by different theorists. On the one hand, his logical unconscious became for writers like Taine and von Hartmann, not to mention Nietzsche, the raw material for a revived theory of the irrational or even supernatural unconscious. Anticipating Nietzsche, Eneas S. Dallas in *The Gay Science* (1866) offered the first theory of art and literature to make systematic appeal to the powers of such an irrational unconscious mind, arguing that a kind of hidden self often guided artistic creation. On the other hand, the first generation of self-styled new psychologists, such as Wundt, *avoided* this ontological unconscious, with its suggestion of a hidden soul, and tried to develop Mill's concept of quasi-logical psychological processes occurring outside consciousness. These experimental psychologists saw psychophysical and reaction-time experiments as a way of empirically determining what Mill could not—the precise basic properties of sensory intuitions. Using a combination of trained introspection and careful experimental control of stimuli, researchers began to try to determine, for example, which aspects of color or spatial vision were innate (sensory) and which were acquired (perceptual). The inconsistencies in the concept of the logical unconscious quickly became apparent to the new psychologists, in the course of serious arguments over what constituted the sensory basis of vision. Although the three greatest nineteenth-century students of perception, Helmholtz, Mach, and Ewald Hering, were engaged in them, these debates remain unresolved, a testimonial to the conceptual inconsistencies at the heart of traditional experimental psychology.

8

The Apotheosis of Positivism

Experimental psychology is often said to have begun in 1879, the year in which Wundt's very productive experimental psychology laboratory was inaugurated in Leipzig. This anniversary is misleading. As we have seen, both the theories and the experimental methods of Wundt (and others in the decade following 1879) had been developed earlier by the associationists and the natural metaphysicians. Nevertheless, the late 1870s mark two important transitions for psychology. The first is institutional: after 1879 "serious" psychological research was increasingly carried out in academic settings, by professionals who identified their work with the lab and the lectern. The second transition was intellectual: the theoretical concerns of earlier generations of psychologists, especially those of the natural metaphysicians, were increasingly set aside in favor of narrower issues, often limited to matters of measurement.

This new psychology of the post-1879 period had shrunk considerably from Shelley's dream, tending to encompass only the phenomena of the mind—where *phenomena* is construed in classic associationist fashion, as atoms of experience. The study of the soul or of the self was set aside by the new psychologists as outside the domain of scientific psychology. Wundt and others who maintained some of the older allegiances of the natural metaphysicians argued that the wider problems should be studied by philosophers, linguists, or anthropologists (as in, for example, Wundt's *Völkerpsychologie*). But already a new generation of psychologists was emerging, even among Wundt's students, who suspected that the older problems were *unreal* precisely because they could not be contained within the narrow compass of mental phenomena.

G. H. Lewes: Transitional Figure

The career of G. H. Lewes (1817–78) is triply instructive with regard to the difficulty of establishing boundaries for the discipline of psychology in the three decades following 1848. First, Lewes was an important thinker whose considerable body of work repays careful study. Lewes strove to integrate contemporary trends in philosophy, psychology, and physiology, as did Bain in his better-remembered work. Lewes's particular contribution lay in showing how contemporary German physiological data could be integrated with British evolutionism and associationism. Second, Lewes was a prolific and effective popularizer. His texts on physiology were read all over Europe. Ivan Sechenov and Ivan Pavlov in Russia credited their reading of Lewes's *Physiology of Common Life* in part with their decision to become scientific psychologists. Lewes's popular biography of Goethe and his even more popular *Biographical History of Philosophy* gave several generations of English-speaking readers their introduction to recent German and French thought, including the work of both Hegel and Comte. Third, although Lewes interacted in important ways with academics, he himself was not an academic but an independent scholar who made his living by writing and editing. His career thus shows how far an independent scientist could go in the middle of the nineteenth century, and it also illustrates the institutional forces that pushed scientific psychology into the academy.

Despite the pivotal position he played in mid-nineteenth-century philosophy and psychology, Lewes is nowadays almost invisible in the history of philosophy and a mere footnote in histories of psychology. E. G. Boring devotes only a passing mention to Lewes, seeing him as an evolutionary associationist of lesser influence than Spencer. Recent histories of psychology either echo Boring or omit any reference to Lewes. Spencer himself credited Lewes, though, with arousing his interest in philosophy and psychology (and Spencer was notorious for never acknowledging any form of intellectual indebtedness), so it may be useful to give some attention to Lewes's contribution.

One difficulty anyone faces in attempting to estimate Lewes's importance is the oddity of the intellectual world of 1848–79, viewed from the confines of the modern academy. Lewes was never a professor or teacher. Nor was this very influential physiologist ever anything more than an amateur experimentalist (albeit one who carried out laboratory work with the likes of Justus Liebig—and thus hardly fits our notion of an amateur, either). Like Spencer, Lewes was primarily a journalist. He was not merely a contributor to the thriving intellectual journals of Victorian Britain but an editor and founder of several important periodicals, including the *Leader*, the *Westminster Review*, and the *Fortnightly Review*. He was also an influential adviser at the birth of *Nature, Brain,* and *Mind*, three of the first British academic journals of importance.

Lewes's interests were broad, and he made real contributions to drama, literature, and biography, as well as to science and philosophy. Lewes's career offers a glimpse at an altogether different kind of intellectual world from the one that has developed since the 1870s. His work does not fit straightforwardly into any single discipline. This point is fundamental: historians of philosophy and psychology cannot assume that the boundaries of their disciplines are or ever were clear, and they certainly should not impose a contemporary view of those boundaries onto the history of their fields.

Lewes was among the first philosophers in Britain to discuss

Hegel and Spinoza. The manner in which Lewes's interest in Spinoza was kindled reveals the danger of treating the written word as the primary vehicle for intellectual expression. In the late 1830s, Lewes, then an aspiring actor and journalist, used to meet at a pub in Red Lion Square in Holborn with half a dozen like-minded people. None of the members of this club were mainstream academics. One, James Pierrepont Greaves, was a mystical anatomist and an educational reformer who influenced some of the founders of Brook Farm. Another member was a bootmaker, and another a typical freethinking bookstall owner. More important, the pub was frequented by a journeyman watchmaker named Cohn, who espoused the philosophy of his coreligionist Spinoza. Cohn worked through parts of *The Ethics* with the group, proposition by proposition, this at a time when no such course was taught — or could be taught! — at any academic institution in the land, or anywhere in Europe, for that matter. Lewes attended the sessions eagerly, because he had heard of Spinoza from Leigh Hunt, who acted as a mentor for many young writers in those days. Hunt, as has been mentioned, knew of Spinoza through Shelley and Shelley's private translations. Lewes also hunted out Spinoza's collected works and began an abortive translation of *The Ethics*. Finally, in 1843, he published an article on Spinoza in the *Westminster Review,* which stands as the first clear nineteenth-century English defense and evaluation of Spinoza. Lewes especially emphasized a doctrine of Spinoza's that came to have great influence on psychology — namely, that spirit and body are merely two aspects of the self and that the soul is our "idea" of the body. If each bodily act produces a set of feelings, as the theory of muscle sense holds, then the entire associated set of all such feelings — our sensory idea of our bodily activity — could be interpreted as the core of our self.

Lewes's visit to Paris in 1842, where he met both Cousin and

Comte, occasioned another fruitful transmission of European ideas to the British islands. Within a year, Lewes was publishing enthusiastic accounts of positivism and discussing plans with Bain and Mill to translate Comte's massive *Cours de philosophie positive* (in the event, the plans fell though, but Lewes was influential in arranging Harriet Martineau's important edition of Comte's works in the next decade). It was at this time (1842–46) that Mill himself was closest to Comte and considered that his own *Logic* represented something like a positivist philosophy of science. Perhaps nothing better illustrates how little our current disciplinary boundaries apply to the previous century than the extensive correspondence of 1842–43 between Mill and Comte, which is taken up primarily with whether phrenology is a scientific approach to studying the mind.

Lewes revisited Comte in 1846, when Comte's great love, Clotilde de Vaux, was dying. Lewes was probably the first British Comtean to turn into a positivist—to focus on the practical aspects of Comte's doctrine, which he began to label positivism, rather than on the man himself and his increasingly eccentric ideas. Beginning in the 1840s, Comte and his closest disciples began to treat his philosophy as a new religious creed, with Comte as pope and his mistress as a substitute for the Virgin Mary. The most important consequence of this unusual development was that positivists across Europe distanced themselves from Comte the person, and tended to generalize his earlier philosophical position into a kind of broad scientific worldview. Lewes pioneered this post-Comtean positivist attitude toward science and psychology, which dominated the European intellectual landscape in the 1870s and 1880s.

In 1845–46 the first edition of Lewes's *Biographical History of Philosophy* appeared, with its substantial discussions of German philosophers, especially Kant, Hegel, and Spinoza, culminating in what can only be called a paean to Comte. (The ending was later toned down and converted into a general positivist credo.) The book was as popular throughout the English-speaking world as any philosophy text had ever been. Thus, the claims of the Oxford Hegelians, widely repeated in histories on the subject, that they brought German philosophy to Britain in the 1870s (after Coleridge's efforts more or less failed) are incorrect. It is also interesting to note that in that widely disseminated text Lewes championed positivism, several years before the revolutions of 1848.

After 1848, Lewes was heavily involved for a time in political journalism, founding the *Leader* with Leigh Hunt's son Thornton. In this context, Lewes began to promote the writings of Herbert Spencer and, a little later, of his longtime companion (he was already married), George Eliot. Even with all this activity, Lewes found time for his third great effort at transmitting European ideas to British soil: *Life and Works of Goethe* (1854), the first comprehensive biography of Goethe. In addition to offering a synoptic view of his writings, Lewes included a useful chapter on Goethe's scientific work, making the work the most complete review of Goethe's broad efforts for years to come.

Perhaps inspired by Goethe, in the next few years Lewes began his series of popular writings on physiological psychology. The books, especially the very popular *Physiology of Common Life* (1859-60), promoted the kind of everyday materialist physiology found in Büchner or Jacob Moleschott but eschewed their anti-idealist ontology. Instead, Lewes's positivist views allowed him to remain agnostic with regard to *how* sensation and feelings accompanied such everyday physiological acts as eating and simply focus on what Lewes believed to be the facts: the correlations of feeling with physiological processes and bodily activity. This invention of a half-Spinozist, half-positivist physiology of mind was Lewes's master stroke.

Before the century was out, this position would come to dominate physiology and psychology across Europe. In this new kind of psychology it is assumed that the mental and the physical are two sides of a single thing: the individual's nervous system. Lewes actually coined the words *neurosis* and *psychosis* to refer respectively to neural processes and their associated subjective feelings. (The words only acquired their later medical connotations in the present century.) Lewes differed from the natural metaphysicians as well as from Wundt and the new psychologists in locating the mind throughout the nervous system, not merely in the brain. He no longer saw the self or the will as transcendent entities that erupt into the phenomenal world; instead, he saw neurosis and psychosis as two different but related sets of phenomena.

In 1864–65 Lewes returned to journalism as editor of the new *Fortnightly Review*. The journal became influential as a mouthpiece for liberal positivism in science, politics, and religion, featuring writers such as Thomas Huxley, Herbert Spencer, John Tyndall, Alexander Bain, Walter Bagehot, and others. A number of important philosophical and psychological essays appeared in this "popular" journal and were widely read. Owing to increasing ill health, Lewes had to resign his editorship after only two years, although by then the *Westminster* was well established. Lewes returned to his home laboratory and decided to write a comprehensive treatise on mind and body, reviewing both his own many experiments and what he believed were his novel ideas about psychology.

Whereas mainstream positivists increasingly espoused a panreflex theory of the mind, Lewes dissented. Already in the 1850s, Laycock and Carpenter were speaking of cerebral reflexes. The notion that even our conscious actions are frequently reflexive became very popular throughout Europe. In the first scene of *Anna Karenina* (1877) Oblonsky, who is cheating on his wife, gives himself away by a false smile, which he himself attributes to a "reflex action of the brain." Lewes admitted that sometimes even the cerebral cortex acts in a reflexive fashion. He objected, though, to the allied notion that spinal reflexes were somehow devoid of subjective feelings—devoid of psychoses, in his terminology. If the reflexive acts of which we have awareness include subjective psychoses as well as objective neuroses, why should this not also be true of, say, the reflexive acts of a frog's spinal column? This question brought Lewes close to Erasmus Darwin's views, although I have found little evidence that Lewes read the elder Darwin.

Lewes had, however, read Whytt carefully, and he replicated many of Whytt's experiments. Like the Scottish doctor, Lewes found that the reflexes of the spinal cord were not mechanically invariable but could adapt, within limits, to changes in both stimuli and the animal's situation. Lewes had concluded already in *The Physiology of Common Life* (p. 134) that the brain was "only *one* organ of the mind" and that every segment of the spinal cord acts "like a little brain." For Lewes, as for Whytt, this implied the existence of some sort of sentience or feeling in the spinal cord, even though the feelings were not accessible by the conscious brain. Whereas Huxley and others invoke the idea of the brain as a reflex machine to discount the importance of subjectivity in human affairs, Lewes used this same idea to argue for the ubiquity of feeling in the animal kingdom and within each animal's body. Perhaps such a debate was inevitable, given the positivists' disinclination to pursue questions about the nature of mind. Once the existence of the two "phenomenal series" (neurosis and psychosis) is granted, they can be correlated in at least these two ways, if not in more. The mainstream positivists focused on the lack of subjective consciousness of the operations of the spine and labeled them purely neural events—yet the positivists themselves inferred the existence of unconscious *cerebral* events, as we have seen. Lewes simply applied the same reasoning in a consistent manner to spinal reflexes, arguing for a kind of unconscious feeling in the spine.

Lewes came to believe that there were three levels of mind: systemic consciousness (for instance, muscle sensibility—a vague and general sense of one's body); sensory consciousness; and rational, or thinking, consciousness. He claimed that his experiments proved that the spine contained at least the first two. To promote this doctrine, Lewes wrote a multivolume series of books, *Problems of Life and Mind* (1874–79). In these books, he uses virtually the same evidence Huxley and others adduced to support the claim that animals are automata—and tries to undermine that claim with his alternative position of levels of psychosis.

Problems of Life and Mind is a consciously magisterial attempt to survey various lines of thought about psychology and to offer a particular program of research as the most promising course to follow. The treatise is divided into three parts: a general philosophy of science as applied to psychology (*The Foundations of a Creed,* in two volumes); a study of mind-brain relations from Lewes's dual aspect perspective, emphasizing the physiology of everyday life (*The Physical Basis of Mind*); and the sketch of a general psychology, describing its scope and limits (*The Study of Psychology,* in two volumes). Lewes did not live to finish this last part; George Eliot edited his manuscript and sent it to press.

Problems shows that the British as well as the Germans could produce multivolume encyclopedic works of philosophical-empirical-physiological psychology. (Probably no book comes closer to Lewes's in scope and conception than Lotze's *Microcosmos,* although Lewes was a far more acute physiologist than Lotze.) In many ways, Lewes's work anticipated trends that have emerged in cognitive science only in the last few decades of the twentieth century: he emphasized the selection of facts from current research (physiological or psychological) to help make a philosophical case, as opposed to the generation of psychological models or theories. Refreshingly, Lewes often pointed out where the available information left issues unresolved, as well as where he believed answers could be found. Perhaps even more remarkably, Lewes, unique among his generation, stressed both the physiological and the social bases of mind. He was adamant in his insistence that a physicalistic account of the mind—which, on the whole, he favored—would prove inadequate without a corresponding examination of the social factors that go into the formation of minds. Lewes also devoted an important chapter of *Problems* to Kant, treating Kantian epistemology as a special case of nativistic psychology. This position, so common among English-speaking writers and psychologists and so removed from nineteenth-century German interpretations of Kant, leaves one to wonder whether Lewes is not the main source of this interpretation.

The two volumes of the third part of *Problems*, Lewes's *Study of Psychology*, represent an uncompleted larger project. The scope of this project—the scope of psychology as Lewes envisaged it—was remarkable. Beginning with taxonomies of mental states (as in Brentano's descriptive psychology), he went on to discuss the parallels between neural states and psychological states, attempting to develop laws of sentience (as Fechner and Wundt had attempted to do). And he went even further by trying to develop a scientific account or logic of feelings-in-themselves as opposed to feelings-as-signs. That Lewes overreached himself is evident when one compares his *Study of Psychology*, published in 1879, with Gottlob Frege's *Begriffschrift*, published that same year, which ushered in the modern science of logic as a science of signs (see Chapter 10).

Despite its excessive length, *Problems* omits much. Lewes seems to have been little moved by the rising tide of experimental psychology on the Continent. He was familiar with Fechner and especially Wundt, whose writings he cites approvingly. But his interest was primarily in Wundt's philosophical position, not in his experimental work. Here Lewes was less prescient than Brentano—the author of another significant work, *Empirical Psychology* (1874)—who acknowledged Wundt's importance, if only to take issue with his concept of inner observation. Lewes (like Lotze) was more of a physiological than an experimental psychologist. He was more at home with his extensive analyzing of the reflex functions of the spinal cord than with worrying about Weber fractions, on the one hand, or sorting out the differences between introspection and inner observation on the other hand.

Lewes's work was in many ways outdated by the time it was published. Professionalization was on the rise, and association with a university and a laboratory was the way to get ahead. Both the theory that animals are automata and Lewes's neo-Whyttian theorizing fit the data, but only automatism pleased the sensibilities of the new professionals, who wanted physiology and psychology to be recognized as physical sciences. Lewes lived just long enough to see the new professional psychology get off the ground. *Mind* began publication in 1876 and *Brain* a year later (the publishers of both sought out Lewes for advice and help). Wundt's lab was already active, and psychological laboratories were even beginning to appear in far-off America, where Peirce had been working at Hopkins on the psychophysics of hue and William James was demonstrating frog reflexes, among other things, at Harvard. The study of the physiology and psychology of everyday life was being abandoned by the increasing array of specialists, each of whom focused on one piece of the puzzle of the human mind: experimental psychologists looked at sensations and reaction times; experimental physiologists analyzed reflex pathways; medical psychologists worked on case studies in hysteria, epilepsy, and stroke. With Lewes's death, the trend toward specialization increased, because he left money to found a studentship on the German model at Cambridge in physiology—a bequest that did much to stimulate an improvement in reductionist physiology in Britain over the next twenty years. In a twist of fate, the greatest proponent of a mechanistic analysis of spinal function (combined with a dualistic interpretation of the brain and mind), Charles Sherrington, was one of three Nobel Prize–winning physiologists whose studies were underwritten by Lewes's bequest.

Lewes's own influence in professionalizing physiological research in Britain was thus a major factor in his ultimate reputation as a transitional or marginal thinker. His dual aspect positivism was immensely popular and became something of a rallying point for experimental and physiological psychologists. But his further argument was simply ignored: that dual aspect theory was consistent with—perhaps even suggested—the idea that psychological states and processes were found wherever neural activity was present. The logical unconscious of mainstream positivism was acceptable to Victorian sensibilities; Lewes's concept of a completely sentient body, with many feelings neither accessible to the self nor under the self's control, was not acceptable and indeed was dismissed without serious consideration. The positivists whom Lewes inspired found it unnecessary to worry about the *meaning* of psychophysical correlations, but only about their *measurement*—this was how to get ahead in the lab. And there is no way of measuring feelings that are unconscious. Yet not all the new psychologists were resolutely dismissive of questions about the meaning of the relations between mind and body. In reviewing one volume of Lewes's *Problems*, the young William James in effect attacked both Lewes and his opponents: "What, indeed, is gained by merely saying that when a man's dorsal [spinal] marrow is crushed his legs still feel, though he does not? What we want to know is *how* they feel, and *who* they are when they feel, and *how* it comes that only when they are in organic continuity with the brain their feelings form part of an ego" (p. 290). James, who was never a positivist in the common acceptance of the term, certainly wanted to know these things, but he was in a decided minority—many others among the new psychologists saw positivism as a golden opportunity for scientific progress.

The Popularity of Positivism

The positivist point of view was enormously popular throughout Europe in the late 1800s. *Everyone* was a positivist, or at least professed to be. Even such unlikely candidates as Freud and Husserl occasionally identified themselves as positivists. Automatists like Huxley and Tyndall were positivists, but so was Lewes, who thought they had gotten everything about the nervous system topsy-turvy. Wundt, with his strict adherence to measurement in experimental psychology (but not in other areas) was a positivist, but even Wundt's most influential opponent, James, who thought issues of measurement the least important part of a scientific psychology, claimed to be a positivist. The overuse of this rubric naturally interferes with the historian's ability to discriminate among different trends. In order to make some sense of the 1880s, I find it useful to restrict the label *positivist* within psychology to theorists who promoted something resembling Lewes's dual aspect view of the mind and body. It was in all likelihood the most popular opinion among proponents of the new psychology, and especially among its popularizers, such as Ribot, whose books on modern English and German psychology brought the positivist gospel to France in the 1870s. Once again, these thinkers viewed the realm of mind and the realm of matter as two separate sets of phenomena, which could be correlated through physiological and psychological experimentation. Qualitative correlations, such as that between a specific stimulus and a specific sensation (say, between a given vibration and a given tone) could be obtained or, better, a quantitative relationship, such as in a choice reaction time. But many of these thinkers went beyond Lewes's philosophy of correlation and argued that enough evidence existed to prove that only one set of phenomena—the phenomena associated with matter—had any causal efficacy. That is, many of these positivists were also physicalists of a sort and denied that mental states had any causal powers.

The metaphor used by Huxley (perhaps drawn from Shadworth Hodgson's *Philosophy of Practise,* 1865) in his lecture on animal automatism (1872) captures the essence of this view very well: "The soul stands related to the body as the bell of a clock to the works, and consciousness answers to the sound which the bell gives out when it is struck . . . all states of consciousness . . . are immediately caused by molecular changes of the brain's substance . . . [but] there is no proof that any state of consciousness is the cause of changes in the motion of the matter of the organism" (p. 242).

Anyone familiar with the earlier debates about the mind and the body, especially with those at the end of the seventeenth century later summarized by Hume, will notice the howler here. Just as there is no proof that mental states cause physical states, so there is no proof, despite what Huxley and others said, of the reverse, that physical states cause mental ones. A physical state, such as a state of nerves in the brain, may be associated with a mental state, such as a feeling, thought, or dream, but we simply have no way of telling whether the physical state caused that mental state. How could a change in nerve activity be the cause of, say, a novel feeling, or of a dream? The problem here lies in trying to understand causality, not in trying to understand the interaction of mind and matter. Most thinkers in the late nineteenth century agreed that physical and mental states were correlated according to certain laws or regularities. Yet correlation is not cause, and we must either (like Hume) reduce all causality to mere association, in which case the causal power flows from mind to body as well as vice versa, or content ourselves with saying that mental and physical states parallel one another, and nothing more. (It is also remarkable that many writers, like Huxley, apparently identified psychological states with conscious states, despite the emerging interest in unconscious mental processes.) Although thinkers like Brentano, Mach, and James quickly called the positivists on this philosophical mistake, it did little to quell the popularity of the positivist position within psychology and the sciences.

I suggest that the broadly positivist position was so popular for three reasons: it was progressivist; it was agnostic; and, despite the protestations of its critics, it was antimaterialist. The progressive facet of positivism was perhaps the only one attributable to its founder, Comte. Comte had maintained that humanity progresses through stages of thought: from the theological to the metaphysical to the positive, each successive stage an improvement over the preceding one. Comte also asserted that natural science had reached a positive stage — it no longer explained phenomena in terms of unobservable forces, much less in terms of deities — but that social thought lagged behind. Positivism thus supplied a simple formula for advancing the social sciences: abandon metaphysical questions. Positivists never acknowledged their own metaphysics, such as dual aspect theory, and adamantly refused to treat their own theories as resting on metaphysics. They insisted, falsely but loudly, that the series of phenomena described by atomist associationist metaphysics were simple fact or pure phenomena and nothing more. Yet they insisted that positive science could be built only on *those* facts. By treating their own metaphysics as science, positivists gained a license to ignore (by shrugging them off as metaphysical and therefore unworthy of being answered) the difficult questions and problems raised by others about positivist assumptions.

In addition, the positivist formula, unlike the spread of materialist science, did not threaten religion. The positivist rejection of theological explanations has often been taken for an antireligious attitude. The worry that positivism was antireligious was certainly widespread at the time, when conservative Christians still attempted to compete with scientists in the realm of explanation. But with the rise of liberal Protestant theology and also of the neo-Thomism of Belgium's Cardinal Mercier, "progressive" Christian thinkers increasingly accepted the idea that religion and science were two separate spheres. In this liberal theologians and mainstream positivists were united. Consider, for instance, Herbert Spencer's reply when the *Non-Conformist* attacked his *Principles of Psychology* as atheistic materialism: "Not only have I nowhere expressed any such conclusion, but I affirm that no such conclusion is deducible from the general tenor of the book. I hold, in common with most who have studied the matter to the bottom, that the existence of a Deity can neither be proved nor disproved."

If the theologians would desist from trying to "prove" their theories scientifically, positivists would meet them halfway by striving to convince scientists that religious hypotheses were beyond the bounds of what science could test. It was Darwin's and Freud's unwillingness to abide by this agnostic truce that made them such dangerous thinkers.

Positivism was not only agnostic with respect to religion, it was also antimaterialist. This antimaterialism was expressed in a very novel way—with reference to the new Erkenntnislehre—

and was widely misunderstood until at least the early 1900s. Indeed, William James spent much of the 1880s attacking the positivist movement in psychology as a combination of fatalism and materialism, a combination that he labeled the automaton theory of the mind.

The antimaterialism of the positivists, as best expressed by du Bois Reymond in Berlin and Huxley and Clifford in London, came not from their dual aspect metaphysics but from their co-option of a certain strand of Erkenntnistheorie. In this regard, Lange's *History of Materialism,* which embodied the first clear statement of the new antimaterialist argument, exerted an important influence in the last third of the nineteenth century. The first generation of self-styled physiological psychologists wanted to argue that physiological states caused mental states, and as we have seen, they showed surprisingly little interest in philosophical subtleties concerning the nature of causation. At the same time, the positivistically inclined among the new psychologists insisted that, in general, scientific claims were essentially restatements of sets of data, redescriptions of the phenomena. Hence, physics, physiology, and psychology alike take as their point of departure whatever phenomena a scientist can obtain through observation and experiment. The simple formula "Brain states cause psychological states" thus requires revision. According to the positivists, the formula must read, "The sets of phenomena known as brain states are correlated with other phenomena, known as psychological states, in such a way that brain states appear to cause psychological states." From this perspective, an assertion like Huxley's that brain states cause mental states is not a claim about matter but a claim about sets of phenomena. Huxley, for example, was always careful to state that it is the *phenomena* described by physiologists as brain states that appear to lead to other phenomena, such as mental states or behavior. Matter for Huxley was just what it was for Mach or Hertz: a set of phenomenal observations made by scientists. It is thus remarkable but true that the most reviled "materialists" of the 1880s—Huxley, Tyndall, and Clifford—were all *phenomenalists* of one sort or another and not materialists at all.

The positivist impulse gave new life to a variety of pan-phenomenalism, one whose adherents were surprisingly un-critical about the analysis of those allegedly basic mental phenomena, sensations. Thus, thinkers as different in outlook and interests as Huxley and Mach, Taine and Spencer, Wundt and Lewes all agreed that the basic "data" on which all science was to be built were sensations. For a while the analysis of sensations tended to proceed along the lines sketched out by Mill, but already in the 1870s and 1880s a number of theorists—especially Mach, Hering, Karl Stumpf, and James—had begun to undermine the consensus by questioning the empirical basis for the assumption that all sensations were simple (see Chapter 11).

Our twentieth-century familiarity with all manner of phenomenalisms should not cause us to overlook how important a development positivist phenomenalism was. Before 1850 or so, perceptual evidence was always taken by scientists at face value: the rock is here, this meter reads thus and so. Now even such ordinary observations were subjected to a kind of skeptical reduction into sensationalist "phenomena": I have sensations from which I infer that the rock is here, or that the meter reads thus and so. Such an intellectual move was consistent with the notion of philosophy as a kind of science of science, as Erkenntnistheorie, but it had and has no other justification. Neither the naturalist nor the experimenter, nor even the theorist, gains by thus undermining observation. Even physiological psychology—the science within which sensationalism was pioneered—

does not benefit from such skeptical maneuvering. How does it assist the psychologist to say, "I had certain sensations, from which I infer that the subject was listening to stimulus X"?

The sole beneficiary of the new positivist sensationalism was positivism itself. If all knowledge of the world results from inferences made on the basis of sensations (à la Mill), then knowledge of mental states is on an exact par with knowledge of physical states. We even infer our own mental reality just as we infer physical reality. Spinoza's unknown substance with two sets of properties, one mental and the other physical, is replaced by Spencer, Lewes, and Huxley's phenomenal realm with two sets of inferred properties, mental and physical. From this new perspective, all attempts to understand what feelings really are, or what gives rise to volitions, or what the nature of thought is—the basic questions of the natural metaphysicians—are misguided. Everything, as Mill had it, is either intuition or inference. Intuition is limited to simple sensations—so simple and unreal that no one is able to observe them, as we saw in the previous chapter—and thus everything else in the whole world, whether rock, animal, star, or emotion, is inference.

Mill's logical unconscious thus took on a key ontological as well as epistemological role within late-nineteenth-century thought. The only thing that can be said to be "behind" phenomena is our basic sensations and the quasi-logical processes from which we infer those phenomena of which we are aware. We cannot be aware of sensations directly, as both Mill and Helmholtz argued, because our experience produces so many "automatic" and unconscious inferences that we are never aware of the original sensations. Hence, Mill's intuitions threatened to become Spencer's unknowable, or even von Hartmann's unconscious: the part of the universe that we suspect exists but that is forever hidden behind the veil of phenomena. Increasingly, the world appeared divided into two sides: the phenomenal and the unknowable.

The Division of the World: Dr. Jekyll and Mr. Hyde

Kant's distinction between noumena and phenomena thus took on new life — and an entirely new connotation — in the second half of the nineteenth century. The world came to be seen as divided into knowable and unknowable, into the phenomenal and whatever lay behind the phenomenal, into light and dark. The phenomenal was knowable and rational, the stuff of science. But perhaps there was more to reality than just this phenomenal side . . .

The European world in the half century following 1848 was a conspicuously divided place. On the one hand, an emerging elite of professionals — bankers, barristers, professors, and doctors — and on the other hand, an industrial working class that knew the bitter degradation of the urban slums. On the one hand, the ideology of empire and the need for "bringing civilization to the world," and on the other, the justification of wanton slaughter and plunder in the name of that civilization.

These divisions have left their mark on the literature of the period. In Dickens's satiric *Hard Times* and Zola's melodramatic *Germinal,* the reader's assumed values are challenged by an unfavorable contrast between slum dwellers and bourgeois. All of Dostoevsky's later novels contain extraordinary attempts to portray the divided minds of people living in the new urban scene.

In stark contrast, the philosophical literature of the period has little or nothing to say about these divisions. In retrospect, we now read Kierkegaard or Nietzsche in large part to try to understand the fissures in the human psyche—but those authors' influence was minimal until the very end of the nineteenth century, and even then, largely outside the academy. The literature of psychopathology, especially after 1880, did reflect the feeling of duality. The idea of a second self, and especially of hidden, dangerous parts of the self, was much discussed. Much of this work, however, came out of, or retained association with, spiritualism and therefore hovered on the fringes of academic respectability; it has been ignored until recently by historians. Positivism served mainstream academics and professionals well by throwing into relief the sober, illuminated, controllable world of phenomena and hiding from view the untidy, ill-lit, unknowable world that might lie behind them.

For all the emphasis given by philosophers in the 1860s and 1870s to the role played by the unconscious in human nature, they devoted remarkably little discussion to what we, in hindsight, find most relevant—the unconscious as a source of irrationality and a vehicle for blinding the conscious mind to the obvious. As we have seen, the new psychologists were more or less forced by their adherence to Millian sensationalism to highlight a kind of logical unconscious. As a group, they were wary of the less rational unconscious being analyzed by doctors, artists, and others at the time. A brief look at one of the most acute late-Victorian literary studies of the unconscious, Robert Louis Stevenson's *Dr. Jekyll and Mr. Hyde* (1889), may help to illustrate the importance of the irrational unconscious.

Stevenson's story is carefully constructed from the outside inward, so that one reads about the external events and other observers' experiences before hearing anything from Dr. Jekyll himself. It may be that other observers are better judges of our unconscious motives than we ourselves are—a disconcerting admission for all psychologies based on introspection. Note also that Mr. Hyde is never allowed to speak for himself until his testament is presented. Thus, in good positivist fashion, the reader learns to correlate two events: Dr. Jekyll's imbibing of a certain potion and the subsequent appearance of an individual, Mr. Hyde, so evil that ordinary souls find it difficult to look at him. In parallel to this, the reader learns of Dr. Jekyll's early struggles—surely familiar to many of his readers—between a dissipated and an upright mode of life. A second correlation may be detected by some readers: the association between Jekyll's inability to give up on "lower pleasures" and his streak of violence. It is easy to imagine the Bohemian Stevenson constructing his story in part to play off on the fears of respectable professionals who indulge occasionally in drink, venery, and other "unacceptable" pleasures but try to keep those pastimes secret and separate from the rest of their lives.

The testimony of Dr. Jekyll, presented as the climax of the tale, puts both correlations in perspective. The reader learns that the potion somehow unlocks one side of Dr. Jekyll's self— that side addicted to "low pleasures." Jekyll claims that he was searching for a way to isolate those lower aspects of his self to set them apart from his otherwise upright life. But as his own narrative intimates to the reader, Jekyll's lower self, once allowed to exercise its energies, began to demand more and more of Jekyll's psychological resources and soon came to dominate his whole life. How much of this Jekyll understands, it is not easy to say. Stevenson's genius allows us to be confident that Jekyll has at least some inkling of this process, but the reader is left to draw his or her own conclusion about whether Jekyll consciously understands all that is happening to him.

Stevenson's story is acutely observed and brilliantly executed, and there is much that could be said about it. It is arguable, for example, that Stevenson meant his tale to be an analysis of addiction to alcohol and its effects on personality. What concerns us here, however, is the unique way in which the two "sides" of the individual are said to relate. They do so through alternation. We are told by Dr. Jekyll that he and Mr. Hyde share memory but no other psychological faculty. Each at first ignores—and later despises—the other's beliefs and tastes. But, the story suggests, so complete a division in attitudes is unstable, and Hyde's predilections come to haunt Jekyll. Thus, a single set of experiences is differentiated by the inferences to be drawn from them, to adopt the terminology of the new psychology. What Jekyll relishes, Hyde detests, and vice versa. Just as the colonizers and the colonized, or the workers and the bosses, might interpret a single set of phenomena in two different ways, so Jekyll and Hyde view the events in this story in a conflicting manner.

Stevenson's "split" perspective on the human soul offers both contrasts and parallels with the positivist psychologies and their view of the unconscious. Each side of the split is looked upon as a coherent set of phenomena, completely observable on the surface. There is little or no hint that, "underneath" Dr. Jekyll, for example, may lurk Hydelike motives, unconscious to Jekyll, but affecting his actions and beliefs. The unconscious is looked on as nothing more than a new, and separate, sphere of phenomena or interpretations of phenomena, which would be just like the conscious mind, if it could be brought to light. It was possible to imagine that one person might "contain" two interpretations of the available phenomena. It was even possible to imagine that one individual might, in some sense, contain two (or more?) persons, each with separate reactions and interpretations of the available phenomena. It was only with Freud's *Psychopathology of Everyday Life* (1900) and James's *Varieties of Religious Experience* (1902) that the concept of a more dynamic and hidden unconscious became popular. In this twentieth-century view, the unconscious is not a separate person, simply interpreting (or reinterpreting) available sensory data. According to the more modern theory, the unconscious is precisely that which is either hidden behind the phenomena (Freud) or that which is always at the fringes of consciousness (James). For both James and Freud, the unconscious may affect the attitudes and beliefs of the individual, behind the scenes, as it were.

Positivism as it manifested itself in the late 1800s was thus a *refusal* to take certain problems seriously. The positivists dismissed the notion that certain wishes and attitudes might be hidden from the self—even while hypothesizing the existence of unconscious inferences as an outgrowth of a metaphysics of experiential atomism. The new psychologists tended to resist the ideas of Freud and James, because the new ideas were not compatible with experiential atomism. Interestingly, these dynamic psychologists of the unconscious often exploited some of the methods of the new psychologists: James, Freud, Jung, and others were very interested in using the methods of word association, not to measure reaction times, but to try to get a glimpse of what they believed were fields of meaning not observable through introspection or direct analysis. Because of their blind spots concerning ontological questions about the mind, their lack of interest in meaning as versus mechanism, the new positive psychologists were unable to assimilate novel applications of their own methods. The story of positive psychology's reticence in dealing with dynamic psychology is well known. Less well known is the positivists' dismissal of evolutionary psychology, even the evolutionary psychology of Charles Darwin, certainly the greatest scientist of the century. In that earlier case, too, the new positive psychology's inability to cope with psychological theories that eschewed sensory atomism proved damaging to the development of scientific psychology.

9

The Anomalous Mr. Darwin

Charles Darwin (1809–82), grandson of Erasmus, was a model scientist who could not and cannot serve as a model for scientists. Among the most influential thinkers of all time, Darwin single-handedly made some of the greatest advances of the nineteenth century in several fields, from geology and biogeography to experimental botany and animal breeding—not to mention evolution and psychology. But this tremendously productive figure was a unique case, not someone whose methods and procedures can be emulated. Independently wealthy, Darwin never had to work for a living and was able to devote virtually every healthy working hour of his adult life to scientific research. Although he was somewhat reclusive, his early successes (stemming from the *Beagle* voyage) made him a leading light of the increasingly London-oriented British biological community (the societies of botanists, geologists, and so on, met in the British capital). Taking advantage of this, Darwin provided himself with an "invisible college" of associates around the world. Among those with whom Darwin was in close contact were many of the most distinguished scientists of his day. By combining this felicitous social arrangement with the extraordinary breadth and depth of his scientific capability, not to mention four decades of exceedingly hard work, Darwin was able to construct a career that remains one of the supreme intellectual achievements of the nineteenth—or any—century.

Darwin's unique career pattern was reflected in the way in which his influence was felt—almost exclusively indirectly, through his writings and other scientists' discussions of them. Darwin never lectured at a university, and his attendance at scientific meetings dropped off as his stature increased, until, after the publication of *The Origin of Species*, he never again spoke at a scientific congress. Thus, the most famous scientist of the century never once gave a public presentation of his revolutionary theory, not even in the form of a classroom lecture! Darwin had no students as such, only allies and followers—many of whom were only too ready to fill the public vacuum created by his diffidence.

The lack of a cadre of Darwin-trained young biologists had a major impact on the so-called Darwinian revolution. For one thing, it allowed thinkers whose grasp of natural selection was shaky to achieve far more prominence than they would otherwise have had. Darwin's famous "bulldog," T. H. Huxley, never could agree with much of Darwin's theorizing about systematics and the nature of species (and often said so). And Herbert Spencer—who was widely thought of at that time as a shining light of evolutionary theory but whose glory, it is easy to tell in retrospect, was largely reflected—was vague or unclear on almost every detail of Darwinian theory. Hence, the vociferous debates about evolutionary theory after the appearance of *The Origin* tended increasingly to focus on general issues surrounding evolution, especially such issues as the evolutionary continuity between humans and animals, and to steer away from concrete or detailed discussion of biological phenomena and processes. Whatever the reason, many of Darwin's advances in the decades following the publication of *The Origin* were little discussed, and even nowadays remain known, if at all, only to specialists. This is unfortunate because, in the twenty-three years left to him after the publication of his famous book, Darwin spent every erg of his not inconsiderable energies on extending and testing his theory in ingenious ways.

Thus, a second consequence of Darwin's failure to create a school of students was the loss to posterity of a clear picture of the overall pattern of Darwin's achievement. Until recently, even serious histories of science presented Darwin as a kind of bemused naturalist, scrutinizing geological strata, plants, and animals and—somehow—arriving at his theory. In fact, Darwin was one of the most dogged experimentalists in European science, often tracking down the smallest implications of his theory through his own experiments, and encouraging others far and wide to help him out. Yet, because he worked as an independent scholar and had no students, no single thinker was familiar with Darwin's overall achievement or grasped its scope. (George J. Romanes might perhaps be considered the one exception to this rule: to some degree, Romanes was an informal student of Darwin's in the last half dozen years of the older scientist's life.)

Histories of the life, behavioral, and social sciences, replete as they are with discussions of Darwin's influence, are thus often misleading and partial. This is especially true of histories of psychology. In them Darwin is presented exclusively as a theorist who thought about some psychological issues on which we now do research—although the emphasis is typically on evolution in general (a subject analyzed by many thinkers, not just Darwin) and rarely on natural selection in particular (which was Darwin's unique contribution to the understanding of evolution). The better histories mention that he was interested in emotional expressions, although I have yet to find one that explains how his interest derived from a need to test the implications of his theory of sexual selection, or that analyzes his novel methodology in detail. Yet Darwin spent perhaps a quarter of his time after *The Origin* came out engaged in experimental research directly related to issues of behavior and psychology, as a brief résumé will make clear. Although Darwin is certainly one of the most famous scientists who ever lived, none of the research mentioned in the next paragraph has been discussed in the literature on the history of psychology—indeed, this work is usually not even mentioned!

Much of Darwin's *The Variation of Animals and Plants Under Domestication* (1868) is concerned with the heritability of behavior, and in the book Darwin pays careful attention to the practices of, for example, dog and pigeon breeders who are trying to select for behavioral traits. It is natural for readers to turn to Darwin's *Descent of Man and Selection in Relation to Sex* (1871) to find out what he thought about human evolution, but there is no excuse for ignoring the several hundreds of pages devoted to the origin and functions of animal courtship and mating rituals, or the analysis Darwin offers of the effects of social interaction on animal behavior and evolution. Several chapters in *The Effects of Cross and Self-Fertilization on Plants* (1876) are devoted to exquisite experiments on bee behavior. Darwin studied both the spatial orientation of bees and their patterns of foraging, discovering that bees will alter how they forage depending on their experience with the flowers and competition from other bees. Darwin's *three* books on plant movement represent the labor of at least two decades and literally hundreds of experiments. Taken together, these epochal works in physiological botany led to the discovery of auxins and other plant hormones. In his last book, *The Formation of Vegetable Mould Through the Action of Earthworms* (1881), Darwin reports several score of experiments on earthworm sensory processes and burrowing behavior.

Darwin was thus a major contributor not only to "scientific" psychology, through his theorizing, but also to *experimental* psychology, through his practice. Yet, despite Darwin's fame, this fact is still unacknowledged. The doyen of historians of psychology, E. G. Boring, in asserting (*History of Experimental Psychology*, p. 453) that "experimental psychology never at any time encouraged by the British universities, was late in making its beginning in England," manages to ignore Darwin's efforts (and the efforts of Lewes and several others) completely, thanks to his focus on the universities as *the* site of research. This ill-considered view has been repeatedly propagated.

The Distressing Mr. Darwin

Darwin's theory of evolution by means of natural selection is in all probability the most important—and certainly is the most famous—scientific development of the nineteenth century. As such it often takes central place in discussions of the intellectual trends of those times. But modern discussions of Darwin have trouble placing him in perspective, precisely because we now realize the profundity of his contribution. At the time— and this really cannot be overstressed—although Darwin was both praised and vilified as a great scientist, his unique contributions were not widely understood, and overall, he was probably less generally influential in the short and middle term than, say, Spencer. In part, as I have just suggested, this circumstance was due to Darwin's anomalous position as an independent scholar. Another reason for the unusual reception of Darwin's work was, of course, the revolutionary nature of his ideas. It is often said that the middle of the nineteenth century was ripe for evolutionary ideas. There is some truth in this allegation— as witness the fact that Spencer's early evolutionary thinking emerged in the 1850s and that Alfred Russel Wallace independently developed a theory of natural selection in that decade as well. It cannot be underscored too strongly, though, that Darwin's work was not *just* about evolution; it was a very radical reconceptualization of the idea of nature and history, based on the implications of the concept of natural selection.

The mid-nineteenth century was a time when most serious thinkers in Europe were eager to hear progressivist accounts of both natural and civil history. Progressivist ideas, which had been associated to a large degree with radical thinkers (such as Erasmus Darwin) now became more widely acceptable. Humans were the most highly developed creatures on earth, were they not? And certain humans (European, male, well heeled) were the best of the best—who could doubt it? Historians and journalists alike promoted this worldview and reacted with savagely racist attacks against anyone who opposed the emerging European consensus on European superiority—Mohammed Ali in Egypt, for instance, or the participants in the great Indian Mutiny of 1857. Darwin's novel theorizing hardly bolstered this chauvinist tendency; correctly understood, it was not progressivist in the then accepted sense. Worse, sexual profligacy, or at least reproductive success, was the engine of natural selection, and that trait was supposedly much more characteristic of working-class, peasant, or "native" families than of the new urban elites.

Darwin's theory was also strongly antiteleological. Because the centerpiece of his thought was an account of the changes in species, Darwin was forced to attack deistic biology (that is, biological theories in which God acts as a creator of the world in any way). Many earlier evolutionary theorists, such as the anonymous author of *Vestiges of Creation* (1844)—a book popular among phrenologists—claimed to be compatible with the creation of the world by an almighty and beneficent deity. Spencer certainly did not rule out the existence of a deity, although his unknowable deity could not be called beneficent.

Darwin's theory went right to the jugular of this sort of thinking: if God exists, Darwin seemed to be saying, He must be a sadist of the worst sort, countenancing waste and profligacy beyond the dreams of even the worst rulers in recorded history and exhibiting an appalling viciousness. Perhaps even more upsetting to mid-nineteenth-century sensibilities was the inescapable inference that any God who could live in Darwin's universe had to be obsessed with reproduction and sex. Whereas Erasmus Darwin's clever euphemisms about the lives and loves of plants had titillated turn-of-the-century readers, his grandson's sober accounts of "fitness" horrified many right-thinking folk who did not want to believe that sexual passion had played a causal role in the formation of most human social emotions, activities, and institutions.

Furthermore, the younger Darwin seemed to do away with the soul as well as with God. One consequence of his theory was a shift in scientific interest, away from the analysis of immaterial principles (such as association) and toward very concrete considerations of variation and the inheritance of variations, including variations in behavior and perception. These were, as Darwin knew, essentially variations in the organization of the nervous system. *Of all the important scientific developments of the nineteenth century, Darwin's was the only one that was strongly materialistic.* It offered little or no purchase for the obligatory antimaterialist arguments, even in their positivist versions. It is striking that in the *Origin* Darwin obsessively emphasized his search for a *vera causa* (real cause) of evolution at the same time that all of the major physicists in Europe were inclined to treat laws as little more than summaries of phenomena. Darwin was by no means above using such a positivist strategy, but even when doing so he stands out from the crowd. For example, his law of pangenesis (in *The Variation of Animals and Plants*) derives in accepted midcentury positivist fashion from a summary of several sets of phenomena, but Darwin stated it with excruciating tentativeness, calling it only a provisional hypothesis, and arguing both publicly and privately that he hoped even here to find the vera causa. Darwin was made terribly uneasy—downright ill, in fact—whenever he could not convince himself he had found the real cause for any element in his theory. Darwin was never susceptible to the blandishments of the positivist worldview. It is striking how he never once wavered from seeking causal explanations for natural facts.

By and large the nineteenth century was prepared to accept evolution, but in no way was it prepared to accept Darwin's theory of evolution by natural selection. Evolution could be "tamed" by making it into a form of historical progressivism, especially if humans and other "good guys" could be seen as standing at the pinnacle of development. But Darwin's theory could not be made to justify such inanities. Evolution was acceptable to the intellectual elite of the Victorian era to the extent that it could be seen as some plan of the deity, especially if God could be said to have planned the course of progress, for that would justify the ways of nineteenth-century civilization. Moreover, vague theories that God had arranged for human beings to evolve a soul or had simply implanted souls in certain animal lineages, could also be seen as consistent with a broadly evolutionary view of the world. Alfred Russel Wallace, who developed the idea of natural selection independently of Darwin, never accepted sexual selection as an important factor in evolution, and ultimately made just this kind of deistic appeal in his account of human evolution. Darwin politely but firmly told Wallace off, both in his private correspondence and in public statements.

When it came to scuttling Darwin's distressing theory of natural selection in favor of a more general evolutionary view, positivism turned out to be a major ally of mainstream thinking. Darwin's unswerving interest in real causes made him an enemy of positivism. When someone proposed theological or metaphysical hypotheses to him, he did not dismiss them as irrelevant to science, as positivists did, but instead tested them just as he tested all other hypotheses. Thus, when the great American botanist (and Darwin's good friend) Asa Gray promoted the idea that God had not created the different animal species but had guided the variations of animals and plants so that certain kinds of evolutionary outcomes would be likely, Darwin took up the challenge. Throughout *The Variation of Animals and Plants* Darwin looked for evidence for and against Gray's hypothesis, ultimately concluding that the evidence was overwhelmingly against it (and Gray in fact conceded this point). A positivist might reply, however, that as Darwin had no direct evidence about either evolution or the causes of variation, his theory was no more than a résumé of the phenomena that left room for other interpretations. Interestingly, this kind of intellectual maneuver was commonly employed by *religious* thinkers in the 1870s—as in the debates among the members of the Metaphysical Society described in Chapter 6. Spencerian evolutionary positivism was an excellent shield against Darwinian thought and its dangers.

DARWIN'S ACCOMPLISHMENTS IN PSYCHOLOGY

Charles Darwin, like his grandfather, did not believe in ghost stories. He did believe in evolutionary continuity, the idea that completely novel characteristics are the exception in evolution. Hence, he looked at psychological characteristics—mental states—as natural entities. He dismissed neither their mental properties nor their physical ones. For example, he saw emotional expressions as the combination of a certain state of feeling with a particular expression of the body or, in the case of humans, the face. In his book *The Expression of Emotions in Man and Animals* (1872) a picture of a cat rubbing against a person's leg is captioned "cat in an affectionate frame of mind." Such statements have been criticized by later psychologists — usually behaviorists — as anthropomorphizations. Darwin would have objected strongly to that description. He would have replied that it was anthropocentric to assume that only humans have affectionate frames of mind. He would also have replied that the behavior in such cases is not independent of the mental state. In particular, he argued that social animals' mental states exert causal powers over their conspecifics — that among social animals it makes a difference whether a creature is in an angry or affectionate mental state, and that both sexual and natural selection operate to favor social individuals who are relatively good at detecting the meanings of emotional expressions. (This idea concerning the causal efficacy of mental states in nature was later taken up by William James as a starting point for his functional psychology.)

Darwin also believed that mental states can be found in very simple animals and perhaps even in plants. He never attributed complex mental operations to these simple organisms, but he did routinely investigate the capacity of simple organisms to be aware of aspects of their surroundings. As reported in his book on earthworms, he performed a number of experiments to determine the sensory capacities of earthworms, for example — there are amusing stories of people blowing bassoons and piccolos at worms in the Darwin estate at Down — and found, among other things, that worms have a sensitivity to bright light. Darwin used a newfangled carbon arc light and demonstrated that most worms will withdraw from such a bright light. Then Darwin asked whether worms have any "power of attention" (as he put it), so he repeated the experiment, this time using copulating worms. None of the copulating worms reacted to the bright light at all, leading Darwin to conclude that they indeed had a "small" power of attention.

Darwin's careful studies of animal psychology, and his evolutionary theory (which allowed him to consider mental states as just another natural feature of organisms) made him disbelieve the positivist account of animals as machines. When Huxley gave his celebrated lecture "The Hypothesis That Animals Are Automata" at the British Association for the Advancement of Science meetings in 1872, Darwin twitted his good friend, saying that he wished the old critical Huxley with his scalpel-sharp wit would review and refute this newer Huxley. And a decade later, in his last letter to Huxley, the dying Darwin gibed that he wished that there were "more automata like you" in the world. In his experimentation, whenever Darwin found an apparently mechanical pattern of behavior, he always looked for the mental state that went along with the behavior and used it to generate experiments in which the behavior was varied. A good example of this kind of methodology is found in his studies on bees' foraging behavior. Darwin proved that bees learn about particular kinds of flowers and, having learned, tend to forage on these flowers in a stereotypical way. Darwin did not believe, however, that bees did this out of some mechanical instinct, but rather out of what might be call their spatial awareness. Instinct motivates the bee to go after nectar, but it cannot and does not help the bee navigate through fields to stands of flowers — that requires a little bit of intelligence, as Darwin put it. To prove this, Darwin showed that when an exceptionally large number of bees are foraging on a single stand of flowers, bumble bees abandon their habitual foraging pattern and actually cut through the base of flowers to gain access to the nectar. This strategy is selected because it represents a time savings for the bees and may cost their competitors time. The bees are not aware of this selective benefit, but they are demonstrably aware of the flower, the location of the nectar, and the competitors, and that awareness makes them change their behavior.

ANOTHER UNAPPRECIATED INNOVATOR: DOUGLAS SPALDING

Was the lack of impact of specifically Darwinian ideas due primarily to the institutional invisibility of Darwin, a private scientist, or to the unpalatability of his ideas? Such questions of comparison are always difficult to answer in historical analyses. There are interesting parallels, however, in the case of an important British experimental animal behaviorist, a contemporary of Darwin, whose work is now recognized as revolutionary but who had little influence at the time. A comparison of the career of Douglas Spalding (?1840–1877) with that of Darwin may help us to determine whether institutional or ideological factors played the bigger role in the resistance to Darwinian thinking.

Spalding offers a stark contrast to Darwin in many ways. Darwin was the offspring of two important English bourgeois families; Spalding, a poor working-class Scot, was born in London but grew up in Aberdeen and first worked as a slater (roofer). He was self-educated but apparently came to the attention of Alexander Bain, who arranged for Spalding to attend his lectures in 1862 without paying tuition. Spalding moved to London, qualified as a barrister, and began to meet and informally to study with some of the intellectual lights of London, such as John Tyndall. Working in London as a teacher and lawyer, Spalding contracted tuberculosis. He traveled to Italy and Spain in hopes of alleviating his condition, eventually meeting John Stuart Mill in Avignon. The two men became close, and through Mill, Spalding met Lord and Lady Amberley, who tried to hire Spalding as a tutor for their son. In the event,

Spalding continued his work as a lawyer until 1873, when he signed on as tutor to Frank, the Amberleys' heir, who now had a one-year-old younger brother, Bertrand Russell. Lady Amberley succumbed to diphtheria in 1874, and Lord Amberley died soon thereafter, in January 1876. The Amberleys had arranged for Spalding to be the guardian of Frank and Bertrand, but their will was broken through the strenuous efforts of Amberley's father, Lord Russell (the former prime minister). Lord Russell's strongest argument was that Spalding was a materialist and an atheist and therefore an unsuitable guardian. Spalding left England, never to return, and died in France in 1877.

The year before going to tutor the Russell children and during his two-year stay at Ravenscroft as their tutor, Spalding undertook a series of experiments on the nature of instinct in animal behavior, experiments that are now recognized as having completely transformed both method and theory in that area of psychology. As was the case with Darwin, his novel research methods most assuredly did not evolve in a university setting. On the contrary, Lady Amberley served until her death as Spalding's research assistant, and apparently the children were involved as well. In June 1874, Bertrand Russell's sister, Rachael, wrote to her grandmother Lady Russell about the disease that later killed both her and her mother: "Thank you very much for the doll and cradle. I am in bed with diphtheria and my throat hurts very much. Spaldy has two rabbits. Spaldy has got robins and a hive of bees in his room." Most historians of science would hesitate to suggest that experimental advances could come from the work of an ex-roofer working as a tutor in the employ of landed gentry, yet this was indisputably the case with Spalding.

Spalding's innovations were many. Most important, he pioneered the design of experiments in which the isolation and control of factors relevant to behavior were perfected. For example, to study whether space perception was innate or acquired, he did not speculate about local signs or specific nerve energies but instead got some fertilized eggs. He waited until they were beginning to hatch, and then "removed a piece of the shell, and before [the chicks] had opened their eyes drew over their heads little hoods. . . . the conditions under which these little victims of human curiousity were first permitted to see the light were then carefully prepared." After depriving them of sight for various lengths of time (up to several days), Spalding then carefully observed, measured, and timed the chicks' reactions to insects, grains of corn, and so on. Spalding's method of "sensory isolation" is one of the most important experimental procedures in this field, even today.

Through his careful and controlled procedures, Spalding also discovered what has come to be called the developmental critical period. He noticed that not only do animals deprived of a sense from birth learn to use it rapidly, "but they can also forget — and very soon — that which they never practised." A chick that has been deprived of hearing other chickens for one day from birth will still learn to orient itself to its mother and thus follow her call (this has come to be called imprinting). A chick reared without such sounds for ten days, however, "hears it as if it heard it not," and the mother hen, despite all her wiles, cannot induce the chick to follow her.

Unlike Darwin, Spalding tried to publicize his work through his personal efforts. He reported on his studies of instinct at the same British Association meeting (1872) at which Huxley proclaimed animals to be automata and later published his paper in *Macmillan's* magazine. He wrote a large number of book reviews, mostly for *Nature,* many of which discussed his views on behavior and the mind. Spalding followed Spencer in his theorizing about biology but not in the latter's philosophy of the unknowable. Spalding was a materialist when it came to psychology and upheld this view even though it led to an estrangement between him and Bain. Spencer's view that a species develops experience in the course of evolution Spalding defended not by theorizing, as Spencer did, but through careful experimental work—hence the rather curious use of *forget* in the quotation describing loss of an instinct. Spalding believed he had shown that chicks were born with some sort of inherited knowledge, which could be forgotten if it were not used soon after birth.

Although he was in no position to attract students, Spalding's work was widely celebrated for a brief time. It was praised by Darwin, as well as by Mill, and G. H. Lewes wrote an article titled "Instinct" in *Nature* (1873, vol. 7, p. 437): "The very valuable contribution to psychology made by Mr. Spalding . . . will no doubt stimulate research and lead to some rational explanation of what has hitherto been enveloped in a mist of metaphysics. Mr. Spalding has not only proved himself an acute thinker, he has shown a rare ability in devising experiments, and we may fairly expect that his researches will mark an epoch." Lewes's remarks sound reasonable and even prescient in the light of modern developments, but Lewes was wrong. Spalding's work stood as nothing more than an isolated example of what could be accomplished experimentally in the study of animal behavior. His work was still widely known as late as 1890, when James referred to "Mr. Spalding's wonderful article on instinct," but Spalding's work and name faded into obscurity soon after that. He has been "re-discovered" once a decade or so since 1950, though, when J. B. S. Haldane first rescued him from an indifferent posterity.

The Unnatural Soul of the New Psychology

It may be that Spalding's work, like Darwin's, failed to exert influence because he had no students; but another possibility is that Spalding's work, like Darwin's, did not fit comfortably with the orthodox assumptions of the new psychologists. Darwin's naturalistic psychology made mainstream thinkers of the late 1800s most uncomfortable. Taken seriously, Darwin's work could not be isolated from sensitive theological issues. It seemed to refute the "hypothesis" that God existed or that human beings have an immaterial soul. Spalding's experiments on inherited experience went further, suggesting that "inborn ideas" might not be God-given but simply another consequence of natural selection.

The areas in which the new experimental psychology thrived were far removed from Darwin's experimental studies of invertebrate behavior and Spalding's studies of mammalian and avian instincts. The experimental analysis of sensory processes or of reaction times or even of remembering and forgetting might at first blush threaten to yield results more antagonistic than Darwin's or Spalding's work to traditional views of human nature. Thanks to the positivist spin put on these studies, however, they were ultimately seen as *compatible* with belief in a soul—the new psychology was the experimental study of mind; it had no commitments to any particular doctrine of the soul. Thinkers such as Darwin and Spalding who naturalized (or even materialized) the soul could not be assimilated into the new science without destroying this tenuous compromise. The new psychology had become not a science to disprove the doctrine of the soul but a discipline that could help thinkers avoid conflict over theories on the nature of the soul. Not only did that orientation make it difficult for the new psychology to assimilate Darwinian thinking, but it also brought it into conflict with another science of the mind—logic.

The Generation of 1879, or How Philosophy Emerged from Psychology

The generation of psychologists who came of age around 1879 transformed the field. Experimental psychology labs sprang up at all the major universities in Germany. Increasingly, and for the first time, scholars began identifying themselves as specialists in psychology—although, in many cases, they also called themselves philosophers or physiologists. Americans in particular flocked to the German laboratories and returned to establish their own; by the late 1890s the center of activity in psychology had already begun to shift to the United States. Britain and France lagged behind, largely because in those countries the universities did not promote research. Alfred Binet in France and Francis Galton in England made major contributions but were unable to find the kind of institutional home available to experimental psychologists in Germany or America.

Yet, as previous chapters have emphasized, this activity was not perceived at the time as the creation of a new discipline distinct from philosophy. Contemporaries perceived a revival and transformation of branches of philosophy and physiology, not the emergence of a separate discipline. Wundt, the self-appointed leader of the new psychology, devoted much of his work in the 1880s to logic, ethics, and metaphysics—efforts never commented on by historians of psychology. William James, the only American to achieve a stature comparable to Wundt's before 1900, transferred from the Physiology Department to the Philosophy Department at Harvard in the late 1870s, teaching a mixture of empirical psychology, clinical psychology, and "purely philosophical" courses. Ribot, the French defender of the new psychology, wrote important works on neurology and on Schopenhauer's philosophy, as well as on experimental psychology. Cardinal Mercier, the Belgian proponent of the new psychology, promoted his revival of Thomism at the same time that he was promoting Wundt's new psychology. Croom Robertson and James Sully, the British thinkers most closely identified with this new generation, are nowadays remembered for their work on Hobbes and aesthetics, respectively. Charles Peirce, who appears to have been the first person to conduct psychophysical experiments in the United States, is nowadays remembered as a pioneer logician, theorist of semiotics, and philosopher.

The idea that scientific psychology emerged out of or split off from philosophy in the decades after 1879 is a false reading of the historical record. The main problem with this widely accepted myth is the assumption that philosophy—which is to say, something we in the twentieth century would recognize as philosophy—*existed* before 1879. It is fairly easy to show that nothing like philosophy—as we now use the term—existed as an institution or even as a distinct academic discipline before approximately 1900. The thinkers we remember nowadays as philosophers were not housed in academic philosophy departments in 1879, and conversely, the people who were housed in those departments are, with a very few exceptions, no longer remembered as philosophers. Wundt was a professor of philosophy but is never read nowadays as a philosopher; Frege was a mathematician; James was still, at least nominally, an associate professor of physiology in 1879; Nietzsche had abandoned the academy; Marx (old and infirm) and Engels (old and sprightly) were, as they always had been, paradigms of independent scholars; Peirce was working for the U.S. Coastal Survey and lecturing at Johns Hopkins University, a position that did not last. Perhaps the most significant exception to this pattern was Brentano, who was professor of philosophy in Vienna in 1879.

The period from 1879 to 1900 was one of considerable change, uncertainty, and transition within this sector of the intellectual world. In hindsight we can see that the universities were experimenting and trying to create modern "professionalized" disciplines. The earlier models of philosophy as ancillary to theology or history were no longer acceptable, nor was the Scottish-American model of philosophy as a guide to right living. One group of philosophers began to follow some of the positivist science-oriented worldviews then popular, and their adherence helped spark the rise of experimental psychology. A different group of thinkers lent their support, though, to epistemology (also derived from positivism), and to the emerging Erkenntnistheorie, the concept of philosophy as a kind of science of science. The group that stressed epistemology came into conflict over "psychologism" in logic with the positivistically inclined group and eventually went on to found the specific fields on which almost all twentieth-century academic philosophy is based—phenomenology and an analytic philosophy allied to symbolic logic.

We should therefore see philosophy in the late nineteenth century as a field in flux, out of which emerged two distinct twentieth-century disciplines, psychology and philosophy. Just as modern scientific psychology has its roots in physiology and medicine as well as in the older philosophical tradition, so modern philosophy has its roots in mathematics and logic as well as in the older philosophical tradition. To reiterate, it is not true that psychology as a science split off from philosophy—this itself is nothing more than a positivist myth. If anything, scientific psychology was much better established by the turn of the century than was philosophy. The two works that helped to define late modern academic philosophy throughout the Western world—Russell's *Principles of Mathematics* and Husserl's *Logische Untersuchungen* (Logical investigations)—were both published at the turn of the century, well after the "new" psychology was entrenched. Russell and Husserl each hoped their books would provide a definitive critique of what they both called psychologism, along with the outlines of a new and special method by which to reinvigorate philosophical work.

Psychologism and Logic

The debate in logical theory over psychologism has its roots in the same part of Mill's theory of logic that gave rise to the theory of the logical unconscious. In many ways it is possible to see the debate about psychologism in logic and philosophy as paralleling the debates over awareness and the unconscious in psychology and philosophy.

Mill's distinction between intuition and inference, and the allied assertion that many inferences can be unconscious, helped to divorce logic from psychology. The notion that logic is a study of the laws of thought that can call on introspective methods is undermined by the doctrine of unconscious inference. It may be, a supporter of the theory of unconscious inference would say, that the patterns of thought accessible to introspection are only a few of the possible patterns, and perhaps not a very representative sample, at that. The logician would then have to study more thought patterns than those available through introspection.

Although Mill himself was not always clear on this issue, many who followed him saw the implications of his distinction. If much of our thinking is unconscious, then a logic that claims to be an introspectively based description of how we think is surely going to be inadequate. One response to this objection is to suggest that logic is an *ethics*, not a physics, of thought. Logic, according to this view, tells us how we *should* think; it does not merely describe how we do think. A number of writers in the 1870s and 1880s argued for this kind of normative logic, but here events in psychology overtook them.

One of the great successes of the new psychology was a novel explanation of sensory illusions, heavily reliant on references to unconscious inference. This account seemed to deal with one of the most perplexing features of such illusions, their persistence even after the "trick" is known to the observer. For example, the classic Müller-Lyer illusion is as follows:

A. $\longleftrightarrow$

B. $\rightarrowtail\!\!\!\!\!\longrightarrow\!\!\!\!\leftarrowtail$

Although line segments A and B are of equal length, we all see B as being greater than A. Moreover, if you take a ruler, measure both segments, and prove to yourself that they are equivalent in length, this will not alter the illusory perception. The *knowledge* that A and B are the same length does not override the *perception* that B is longer.

Theorists of unconscious inference, largely following the immensely influential Herman von Helmholtz, argued that the resistance of illusory perception to conscious thought was due to habitual unconscious inference. On the basis of prior experiences and associations, we have developed certain unconscious ways of interpreting the world, and these will resist conscious modification. (The question of what experiences generate the Müller-Lyer illusion turns out to be a thorny one and has still not been resolved, incidentally.) The weaknesses of the theory are glaring: If the unconscious inferences are based on prior experience, couldn't they be changed through re-education or proper early training? Still, the theory was very popular throughout the 1880s and 1890s and seems to have withstood serious attacks from both Hering and James. Relevant here is that if unconscious inference can, and often does, lead to illusion, then the thought patterns it establishes are not good candidates for normative laws of thought. The theory of unconscious inference might yield a logic of illusion instead of a logic of truth—an idea at least considered by Nietzsche, who seems to have been much taken with Helmholtz's theory.

The problems with the model of logic as either a physics (descriptive account) or an ethics (normative account) of thought slowly led to a new conception of what logic should be. In the latter part of the nineteenth century, the idea emerged that logic could be a study of *possible patterns of thought,* not of actual patterns. These patterns of thought would not be the actual subjective states of individuals but only potentially subjective states, thinkable ones. Logic would be the study of such possibilities and their patterns, whereas psychology could concern itself with what happened when people actually did think these or any other thoughts.

Three distinct versions of this approach to logic were proposed after 1879: Frege's logic of abstract contents, along with his technique of a concept script for manipulating the possible thoughts (it later became the symbolic algebra of logic); Peirce's logic of relatives and his semiotic approach to manipulating those potential thoughts; and finally Husserl's early phenomenology, with its strong separation of thought as essence from actual thoughts.

The creation of a separate and abstract discipline of philosophy required a methodological innovation along such lines. To gain access to the newly available academic resources, philosophers would have to show that they had a valuable method, unique to them, for obtaining results. Unless philosophers could show that what they did was different from the analysis of actual thoughts and subjective states, philosophy would continually be threatened with annexation by psychology. Logic would disappear and the psychology of reasoning would triumph. How well these options were understood at the time is difficult to say. Certainly, Frege, Husserl, and Peirce all spoke consciously of starting a new discipline and of inventing a new method, and each produced a substantial body of work detailing precisely the scope and meaning of the projected discipline. Few subsequent thinkers, however, found themselves able to adopt those proposals in anything close to their original form. In contrast, scores of thinkers found considerable use for the methodological innovations championed by Frege, Husserl, and Peirce, and adopted their new methods while eschewing their philosophical positions. It is not too much to say that after World War I the practice of philosophy within the academy came to be dominated by the methods invented by these three thinkers—and that this methodological innovation played a major role in shaping twentieth-century philosophy as we know it.

LOGIC, PSYCHOLOGY, AND NOTATION IN FREGE AND PEIRCE

What modern logicians refer to as the first-order predicate calculus was invented independently in the 1870s by Charles Peirce and Gottlob Frege. Frege was a mathematician, and Peirce was an applied scientist who later eked out a meager living in intellectual journalism of all kinds. For a few brief years around 1880, however, Peirce secured a position at Johns Hopkins University that enabled him to work with graduate students and publish some of his logical work in the *American Journal of Mathematics* (before he offended its editor). That was the last time in his career that Peirce had an academic affiliation; nevertheless, his publications in the field of logic (only an extremely small proportion of his total writings on logic) achieved sufficient recognition to influence the next generation of logicians—Leopold Löwenheim, Bertrand Russell, and Ernst Zermelo, among others—before Russell "discovered" Frege.

The systems of logic invented by Peirce and Frege were designed to overcome psychologism and introduce a radically new methodology. Frege remained resolutely antipsychological throughout his career. Peirce, once he had clarified to his own satisfaction how to do antipsychological logic, tried to develop a theory of the relationship between psychology and logic, because he was as interested in the psychological processes involved in apprehending logical inferences as he was in the inferences themselves. In modern parlance, we might say that Frege's interests centered on formal logic, whereas Peirce's interests encompassed informal logic, the logic of the sciences, and even the psychology of the scientific process.

Throughout his writings, Frege always urged the separation of logic from the analysis of thought. "The business of the logician [is] to conduct an unceasing struggle against psychology." His basic insight is that something about a thought must be independent of that thought, and beyond all of its subjective aspects. Frege called this the *content* of a thought. "If other people can assent to the thought I express in the Pythagorean theorem, just as I do, then it does not belong to the content of my consciousness, I am not its owner; yet I can, nevertheless, acknowledge it as true." For Frege, no psychological process can make something true. The subjective processes of judgment may help me to find a truth but to not construct one. Psychology provides us with a causal account of thought and judgment, but logic provides us with an inferential account of that which is independent of the subjective aspects of thought, namely, the contents of the thought. Logic is about what is true, not about concepts.

The great mistake of the psychological logicians, Frege wrote in his *Basic Laws of Arithmetic* (part 1, sec. 18), is to assume that what is not real or objective must be subjective. That could be true if all knowledge came through the senses, but Frege denies this. Frege speaks of a "domain of what is objective which is distinct from that of what is real" or from that which resides in the external world. Nonphysical objectivity is what "is exactly the same for all rational beings, for all who are capable of grasping it." This Fregean sense of the objective is different from prior uses of the term. External (perceptible) objects are not objective, because they are not the same for all perceivers; psychological states are not objective, either. Only the contents of propositions, such as the meaning of the Pythagorean theorem, can be objective.

But how can we know anything about this special objective realm? My own thought about the Pythagorean theorem is not the content but merely my thought about that content. And when I express my thought to you, it is necessarily couched in language that when it is interpreted, is again not the content as such.

Frege's agenda was set by his understanding of this problem —a problem never before articulated so clearly. His suggestion was that the goal of logic was the search for truth, not truths. Frege started from the assumption, based on the wide intersubjective agreements we find in mathematics, that a realm of the true exists, an *objective* realm, in his special meaning of that term. Because ordinary language and thought obscure objective contents, though, Frege saw the need to create a technique for expressing and manipulating contents without distorting them —a notation for logic. This notation he called the *Begriffschrift*.

Peirce separated logic from psychology almost as sharply as did Frege, but without appealing to Frege's realm of objective contents. Like Frege, Peirce emphasized that intersubjective agreement seemed to imply that the contents of thought were, at least to some degree, independent of thinkers. Peirce spent much of his life searching for an accurate expression of this metaphysical realist insight, but with little success. After noting his position, then, we can leave aside the (unsettled) details of Peirce's realism to focus on his theory of logic.

As early as 1869 Peirce was arguing for a separation between psychology and logic: "The syllogism . . . is intended to represent the mind . . . only as to its relation of different judgments concerning the same thing. And it should be added that the relationship between syllogism and thought does not spring from considerations of formal logic but from those of psychology. All that the formal logician has to say, is that if facts capable of expression in such and such forms of words are true, another fact whose expression is related in a certain way to the experience of these others is also true." Awkward as this phrasing is, Peirce is emphasizing that logic focuses on the facts (Frege's objective contents) and the contents' relation, not on their expression or our comprehension of these facts.

With this in mind, and like Frege, Peirce argued that logic required a system of notation that pointed to the contents of propositions, not to their form or subjective interpretations. Peirce himself developed at least two kinds of notation systems, one an algebraic system and the other a quasi-geometrical system based on Venn diagrams. Here is an important difference between Frege and Peirce. Frege's logical notation was algebraic and intended to remove all need for the logician to use his or her "intuition" in assessing the significance of the symbols. Peirce believed that trained observers could recognize that a certain pattern constituted a valid inference—that, properly educated, intuitive, subjective processes could help in our search for truth—and he designed his notation system to take advantage of this capability.

Peirce saw the Fregean realism of objective contents as something that human observers might eventually be able to apprehend. Despite all his personal setbacks, Peirce was an optimist who believed that in the long run our very processes of thought might come to conform to patterns of logical inference. For Peirce, inferences were psychological processes; they mark the psychological transition from one judgment to another. And Peirce spoke of the "faith of the logician" that all these psychological processes are "adapted to an end, that of carrying belief, in the long run, toward certain predestinate conclusions which are the same for all men." It seemed to Peirce that logical notation guides and corrects our "cerebral habits" so that they will conform to the truth. Frege could agree with this up to a point — the point being Peirce's progressive metaphysical realism, with its implication that human thought can and will asymptote to valid inferences. Frege obviously believed that properly trained logicians could learn to make, express, and even discover valid inferences. He did not, however, go so far as Peirce, who seemed to see the objective realm of thought contents as a goal toward which human thought is approaching.

FROM GESTALTEN TO PHENOMENOLOGY

The attack on psychologistic logic that so aroused Frege and Peirce was not confined to logical theory. Indeed, the problems revealed by the critique of psychologism seemed to be central to the enterprise of the new psychology. If knowledge of the world can come only through sensations — as the new psychologists for the most part argued — then is it even possible to have logical, mathematical, or scientific knowledge? How can sensation-based knowledge support the absolute certainties of, say, mathematical proof? Descartes's solution to this problem — to claim that God has given us innate knowledge — did not seem reconcilable with an evolutionary perspective. Hence, Frege, Peirce, and others tried to specify a completely different way of looking at the problem and in so doing, separating logico-mathematical knowledge from empirical (sensation-based) knowledge.

A different response to these same problems emerged alongside of Frege's and Peirce's work. By the late 1880s, a number of theorists were disputing the new psychologists' account of sensations and their relation to knowledge. Some theorists, like Mach and James, contrived to talk of sensations but radically altered the meaning of that term. Other theorists, many of them students of Brentano or scholars associated with him (such as Stumpf, Meinong, Ehrenfels, and von Hornbostel), began to refer to entities other than sensations as sources of empirical knowledge. One strand of this critique of the new psychology evolved into Gestalt psychology, and a different strand evolved into Husserl's phenomenology. A complete history of these developments belongs properly to a history of early twentieth-century thought, but I will give a very brief sketch here to show how phenomenology, the second major new methodology in philosophy (after symbolic logic), also had its origin in the revolt against psychologism.

Stumpf, like his friend James and his teacher Brentano, was a critic of the new psychology. In his *Über den psychologischen Ursprung der Raumvorstellungen* (1873) he criticized both Wundt's and Helmholtz's theories of perception for being based on unconscious inference. In particular, he criticized the new psychologists' sensory atomism, and offered a novel way of thinking about the elements of experience. Stumpf analyzed experience as a whole as being made up of contents (*Inhalten*). It should be stressed that this use of the word is entirely different from Frege's. Some contents of experience, Stumpf argued, are *independent,* meaning that they can be experienced separately and independently of other aspects of experience. Many aspects of experience are not independent, however, but constitute what Stumpf called *partial contents* (*Theilinhalten*). Neither in real nor in imagined experience can a partial content appear all on its own. For example, it is impossible to have the experience of color without an experience of extension, or vice versa. One cannot even imagine color without extension of some kind. Many of Stumpf's explanations of what counted as partial contents have proved incorrect; nevertheless, his distinction has been useful. Stumpf believed, for example, that visual motion was a partial content, that one always had to see some object in motion. Max Wertheimer, one of the early Gestalt psychologists, turned this argument around by showing experimentally that in certain cases of apparent motion there is a pure perception of visual motion, independent of all other elements. Thus, although Stumpf was wrong about the details, his idea of searching for separable features of experience proved so fruitful that it could actually be used to refute his theory about the independence of visual motion.

Stumpf's analysis suggested that the basic sensations inferred by the new psychologists either do not exist or do not exist in the atomistic form proposed by Wundt and others. Experience may have independent contents, but these are not the elementary sensations of color or sound the new psychologists conceived of. Twelve years later in his *Analyse der Empfindungen,* Mach redefined sensations in a holistic manner; essentially they corresponded to Stumpf's *contents.* Stumpf had been professor of psychology at Würzburg and then at Prague in the 1870s and 1880s (later moving to Halle, Munich, and finally Berlin), and Mach was professor of physics at Prague before moving to Vienna in 1893. Brentano, who taught philosophy at Vienna, was keenly aware of the emerging Austro-Hungarian critique of the (largely North German) new psychology. In the event, it was two students of Brentano, Christian von Ehrenfels (1859–1932) and Alexius Meinong (1853–1920), who took the next step in the attack on sensationalism.

Ehrenfels noted that some aspects of experiential content seem to be tied to particular sensory variables, whereas others are not. The classic example is a melody. Each element of a melody is a tone—a particular auditory sensation. But the melody as an aspect of experience is not an auditory sensation, nor even tied to any particular group of sensations. This is demonstrated by the fact that a melody transposed to a different key—that is, to an entirely different set of notes—can easily be recognized as the same melody. Ehrenfels conceived of a melody as a form in time, as a relationship that obtains among acoustic events and is not necessarily tied to any particular auditory sensation. Ehrenfels also argued that there are spatial, as well as temporal, forms: the squareness of a square is to the four line segments it comprises precisely as the melody is to its component notes: squareness can be preserved even if the lines change in many ways (color, size, rotation).

Form qualities, or *Gestaltqualitäten,* as Ehrenfels called them, fit Stumpf's definition of independent contents, but they are certainly not sensations. Thus, whereas the sensationalists assumed that the basic independent contents were sensations, Stumpf's and Brentano's students used phenomenological analysis to find other kinds of independent contents. Ehrenfels argued that gestalt qualities are apprehended by a special mental act, different from sense reception.

At Graz, Austria, Meinong took Ehrenfels's analysis as his starting point and argued for a distinction supplementary to Stumpf's. In addition to independent and partial contents, Meinong argued, contents can be further separated into found-*ing* and found*ed* contents. Founding contents are akin to Mach's sensations (not to Wundt's sensory atoms) in that they are based on sensory qualities. Founded contents emerge from the form or pattern of sensory qualities. Hence, sets of very different founding qualities can be perceived as having a founded content in common—as when one hears a melody played in the key of E-flat on the clarinet and then in C on the piano. (The melody is the single founded content; the two sets of notes—each yielding the unique auditory sensations of the instrument on which they were played—are the founding contents.)

Stumpf's first pupil after he arrived in Halle in 1884, a young mathematician named Edmund Husserl, was recommended to him by Brentano. From about 1885 until the turn of the century, Husserl worked on the problem of mathematical knowledge and tried to assimilate the "Austrian" critique of the new psychology into a critique of logic and the foundations of mathematics. The existing arguments against both empiricism and psychologism were generally based on psychological logicians' assumption that all logico-mathematical knowledge derived from sensations, in the sense of sensory atoms. But perhaps the empirical basis of mathematics lay not in sensations but in the gestalten and founded contents—the relatively complex patterns—that characterize our experience of the world. Husserl's early work culminated in his *Logische Untersuchungen*, in which he argued strongly against the psychology of sensory atomism, suggesting instead that human beings are capable of a very different kind of apprehension of the world—awareness of its gestalt aspects.

For Husserl, logical judgment and inference take place independently of psychological processes. The new concepts of contents and founding seemed to him very helpful for his argument. If some mental contents are not always tied directly to sensory atoms—if founded contents, to use Meinong's terminology, were important to thought—then manipulation of those contents can and should be kept distinct from the apprehension of simple sensory elements. The psychologists' laws of thought and experience would have to do with what makes certain contents independent and others partial, or what is involved in the process of founding. Husserl claimed that such processes were nothing like the simple associative processes of the psychologists. The laws of logic, he argued, should be understood as abstract patterns relating founded contents and should in no way be tied to particular details of any sensory processes.

After 1900, in his logical writings and in the texts that became *Ideen* (Ideas) Husserl further developed his new methodology, not just for logic but for all of philosophy. The new approach, which he christened phenomenology, took as one of the basic methods of philosophy a "bracketing" of experience, in which the founded contents of thought can be treated as the objects of philosophical analysis, independently of their relation to the "objects" of everyday life or of science. Phenomenological philosophy, which Husserl envisaged as a science, would place the study of bracketed experience as such first, prior to questions about ontology or psychology. Ontological and psychological questions are legitimate, Husserl admitted, but not necessary within the basic sphere of philosophy. For Husserl, philosophy became the analysis of the world of contents independent of their causation and also independent of their relation to any ontology, whether scientific or everyday. To some degree, Husserl was attempting to create a philosophical methodology suitable for studying the "stream of consciousness" that William James had placed at the heart of psychology. Husserl recognized, as few self-described psychologists did, that James's psychology was incompatible with the ideas and methods of the new psychologists.

Although it is common enough to read about how psychology emerged from philosophy, one rarely reads about how modern philosophy emerged from psychology. Yet the two most fundamental methods of modern philosophy—methods that arguably define most of twentieth-century philosophy—both developed in response to the perceived successes of the new psychology. Without "psychologicians" such as Wundt and Theodore Lipps, and their allies in epistemological theory, such as Helmholtz, the development of both symbolic logic and phenomenology would have been radically different. Modern philosophers have obscured this history by creating a canon for their field that stretches back through Kant and Hume to Descartes and others during the scientific revolution. Yet psychologists have just as good a claim to this canon—perhaps a better one.

Both modern psychology and modern philosophy—as academic disciplines comprising professional scientists or scholars—began to emerge toward the end of the nineteenth century. Psychology in this sense preceded philosophy by at least ten years, although it tended to be housed within philosophy departments. Obviously, a great deal of jockeying for position, power, prestige, and influence took place. In the United States it was only in the 1890s that philosophers sought to organize specialized journals and started to think about founding a professional society (which did not begin functioning until 1901). In these activities they lagged at least a few years behind the psychologists, and many of the founding documents of "strictly philosophical" institutions explicitly refer to the successes in psychology as one of the reasons for establishing such distinctively philosophical entities. Small wonder that the new professional philosophers latched onto the most provocative antipsychological methodologies available, phenomenology and logic, as defining the activity of members of their emerging discipline.

William James:
Psychology as a Science of Experience

William James is both a major figure in the history of American thought and an anomalous one. In standard accounts he is treated as the first major American philosopher and also as the father of psychology in America. Acclaimed as the father of two academic disciplines, James nevertheless deplored academic specialization, as he made clear in his critical article "The Ph.D. Octopus." Furthermore, the projects on which he expended the most labor—his stream-of-consciousness psychology, his studies of psychic powers, his analysis of religious experience and conversion—have never been taken up seriously by those who claim to be his heirs in philosophy and psychology throughout the United States.

Especially in psychology, James's towering figure is oddly blurred or even doubled. On the one hand, he is said to have brought the new experimental psychology to the United States; by founding a psychology laboratory at Harvard in the 1870s, he certainly made a major contribution to this trend. Yet James was never comfortable with the new psychology and always maintained his intellectual distance from it.

Thus, although James is widely cited by modern psychologists as an inspirational father figure, he would have denied his paternity of anything resembling modern experimental psychology. James's best psychological work, spanning the last twenty-five years of the nineteenth century, offers a remarkable synthesis of earlier thinking and results, yet he took issue with nearly all the major themes of nineteenth-century psychology. In a number of ways he attempted to resurrect the Shelleys' natural supernaturalist psychology in a new form—a psychology of "wide circumference." But his efforts toward this end have rarely been understood or appreciated, in large part because so many modern academic schools and disciplines have insisted on claiming him as their ancestor.

JAMES'S CRITIQUE OF THE NEW PSYCHOLOGY

The recognition of James as an important thinker coincided with the arrival of the new psychology and its laboratories in Europe. His first major essays dated from the end of the 1870s, and much of the early work revolved around criticisms of this psychology, especially the influential British version, which was based on Spencerian evolutionary associationism. James's essays in criticism were collected, organized, reworked, and amplified in *Principles of Psychology* (1890), but I shall focus here on the outlines of his ideas found in somewhat rawer form in the original articles.

At least five points were at issue between James and the new psychologists. First, the new psychology was evolutionary only in Spencer's sense; it did not take into account Charles Darwin's theory of the combination of chance variation with competition to yield natural selection. Second, the new psychology tended toward an updated associationism, focusing on the supposedly elementary sensory states—mental atoms, as it were—and ignoring, or so James claimed, the transitive, relational, and fluid elements of mind. Third, as a consequence of that mental atomism, the new psychologists were forced to postulate unconscious mental processes. James simply did not believe in these and, as a kind of a test case, spent a great deal of effort working out a theory of space perception that obviated the need for unconscious inference. (James's persistent disbelief in the logical unconscious of the new psychologists did not, however, entail disbelief in fringe consciousness or subconscious phenomena, both of which he studied extensively.) Fourth, the supposedly antimetaphysical positivism of the new psychology turned out to be, James asserted, just another metaphysics, but one biased in favor of a kind of cognitive atomism. James offered a strikingly different picture of the relation between psychology and metaphysics. Finally, James believed that the new psychology was yet another version of traditional Christian monotheism: that it postulated a unified soul in some way reflective of a monotheistic deity. This proposition seemed to James an extreme distortion of the phenomenology of religious experience. It is in regard to this last point that James's striking originality is apparent—who else chose to challenge the new psychology because of its empirical inadequacy vis-à-vis religious experience?

Much of the new psychology ignored the intellectual battles over evolution. To students grappling with testing mental reaction times it did not much matter whether the nervous system had evolved via natural selection. But because of the enormous prestige of Spencer's work, in the English-speaking world the new psychology was commonly regarded as an integration of the new evolutionary theory with the principles of associationism.

Spencer's formula that the mind constituted an inner world that needed to be adjusted to the outer world enjoyed a tremendous vogue in the 1870s and 1880s. Doubtless some of its popularity was due to the ambiguity of its basic precept—what fact could possibly *resist* being counted as an instance of the "adjustment" of an animal to its surroundings? Spencer's formula was also vague enough to be seen as a continuation of the British tradition in epistemology that ran from Locke through the two Mills. Spencer's adjustment was conceived largely as a

shaping of *ideas* (through association) to *reflect* the world outside them. Finally, Spencer's formula served as an updated form
of Montesquieu's ever-popular doctrine, climate shapes character. One could simply add an evolutionary time frame to the
mechanisms whereby the mind was supposedly shaped by climate and geography.

James was far too acute a Darwinian to let this Spencerian
sloppiness pass as the "evolutionary" approach to psychology.
The only prominent psychologist of his day to have studied
comparative anatomy, James had been a pupil of both Jeffries
Wyman and Louis Agassiz at Harvard during the 1860s, when
they were in the middle of their heated debate over Darwinism. Wyman was the second most important Darwinian in the
United States after Asa Gray, who was also at Harvard and
also part of this vicious intellectual battle. Agassiz was perhaps America's most distinguished naturalist, and certainly its
fiercest anti-Darwinian. When James joined Agassiz in a col-
lecting expedition in Brazil in 1865–66 (designed in large part
to prove Agassiz's theory of fish taxonomy against Darwin's —
a goal that could not be, and was not, met), he was repelled
by Agassiz's unwillingness to consider Darwin's views. Thirty
years later James still remembered a verbal tongue-lashing the
distinguished professor gave to the twenty-three-year-old who
dared defend Darwin.

One of James's first important essays is his "Remarks on
Spencer's Definition of Mind as Correspondence" (1878),
which is a full-scale Darwinian critique of Spencer. Here James
made his often-misconstrued point that "the knower is not
simply a mirror floating with no foothold anywhere, and passively reflecting an order that he comes upon and finds existing.
The knower is an actor, and co-efficient of the truth on one
side, whilst on the other he registers the truth which he helps
to create." Absent the Darwinian context, James's point about

knowers helping to make their own truths can easily be misread as a version of idealism, such as Wundt's concept of the mind as unconsciously acting to create a model of reality. But James did not attack Spencer in order to fall into the arms of Wundt. When James says that the knower is an actor, he has in mind the activities of life, not of the Kantian mental "sausage factory" (James's favorite epithet against all active idealisms).

For James the key point here is that knowers are evolved animals, making their way in a competitive natural world. Unlike Spencer's knowers, they are creatures who feel as well as know; also unlike Spencer's knowers, they are creatures who are each born with a unique set of abilities and inclinations. Variation is fundamental, ubiquitous, and random. Hence, some of the most important aspects of a mind may be shaped by its inherited tendencies, rather than the solicitations of the environment. As James put it in another critique of Spencer and his epigones, "Great Men and Their Environment" (1880): "No geographical environment can produce a given type of mind. It can only fasten and further certain types fortuitously produced, and thwart and frustrate others."

James argues that these basic inherited mental variations differ not in their cognitive powers but in their *selective* powers. He recognized that no living, flesh-and-blood animal could merely mirror the world. Active creatures must select aspects of their surroundings to attend to and act on, even transform. The idea that they mirror all of reality, or even a part of it, is irrelevant. Even in "remarking" on Spencer in his early essay, James emphasizes that the knower is not passively reflecting but actively selecting. The environment serves, James suggests, to "awaken an interest" in each knower. But the only interest recognized by Spencerians is survival, or self-interest. Hence, they believe that "the embodiment of the highest ideal perfection of mental development [is] a creature of superb cognitive endowments, from whose piercing perceptions no fact was too minute or too remote to escape; whose all-embracing foresight no contingency could find unprepared . . . but in whom all these gifts were swayed by the single passions of love of life, of survival at any price."

James replaced this—the very image of Shelley's shrunken perimeter—with a more encompassing ideal, in which survival is but one of many interests. In James's Darwinian psychology, the knower is by no means omniscient. Each effort at knowing or guiding action involves a corresponding ignorance, a closing off to part of the world in order to deal better with the things of interest. Animals whose interests, shaped by inheritance as well as experience, are either too narrow or inappropriate will find their actions "thwarted" and "frustrated," James suggested.

In his now-famous essay of 1879, "Are We Automata?" James took this argument a step further. Here James enunciated his controversial doctrine that because consciousness has evolved, it must have a function. Stated thus—and it is usually so stated—the argument is an example of the adaptationist's fallacy. One could just as easily say, because appendixes (or earlobes, or ingrown toenails) have evolved, they must have a function. But nowadays appendixes are good for little more than appendicitis, a dubious "function." It is noteworthy, therefore, that James's argument for the evolution of consciousness is not this typical adaptationist claim but something else again, something based on his critique of Spencer.

James's argument in "Are We Automata?" takes up his account of an interest-based selection where he left it in his critique of Spencer. James's point is that according to a Darwinian view, interest—a mental state—must be conceived of as part of nature. He reviews the standard arguments made by the new psychologists about the evolutionary value of cortical or conscious guidance superseding mere reflex response.

Such concepts as "useful [nervous] discharge, appropriate direction, right-reaction, and the like" are precisely how the new psychology distinguishes higher from lower psychological processes. But, says James, these "all presuppose some Good, End, or Interest to be the animal's." The interest must be the animal's rather than the observer's because whenever any choice is involved, the determining factor must be what the animal selects as better, more interesting, more appropriate, more needed. Yet such interests "cannot be posited at all so long as we consider the purely physical order of existence. Matter has no ideals. . . . Good involves the notion of less good, necessitates comparison, and for a drop of water either to compare its present state with an absent state or to compare its total self with a drop of wine, would involve a process not commonly thought of as physical." If there is one thing in a Darwinian universe that is not part of our typical idea of a mechanical, physical universe, it is this—the interests of the individual.

James is arguing here that his Darwinian psychology of interest *brings mental states into the natural world,* an idea that is completely absent in Spencer and in the positivistic new psychology. As James put it in his "Remarks": "The mind, according to [Spencer's] philosophy, should be pure product, absolute derivation from the non-mental. To make it dictate conditions, bring independent interests into the game which may determine what we call correspondence and what not" goes against Spencerian theory. And each of these acts of interest-based comparison, James says, "is known as a consciousness"—not mere sensations or feelings, but selections and choices.

Thus, when James calls the mind active and claims that it helps to create the true, he is referring not to an activity outside of nature—as consciousness has often been conceived—but to a natural activity, the psychological process of selection based on interest. The psychological realm is not a new world of mind or spirit or even of ideas but an evolution of the natural world, in which certain factors are isolated, compared, and combined, often in novel ways.

JAMES AGAINST THE ATOMISTS AND PSYCHIC STIMULISTS

James visited both Mach and Stumpf in Prague in 1882, discussing with them their separate but parallel attacks on the atomistic sensationalism of the new psychology. He took their critiques seriously, but he himself developed yet a third, and perhaps more powerful, criticism of psychological atomism. Following his visit to Prague, in the winter of 1883, James wrote "On Some Omissions of Introspective Psychology," an essay that contains the outline of his critique of sensory atomism and the beginnings of his own stream-of-consciousness psychology.

In the essay, James distinguished between the substantive and the transitive parts of the stream of consciousness. (He thought of these as two ends of a dimension, although he often wrote of them as if they were categorical opposites.) The substantial parts were the psychologists' "sensations"—or, better yet, Mach's sensations and Stumpf's contents. But the transitive parts had not been given their due by psychologists. They are the experiences of relation and process that make up most of our stream of thought. "We ought to say a feeling of *and,* a feeling of *if,* a feeling of *but,* and a feeling of *by,* quite as readily as we say a feeling of blue, or a feeling of cold, yet we do not." As far as James was concerned, the failure of introspective psychology to recognize these feelings of relation and process is the worst sin of the new psychologists. "What God has joined together, they resolutely and wantonly put asunder."

If there are genuine feelings of relation, then many of the mental entities supposedly created by association may be nothing of the sort—they may simply be elements (relational elements) of experience. And, similarly, some of those mental entities ultimately called Gestalt qualities or founded contents by the Austrian school may also better be understood as feelings of relation. "The demand for atoms of feeling, which shall be real units, seems a sheer vagary, an illegitimate metaphor. Rationally, we see what perplexities it brings in train; and empirically, no fact suggests it, for the actual content of our minds are always representations of some kind of an *ensemble*."

In opposition to James, the new psychologists claimed that their theories of associationism and unconscious inference were based as much on neurophysiological facts as on facts of introspection. It had become clear, as we have seen, that claims about unnoticed sensations and the like could be supported only through such arguments. If the eye and brain are so constructed that they must yield atomic sensations as the first step in the perceptual process, then James's introspective critique of the new psychologists' introspection is irrelevant.

James was well aware of this response and had a rejoinder ready as early as the 1883 essay. He argued that the emerging consensus in neurophysiology was also against atomism. "The whole drift of recent brain-inquiry sets towards the notion that the brain always acts as a whole, and that no part of it can be discharging without altering the tensions of all other parts." In short, brain inquiry supports James's stance against the ideas of the new psychologists: the basis of our awareness is a complex stream of consciousness with subtle and continual changes in its elements, paralleling (in some way that we do not understand) the activities of the nervous system as an ensemble.

Several years earlier, James had begun to develop an inquiry into the nature of space perception as a test case for his relational theory. In "The Spatial Quale" (1879) he offered the first version of an empirical critique of the new psychology that ultimately became a leitmotif of *The Principles*. If the elements of our spatial awareness are sensory atoms—substantive, not relational elements in the stream of consciousness—why is this not reflected in our experience of space? "Any space which I can take in at one glance comes to me as an undivided plenum. Were it built up . . . out of a vast number of perceptions of position fused together, I do not see how its quality could escape retaining something of the jerky, granulated character of its composite source. The spaces we do construct by adding together related positions—those, namely, which are too vast to be taken in at one glance—are, in fact, presented to consciousness in this jerky manner."

Consider, says James, how you apprehend the space in front of you: from where you are sitting, say, to the wall—it is smooth, taken in at a glance. Then consider the space between you and San Francisco: this has a certain granularity, being composed of many separate scenes and situations. Taken together, the contrast between these two experiences suggests to James that each of our sensations has a certain intrinsic spatial quality (a transitive rather than substantive quality). "I say that the feeling arising from the excitement of any extended part of the body is felt as extended." From the point of view of traditional psychology, this is the heresy of maintaining that the soul is extended (a heresy with which both Robert Whytt and Erasmus Darwin were charged). From the point of view of the new psychology, this is the heresy of attributing to the body and feeling the work of the mind and thought.

According to James, there are three possible theories of spatial awareness. First is the theory that there is no real spatial perception at all, space being just a symbol of the succession of certain sensations. This was probably Berkeley's view and it was, as we have seen, the doctrine of Brown's that was most influential, especially in Britain—both Mills and Bain endorsed it. Second—James's own view—there is a spatial quale (property) in (at least some) sensations, from which our appreciation of space derives. And third, the spatial quale is produced outside the mind and attributed to certain sensations. As James notes: "This last is the Kantian view. Stumpf admirably designates it as the 'psychic stimulus' theory." One of the major motivations behind James's psychology is to undermine the psychic stimulists, who until then had dominated the new psychology. Time and again James would claim to find within the stream of consciousness what these psychic stimulists insisted was not in direct awareness but only elicited from the mind by sensory events.

Antimetaphysics and Metaphysics

Given the philosophical controversy between James and the new psychologists, we can see why he was so irritated at the claims of the new psychologists that theirs was a "positive" psychology, shorn of metaphysics. James rightly complained that this positivism was little more than a smokescreen for a generally atomistic view of the world. And unlike Fechner's holistic atomism (of which James approved), the mainstream of new psychology was resolutely reductionist.

The nineteenth-century positivism with which the new psychologists allied themselves was, in fact, very atomistic—or, to use James's language, thinkers like Wundt tended to emphasize substantive elements to the exclusion of transitive ones and thereby dismiss the stream of consciousness. Sensations of color or intensity or weight they willingly granted, but they balked at sensations of movement or form. For James, the test case for this branch of positivism was not the theory of spatial perception but the analysis of belief or "the perception of reality" (as he later put it). James opened his discussion of these issues in his first serious analysis of volition, "The Sense of Effort" (1880), and he continued it in "The Psychology of Belief" (1889), which was reprinted in *The Principles* as "The Perception of Reality."

Here James identified a remarkable gap in traditional associationist thought. Starting with James Mill's *Analysis of the Phenomena of the Human Mind* (1829), nineteenth-century associationists had attempted to treat volition as on a par with all other mental events—that is, to treat intending to do x as having a certain kind of idea of x. Now, in general, when we accept an idea, we can be said to believe it; but in one case only, our acceptance of an idea requires something to happen in the world—when we voluntarily intend to do something. The associationist analysis treats all ideas as equally real for the mind, and adds that volitional ideas become real for the body, and even the world, if and when they are carried out.

Yet in the case of belief—or, better, the perception of reality—an idea (to continue speaking in associationist terms) is held to be true of the world, not just true for the mind. It is one thing to have an idea (that today is sunny) and quite another to believe that idea to be true of the world. John Stuart Mill identified this problem in associationist theory in his notes to his edition of his father's *Analysis* (1869), in a passage that James quotes in both "The Sense of Effort" and "The Psychology of Belief." Mill asks:

> What is the difference to our minds between thinking of a reality and representing to ourselves an imaginary picture? I confess I can see no escape from the opinion that the distinction is ultimate and primordial. . . . I cannot help thinking, therefore, that there is in the remembrance of a real fact, as distinguished from that of a thought, an element

which does not consist . . . in a difference between the mere ideas which are present to the mind in the two cases. This element, however we define it, constitutes belief, and is the difference between memory and hallucination.

James's analysis of willpower starts from the element, however we define it, that constitutes belief.

According to James, volition is a process of choice among ideas, as he makes clear in "The Sense of Effort." The ideas among which we choose are ideas in James's nonassociative sense, so they are for the most part ideas of relations, including ideas of my relation to the world around me. Deliberation or reflection is "a conflict between many ideas of possibility," and throughout the period in which this conflict plays out, the ideas must be held as possibles, not realities. "The conflict [of ideas] is over when the sense of reality returns, like the tempered steel, ten times more precious and invincible for its icy bath in the waters of uncertainty."

But why does the sense of reality return? Do our efforts of will tip the competitive balance in favor of one idea or another? Or does the strongest idea simply win out on a purely mechanical basis? This contrast between a kind of fatalism and a belief in the efficacy of the will was the fundamental philosophical question for James. He has prepared his answer through his psychological doctrine of the natural reality of interest: part of what sways the battle of competing ideas will be the interests of the individual, as unfolded in his or her life—and, if these have efficacy, we can then say that mind and will have some sway over choice and selection.

With his naturalistic theory of the mind as a basis, James makes a clever dialectical move by applying his analysis of belief to the question of fatalism. Here we have a competition of ideas (one that goes back to ancient times) between the idea of free will and the belief that the will is predetermined. By an effort of the will, James asserts that he will choose to believe in the "alternative of freedom" — *because it is in his interest to do so.* He thus instantiates the efficacy of free will in part by raising the question of whether the will be free or no.

Of course, the positivists (among others) cried foul at this dialectical dance. If the question of free will is not (yet) decidable by evidence — and the positivists asserted that it wasn't — then it must be left undecided. Yet isn't leaving the question undecided an example of allowing a different set of interests to sway the decision? The interests may be those called empirical, or rational choice, by the positivists, yet interests they are, nonetheless. But James went beyond simply playing dialectical tricks with free will. If we have ideas of relation, as James kept insisting against the positivists, then do we not have ideas about our relation to the world? Indeed, throughout the 1880s James championed the argument that our motor ideas, our ideas of volition, efficacy, and action, derive from our perception of our actions (via musculoskeletal sense, or kinesthesia). Wundt and his followers denied this, claiming that the sense of effort was not relational but substantive, based on our brain's commands to the muscles.

James perpetrated a second slick dialectical maneuver. He coopted (at least in *The Principles*) the lingo of the positivists. He replaced their atomistic sensations and ideas with his relational and complex sensations and ideas, but he still called them sensations and ideas. He replaced the positivists' atomism with his own holistic natural history, but he still used the vocabulary of associationism. He even proclaimed that his book was "positivist" in the sense of emphasizing the phenomena of experience (in James's meaning of the term) and that his was a "psychology as a natural science." He chastised the positivists for endorsing a particular brand of metaphysics (atomism and physicalism) and claimed the neutral high ground for himself, although he certainly hinted at his own metaphysical predilections. This oversubtle maneuver was a mistake. True, once the reader understands how James is using words, he or she will probably agree with him. But very few readers actually do understand James's subtleties of language and logic. Countless readers have (mis)interpreted *The Principles* as propounding a variant of the new positivist psychology when it was in fact an all-out assault on the turn psychology had taken in the 1870s.

James's decision to avoid metaphysical argument in *The Principles* had the unfortunate consequence of separating some of his philosophical ideas from his work in psychology in the popular mind. (Indeed, the fact that some of his work is typically labeled *either* philosophy *or* psychology underscores this view, and the editors of the collected *Works of William James* have perpetuated the problem by separating his so-called essays in psychology from his essays in philosophy.) At about the same time that he was developing his arguments about belief and volition, James was also exploring a further implication of his theory of relational states of mind. In "Reflex Action and Theism"—a talk given in 1881 to the Unitarian Ministers' Institute in Princeton, New Jersey, and reprinted in James's collection of essays *The Will to Believe* in 1897—James began to develop his pantheistic metaphysics on the basis of his new psychology. It is the non-Christian (even non-Western) religious metaphysics that most decisively distinguishes James from the other new psychologists (as well as from Freud). Because James left these arguments out of *The Principles,* though, their connection with his psychological work has not been appreciated.

That James had the new psychologists in mind is obvious from the title of his talk, "Reflex Action and Theism," which sounds like the essays on the new psychology penned in the same decade by G. Stanley Hall, James Mark Baldwin, and John Dewey (discussed in Chapter 1). But James begins with a joke that turns the Protestant pieties of the new psychologists upside down: "One runs a better chance of being listened to to-day if one can quote Darwin and Helmholtz than if one can only quote Schleiermacher or Coleridge. I almost feel myself this moment that were I to produce a frog and put him through his physiological performances in a masterly manner before your eyes, I should gain more reverential ears for what I have to say." And he concludes: "The latest breeze from the physiological horizon need not necessarily be the most important one."

James proceeds to develop his naturalistic theory of volition, telling the ministers that in evolved beings like ourselves action dominates cognition: "The willing department of our nature . . . dominates both the conceiving and the feeling department." Although our sensory apparatus and our brains are marvelously acute instruments of apprehension, we cannot simply soak in and "appreciate the [whole] given order" of the world. Minds are not internal realities that reflect the external ones, as Spencer claimed; they are parts of living organisms and aid in the process of selection, as Darwin intimated. We are forced to select what we do and what we attend to, and this selection is based largely on interests and needs tied up with action.

But interests and needs emerge from our relation to the world—and such relational entities have been filtered out of the universe by positivist psychologists. Characteristically, James couches this crucial charge in a lively image:

> The whole array of active forces of our nature stands waiting, impatient for the word which shall tell them how to discharge themselves most deeply and worthily upon life. "Well," they cry, "What shall we do?" "Ignoramus, ignorabimus!" says agnosti-

cism. "React upon atoms and their concussions!" says materialism. What a collapse! The mental train misses fire, the middle fails to ignite the end, the cycle breaks down . . . and the active powers, left alone, with no proper object on which to vent their energy must either atrophy . . . or else [unleash] pent up convulsions.

As far as James is concerned, the atomistic and agnostic positivists are promoting yet another metaphysics. But theirs has the disadvantage of denying belief in realities James claims are obvious and basic to all who experience: needs, interests, and powers of all kinds.

THE SOUL IN PSYCHOLOGY

Traditional associationism had need of the soul because something had to hold all the sensations and ideas together. The new psychologists and positivists denied the problem, saying that the phenomenon of aggregation was sufficient and that we cannot know whether a soul exists because there is no sensory atom to tell us whether it does.

James, too, denied *this* soul's existence—but for very different reasons. James's relational elements of consciousness provided the "glue" for which the associationists had always looked to the soul. But this new, Jamesian universe also included powers and relations of other kinds. As James was to emphasize in his Ingersoll Lectures on immortality (1898) and again in his *Varieties of Religious Experience* (1902), our experience discloses no single source of power and agency or even of goodness, but rather a plurality of such sources. James could agree with the new psychologists that the soul was nonexistent—or at least that no one could prove it existed—and he could agree to their similar arguments about God. But he could not and did not agree that humans lack all soul-like powers of agency, even though those powers are often diffuse and evanescent. Similarly, he could not agree that the universe lacked all power and agency. Indeed, he felt sure that his experience disclosed such external powers every bit as much as it disclosed the efficacy of his own will. In contrast to the other founders of modern psychology, James was a pluralist with regard to the soul and also with regard to the gods. Perhaps that is why he still speaks to readers in such a fresh voice.

As a child, William James's younger brother Henry complained that he found it difficult to keep up with Willy, who was always down the street and around the corner. For the mature Willy, the gods were always down the street and around the corner: at the edges and margins of our experience, perhaps, but believable and real all the same.

A Science of the Soul

James's concept of experience, which stood at the center of his diverse ideas, never caught on. Philosophers rejected it in favor of the associationists' concept of elementary sensations or, in our own century, for the analytic philosophers' hypothesis about logical elements. Psychologists, too, at first rejected James's concept of experience, for the more elementary and less fluid notions of associationism; later, in accordance with the principles of behaviorism, psychological theory substituted stimuli and responses for experience altogether. James's fundamental critique of the new psychology, embodied as it was in his radical concept of experience, was thus lost. Like some of the Romantics, especially the Shelleys, James urged that a scientific approach be taken to all aspects of human experience, including the mystical, the marginal, and the inchoate—the "fringe," as James often called it. Subsequent thinkers rejected his broad view of psychological science, and as a result modern psychology, to the extent that it remains true to the goals of science, has been increasingly unable to grapple meaningfully with the experiences of ordinary people.

At the outset of the industrial revolution many humanistic thinkers believed that science offered us the best hope for understanding the meaning of life; nowadays, as the twenty-first century approaches, few thinkers—and very few nonscientists—look to science for such insights. Poets like Wordsworth, Keats, and Shelley all embraced Erasmus Darwin's view that science was a boon to mankind, a means of furthering not only our material aspirations but also our spiritual longings. It is a myth that the Romantics rejected science; on the contrary, most of them nurtured hopes for science that those of us living in the world after Hiroshima can scarcely comprehend.

The Romantics' expectations for science were brought low by many factors, most of them political and economic, as the industrial revolution created not a new golden age but the dirty and depressed urban industrial centers so vividly portrayed by Dickens, Zola, and others. Yet in one way at least, science itself failed to meet the Romantics' aspirations for a new understanding of life: with the rise of the new psychology at the end of the nineteenth century, the dream of a science of the soul was soundly defeated. The science of the mind triumphed instead.

The new psychology divided what had been the soul into three parts: the mind, the unconscious, and the body. That this new science could not adequately relate the three was not considered an insurmountable problem: at least the animal-like activities of our bodies and unconscious selves could still be kept separate and distinct from our minds. This separation fit well into the increasingly dominant liberal Protestant views of American and European elites at the turn of the century.

The twentieth-century legacy of this new science of the mind is a discipline deeply divided against itself, split into myriad subdisciplines. Some of these subdisciplines focus on aspects of the mind, such as cognition or emotion; others focus on aspects of the body, such as neurotransmitters or reflexes; still others, such as psychoanalysis, focus on the unconscious. From James's point of view these foci are all, equally, abstractions drawing us away from the reality of living, breathing, acting, and experiencing.

A *science* such as James advocated, one based on concrete, lived experience, remains conspicuous by its absence. The vacuum has been filled in the twentieth century by all manner of biased and unsystematic beliefs, religious, spiritual, racial, and ethnic. Because scientists have withdrawn from James's wider realm of experience into a much narrower domain, they have repeatedly ceded much of the important territory connecting everyday experience with meaningful self-understanding to religious, nationalist, and populist leaders who are often no more than demagogues.

I believe that the Romantics were right to call for a science of the soul, and that James was right to seek to implement this idea through his science of experience. Once the science of psychology arrogates the right to reject out of hand the content of a person's experience—because it is too inchoate, mystical, or whatever—it can no longer pronounce on the meaning of that experience. Psychology in its present divided state applies at best intermittently and incompletely to the lives most of us lead. It is my hope that in tracing how psychology came to impose these limitations on itself, this book will set the stage for a reevaluation of the mission of psychology and perhaps even lead to a rebirth of the Romantic dream of a science of the soul.

Bibliographic Essay

This book is an essay, not a comprehensive history. It was written in the belief that what the history of psychology needs is more essays and fewer histories—that we need to discuss what should count as the important issues and to be more explicit about the historical hypotheses animating our research and writing. For this reason I have based as much of my thinking as possible on primary sources. The sad fact is that most secondary sources, at least in this area, are partial and misleading at best. Especially in the English-speaking world, historians of philosophy and psychology have had a very narrow gaze, focused on a remarkably small set of actors and events. For example, although Fechner is universally acknowledged to be a key founder of psychophysics, serious discussion about whether his pantheism might be related to his psychophysics is nearly absent from the secondary literature.

Of course, I have not altogether abjured secondary sources. My greatest debt is to those historians who have taken a fresh look at aspects of my period, such as M. H. Abrams, Henri Ellenberger, Eric Hobsbawm, and Maurice Mandelbaum. It is striking is that these writers (with the partial exception of Ellenberger) do not consider themselves historians of psychology, nor are they typically cited in specialized texts on the history of psychology and philosophy. I have also made an effort to find nineteenth-century secondary sources that provide some insight into how contemporaries viewed the thinkers and ideas I discuss. This procedure has led to some important historical hypotheses. I have no doubt, for example, that the common assumption of twentieth-century historians that thinkers like Huxley and Tyndall were "materialists" stems entirely from misleading attacks made on them by their contemporaries. The perpetuation of these misrepresentations in modern historical surveys can be accounted for only by a general unfamiliarity with the originals.

I want also to be clear about resources I have *not* used. I made a conscious decision not to use archival resources or other material that dates from this period but was not published during the nineteenth century. Doubtless, many new insights can and should be gleaned from such material, but I think we need to become more aware of and knowledgeable about the important public trends before working on private happenings and motivations. If the argument I present in this book is correct, we do not yet have a clear picture of what happened to public thinking about the soul after 1800. At any rate, I have made the establishment of a clearer description of intellectual events and their underlying tensions my primary goal.

A second reason for not using archival material is pragmatic: I found myself busy enough within the limited scope of the present task. One can find plenty of important gaps in the current understanding of the history of psychology without going to any archives. Indeed, anyone who has tried to read systematically in nineteenth-century psychology or philosophy of mind knows that no single human life span could possibly suffice to enable a person to absorb all the published primary material! Although I have been reading for this project for more than twenty years, I make no pretense of having done more than skim the periodical literature, except to track down information on certain crucial periods and individuals. Moreover, I have never had access to a good file of German periodicals and am sure this lack has limited some of my conclusions. Nevertheless, as the following bibliography attests, I have read broadly in English-, French-, and German-language sources. The purpose of the present study is to understand a trend in *European* thought, not merely trends in a single country.

GENERAL STUDIES

The first thing a reader notices when comparing histories of the nineteenth century against histories of philosophy or psychology is that histories of psychology or philosophy rarely mention events highlighted as crucial in general histories of the period. Napoleon and Bismarck do not even make offstage appearances in most histories of psychology or philosophy; nor does the tremendous midcentury revolution in communications and transportation throughout Europe, despite the growth of scientific societies, congresses, and periodicals that resulted from it. Finally, no history of psychology devotes any serious discussion to the development of the novel alongside that of psychology as a science. I hope that my effort here will be taken for what it is: a very small first step toward rectifying this lack of integration in our historical understanding.

The best place to begin any study of the nineteenth century is Eric Hobsbawm's brilliant trilogy: *The age of revolution: 1789–1848* (New York: New American Library, 1979); *The age of capital: 1848–1875* (New York: New American Library, 1979); and *The age of empire: 1875–1914* (New York: Vintage, 1989). Hobsbawm not only offers a grand synthetic overview of what is known about the period but includes a number of truly perceptive hypotheses about particular cultural and scientific developments as well. Because of its popularity, I feel obliged to caution readers about Paul Johnson's synoptic *The birth of the modern: World society, 1815–1830* (New York: HarperCollins, 1991). Throughout the book, Johnson's conceit that Napoleon was a kind of proto-Stalin undermines his judgments about both cultural and political events. Readers should always compare Johnson's claims with those of other writers.

M. Mandelbaum's *History, man, and reason* (Baltimore, Md.: Johns Hopkins University Press, 1971) offers an insightful overview of nineteenth-century trends in philosophical perspectives. Although he does not claim to be giving a comprehensive history of psychology, he in fact offers good, detailed accounts of Schopenhauer, Comte, Marx, and other "historicists." Mandelbaum is however very weak on traditional metaphysics of the sort that was taught officially in most countries before 1830. His book is thus usefully supplemented by E. Bréhier, *Histoire de la philosophie*, vol. 3, *XIX–XXe siècles* (Paris: PUF, 1932), and J. McCosh, *The Scottish philosophy* (Hildesheim: G. Olms, 1966 [1875]). H. W. Schneider's *History of American philosophy* (New York: Columbia University Press, 1964) is a model of its kind: it provides clear, concise, and consequential accounts of changes in intellectual content and style. The sections on the Scottish influence in America and the pragmatist–neo-Realist developments around 1900 are exemplary. A. A. Roback's *History of American psychology*, rev. ed. (New York: Collier, 1964), is also useful, especially on the first half of the nineteenth century.

Without a doubt, E. G. Boring's books, despite their many problems, still rank as the classic texts in the history of psychology. His *History of experimental psychology* (New York: Century, 1929) underwent significant alteration in the second edition of 1950, and careful students will want to use both volumes. Boring's *History of sensation and perception in experimental psychology* (New York: Appleton-Century-Crofts, 1942) is important because so much of the early history of experimental psychology revolved around psychophysics and sensory physiology. Most of the limitations of Boring's work stem from his two strong biases: the assumption that psychology was at its origin a German science, and the assumption (inherited from his teacher Titchener) that Wundt was some sort of positivist. Later historians have done much to correct these biases, as we shall see, but no one has as yet created a new synthesis of the entire history of psychology to match the scope and weight of Boring's.

E. S. Clarke and L. S. Jacyna's *Nineteenth-century origins of neuroscientific concepts* (Berkeley: University of California Press, 1987) is perhaps the best introduction to the activities of physiologists of the nineteenth century who worked on the nervous system. Surprisingly, though, it makes little effort to integrate the discussion of physiological work with philosophical or cultural issues. In some ways F. Fearing's *Reflex action: A study in the history of physiological psychology* (New York: Hafner, 1964 [1930]) is still the best entry point for readers who want to understand how neurophysiology and psychology began to intersect in the 1800s. Fearing's book is now usefully supplemented by R. Leys's detailed study of what might be called the Scottish school of medicine and its impact on studies of the spinal reflex in the first part of the nineteenth century, *From sympathy to reflex: Marshall Hall and his opponents* (New York: Garland, 1990). Leys shows how the modern theory of the reflex arose in large part out of Whytt's and Cullen's theories of "sympathy"—of a special soul they considered to be embodied in the spinal cord.

Henry Ellenberger's magisterial *Discovery of the unconscious* (New York: Basic Books, 1970) is unsurpassed for its insights into the tangled relations of mesmerism, medicine, and psychology. Much of dynamic psychology—the psychology of motives, feelings, and thoughts that are not accessible by the individual who seems to have them—has its roots not in mainstream philosophy, medicine, or science but in the various groupings associated with hypnotism, spiritualism, and other still poorly understood phenomena. A. Gauld's *History of hypnotism* (Berkeley: University of California Press, 1994) is an exhaustive survey. G. F. Drinka's *The birth of neurosis* (New York: Simon & Schuster, 1984) is also useful for showing how deeply intertwined late nineteenth-century psychiatry was with spiritualism, unorthodox theories of electricity and magnetism, and hypnotism.

The nineteenth century in Europe was a time of significant demographic change. In Central Europe the various German-speaking principalities coalesced into Prussia and Austria; in southern Europe Italy emerged as a more or less unified nation-state in the 1860s. The industrial revolution gave rise to considerable migrations of people from rural to urban areas, and significant growth occurred in large cities—cities that began to be central hubs for both nation-states and their overseas economic activities. Large cities became centers of cultural activity, and it is often in and around them that modern scientific institutions arose. The institutions included not only universities and laboratories but also medical and scientific societies, their meetings, and their periodicals. The most important cities for the growth of psychology as a science were Berlin, London, and Vienna. Two smaller cities, Edinburgh and Leipzig, were of nearly equal importance to these and, perhaps surprisingly, of greater significance than Paris. Hobsbawm's discussion of these demographic trends is an excellent overview and very provocative, but for more information the reader will want to consult N. J. G. Pounds's *Historical geography of Europe, 1800–1914* (New York: Cambridge University Press, 1985).

As mentioned earlier, I have used a number of contemporary secondary sources, in part to guide me concerning what nineteenth-century thinkers found to be the important issues of the day. The most general studies I consulted were: R. Blakey's

History of the philosophy of mind: Embracing the opinions of all writers on mental science from the earliest period to the present time (London: Longmans, 1850), vol. 4. Blakey was a minor offshoot of the Scottish school, teaching at Belfast. His book is essentially a compendium of brief notes on a plethora of writers, but it is indispensable in helping us to see what thinkers were considered important in 1850 (and which thinkers were not!) as well as for providing leads to thinkers who have been forgotten. J. T. Merz's *European thought in the nineteenth century* (Gloucester, Mass.: Peter Smith, 1976 [1903-12]), 4 vols., is a synopsis of European thought, written from a more or less positivistic view. A similar compendium, which is very useful because of its allocation of a great deal of space to traditional metaphysicians who are not well known nowadays, is C. S. Henry's *An epitome of the history of philosophy: Being the work adopted by the University of France for instruction in the colleges and high schools* (New York, Harper, 1842), 2 vols.

J. M. Baldwin's *History of psychology: A sketch and an interpretation* (London: Watts, 1913) is not a work of scholarship but nevertheless records the opinions of one of the most astute "new psychologists" in North America. G. H. Lewes's *Biographical history of philosophy* (Manchester, Eng.: Routledge, 1893) was widely used, beginning with its first edition in 1845-46. (I consulted the eighth edition.) Lewes's popularity, combined with his high evaluation of Comte and the positivists, led to a reaction, at least in Britain, of strenuous attacks on positivism and materialism. Elie Halévy's *The growth of philosophic radicalism* (Boston: Beacon, 1960) was first published in the 1920s and is in some senses a contemporary's view of the evolution from early associationism to utilitarianism and "radicalism." Halévy is such a great historian, however, that this work still holds up well and should certainly be read by anyone who wants to understand the origin of James and John Stuart Mill's ideas.

CHAPTER 1: IN SEARCH OF PSYCHOLOGY

J. B. Dods's *Electrical psychology* (New York: Fowler & Wells, 1850), 2d ed., is still to be found in many municipal libraries, at least in the northeastern United States. Fowler & Wells was perhaps the biggest publisher specializing in phrenology and mesmerism; a study of its publications would go a long way toward clarifying what ideas about the mind were widely disseminated in the United States in the latter part of the 1800s. The Lotze quote comes from the author's introduction to his *Microcosmos*, p. xv. It is perhaps worth noting that the English translation of the book was carried out by the daughter of Sir William Hamilton: *Microcosmos: An essay concerning man and his relation to the world* (New York: Scribners, 1887), 2d ed.

Peter Bowler's *The eclipse of Darwinism: Anti-Darwinian theories in the decades around 1900* (Baltimore: Johns Hopkins University Press, 1983) is, surprisingly, one of the few scholarly studies of the anti-Darwinian trend of scientific and philosophical thought in the late nineteenth century. I say "surprisingly" because almost everything published in English between 1890 and 1930 was anti-Darwinian in spirit, content, or both. This anti-Darwinian tendency was less pronounced in German or Italian works, but much worse in French, of course.

Similarly, habitués of the medical sections of libraries and used bookstores know that most "medical" publications in the late 1800s were put out by people who were later classified as "cranks." Nevertheless, academic historians have acted as if most of this literature were somehow nonexistent. D. & E. Armstrong's *The great American medicine show* (New York: Simon & Schuster, 1991) is a compendium of information about so-called alternative theories in medicine. (But alternative to what? Modern allopathic medicine was simply not mainstream until this century.) The book includes thumbnail sketches of mesmerists, mind healers, electrical therapists, and others. The authors' cynicism about these practitioners prevents serious analysis of their ideas; nevertheless, the book is unique in bringing together many widely disseminated ideas related to mind and health.

The conflict over materialism in the German speaking world of the 1850s gave rise to a whole host of misreadings and misconceptions. The best introduction to this episode is F. Gregory, *Scientific materialism in nineteenth-century Germany* (Boston: North Holland Publishers, 1977). In light of the later controversies over Darwin, it is interesting to note that the ideas that seemed to generate the most opposition were those which tended to "naturalize" the study of humankind, not necessarily ideas that would properly be called materialist in a philosophical sense.

Hobsbawm's *Age of revolution* is a good introduction to the politics of the Napoleonic era and the repressive policies of the Concert of Vienna, which ended it. R. R. Palmer's *The age of democratic revolution* (Princeton: Princeton University Press, 1964), 2 vols., is still the most readable and reliable survey of the political events in Europe and the European colonies. H. Nicolson's *The concert of Vienna* (London: Macmillan, 1946) is probably dated, but a good read. For a detailed introduction to the methods and habits of early modern police states, see D. Emerson, *Metternich and the secret police: Security and subversion in the Habsburg monarchy* (The Hague: M. Nijhoff, 1968). E. Halévy's classic *History of the English people* (New York: Barnes and Noble, 1961) is also probably dated, but I found volumes 2 and 4 the clearest account of the British government's response to the French Revolution and the subsequent acts of repression, especially in the crucial years from 1815 to 1819. The same history is told "from the bottom up" in E. P. Thompson's modern classic, *The making of the English working class* (New York: Vintage, 1968). The quote from James Sheehan appears on p. 555 of his monumental *German history: 1770–1866* (New York: Oxford University Press, 1989).

G. Stanley Hall's "The new psychology" appeared in the *Andover Review*, 1885, 3, 120–35, 239–49; John Dewey's "The new psychology" had appeared in the *Andover Review* a year earlier and is reprinted in *John Dewey, the early works* (Edwardsville: University of Southern Illinois Press, 1989), vol. 1. James Mark Baldwin's "The postulates of physiological psychology" appeared in *The Presbyterian Review*, 1887, and his essay on the soul appeared in the same journal, slightly renamed, *The Presbyterian & Reformed Review*, 1890; both essays were reprinted in Baldwin's *Fragments in philosophy and psychology* (New York: Scribners, 1902). G. M. Marsden's *The soul of the American university: From Protestant establishment to established unbelief* (New York: Oxford, 1994) is very good on the pervasiveness of liberal Protestant theology throughout academia in the 1870s and 1880s. Marsden reads the liberals' abandonment of specific elements of Christian apologetics, however, as a move toward secularism, whereas I would argue that Hall, Dewey, and others were in fact attempting to unite their interpretation of Christianity with a form of naturalism.

For William James's life and career the best source is still R. B. Perry, *The thought and character of William James* (Boston: Little, Brown, 1935). Jean Strouse's *Alice James* (Boston: Houghton Mifflin, 1980) is a most revealing study of James's relationship with his younger sister.

R. K. French's *Robert Whytt, the soul, and medicine* (London: Wellcome, 1969) is the only biography of this important Scottish Enlightenment figure, but it hardly begins to do him justice. It was Whytt, more than anyone else, who set the basic assumptions of scientific psychology in motion, with his invention of the doctrine of the stimulus and of unconscious sensations. For Whytt's crucial place in the "prehistory" of psychology see E. S. Reed, "The corporeal ideas hypothesis and the origin of scientific psychology," *Review of Metaphysics*, 1982, 35, 731–53, and also my "Theory, concept, and experiment in the history of psychology: The older tradition behind a 'young science,'" *History of the Human Sciences*, 1989, 2, 333–57. K. Figlio's "Theories of perception and the physiology of mind in the late eighteenth century," *History of Science*, 1975, 12, 177–212, is also useful.

For Lewes, see the bibliographic notes for Chapter 8 and for Erasmus Darwin and the Shelleys see those for Chapter 3. For Reid and Kant see the bibliographic notes for Chapter 2.

F. A. Lange's *History of materialism and criticism of its present importance* (Boston: Houghton Mifflin, 1881), 3 vols., began to be published in German in 1869 and is one of the few products of the "materialism crisis" of the 1850s and 1860s that is still, at least occasionally, read. Lange tells a simple story: Kant had already figured out why materialism did not hold true, but later materialists did not understand Kant. Fortunately, Helmholtz and his school had assimilated Kant's lessons and showed how the new psychology refuted materialism. Despite the fact that this book was widely read throughout Europe, many opponents of the new psychology (including even William James) tended to associate it with materialism, and to this day historians of psychology have not understood that the success of the new psychology in Germany was in large part based on its being a successful riposte to materialism. L. Büchner's *Force and matter* (London: Trübner, 1870), 2d English ed., from the 10th German ed., was among the most widely printed and read scientific books of the late nineteenth century but is rarely discussed today. Although Büchner was one of the German "vulgar ma-

terialists," he appears to have been something of a phenomenalist and a positivist, working along the lines more clearly developed by Heinrich Hertz and Ernst Mach.

J. Müller's *Elements of physiology* (London: Murray, 1838),
2 vols., is one of the classics of nineteenth-century science. In
many ways it marks the transition from descriptive anatomy-
cum-physiology to the more experimental work of Müller's
students, such as Helmholtz and du Bois Reymond.

Although I do not discuss the work of Sigmund Freud here
at any length, readers will doubtless want to think about his
place within this new history of psychology. A good place to
begin would be the chapter on Freud in Ellenberger's *Discovery
of the unconscious* (cited earlier). F. Sulloway's *Freud: Biologist of
the mind* (New York: Basic Books, 1979) is very good on Freud's
early career and on his scientific training. Peter Gay's *Freud: A
life for our time* (London: Dent, 1988) is the best available biography, although Gay's critical acumen is occasionally overcome
by his admiration for his subject. Freud's own view of the relation between his theory and the new psychology can be found
in *The interpretation of dreams* (New York: Avon, 1965 [1900]),
chap. 7, and in *The question of lay analysis* (New York: Norton,
1969 [1927]), *passim.*

CHAPTER 2: THE IMPOSSIBLE SCIENCE

The category *traditional metaphysics* is of my own making, so
there are no historical studies of it per se. It is interesting that
the thinkers who worked in this tradition tend to be under-
played in most texts in the history of philosophy—undoubtedly
an inheritance from the Hegelian assumptions of much of modern history of philosophy. The "story line" of Hegel's *Lectures
on the history of philosophy* (New York: Humanities Press, 1963
[1827]), 3 vols., is widely followed: that European philosophy

before Kant divided into "rationalists" (primarily Continental) and "empiricists" (primarily British) and that Kant integrated the two traditions and ultimately transcended them. This story is largely fictional. For instance, it simply ignores the fact that most French philosophers after 1730 were heavily influenced by Locke, or at least by Voltaire's Locke. (It is often expedient not to count certain people as philosophers, so Helvétius, Condillac, d'Holbach, Diderot, and D'Alembert are typically allotted a very small amount of space in non-French histories of philosophy.) The standard story also conveniently ignores such influences as that of Malebranche on Hume, or the pervasive influence of Pierre Bayle. L. Loeb, *From Descartes to Hume: Continental metaphysics and the development of modern philosophy* (Ithaca, N.Y.: Cornell University Press, 1981), is a good antidote to these misreadings of the early eighteenth century. See also C. McCracken, *Malebranche and British philosophy* (New York: Oxford, 1983). Peter Gay's *The Enlightenment: An interpretation* (New York: Norton, 1969), 2 vols., is also to be recommended for taking seriously the considerable variety of opinion among the so-called *philosophes*.

There is a real need for a comprehensive modern account of "the Scottish philosophy," especially one that does not simply assume that the post-Reidians actually read or followed Reid. None of the available books is sufficiently comprehensive or critical. These texts include: D. S. Robinson, *The story of Scottish philosophy* (New York: Exposition Press, 1961); James McCosh's *The Scottish philosophy* (Hildesheim: Olms, 1966 [1875]). D. Robinson's "Thomas Reid's critique of Dugald Stewart," *Journal of the History of Philosophy,* 1989, 28, 405–22, is a good place to begin when studying the Scottish school, as it quickly clarifies how far Stewart deviated from Reid. (Thomas Brown deviated further from Stewart and Hamilton further still.)

Some of the primary Scottish sources I used in writing this

chapter were: J. Abercrombie, *Inquiries concerning the intellectual powers and the investigation of truth,* Jacob Abbott, ed. (New York, Collins & Brother, n.d. [1840?]); Anonymous, "Reid and the philosophy of common sense: An essay-review of William Hamilton's edition of *The works of Thomas Reid,*" *Blackwood's Edinburgh Magazine,* 1847, 239–58; C. Bell, *The hand: Its mechanism and vital endowments* (Philadelphia: Cary, Lea, & Blanchard, 1835); T. Brown, *Observations on the nature and tendency of the doctrine of Mr Hume, concerning the relation of cause and effect* (Edinburgh: Mundell & Sons, 1806), 2d ed.; W. Hamilton, *Lectures on logic and metaphysics* (Boston: Gould & Lincoln, 1865), 2 vols; J. Haven, *Mental philosophy: including the intellect, sensibilities, and will* (Boston: Gould & Lincoln, 1873); T. Reid, *The works of Thomas Reid, now fully collected, with selections from his unpublished letters* (Edinburgh: Maclachlan & Stewart, 1872), 7th. ed, 2 vols. (this is Sir William Hamilton's widely published edition of Reid); P. M. Roget, *Treatises on physiology and phrenology* (Edinburgh: Black, 1838); D. Stewart, *The works of Dugald Stewart* (Cambridge: Hilliard & Brown, 1829), 7 vols.; F. Wayland, *The elements of moral science* (Boston: Gould, Kendall, & Lincoln, 1839), 11th ed; O. Wight, *Sir William Hamilton's philosophy* (New York: Appleton, 1857); H. Winslow, *Intellectual philosophy: Analytical, synthetical, and practical* (Boston: Brewer & Tileston, 1864), 8th ed.

To a great degree, America at this time was largely an outpost of Scottish philosophy, as is made clear in H. Schneider's *History of American philosophy* (see under the earlier heading "General Studies"). See also D. W. Howe, *The unitarian conscience: Harvard moral philosophy, 1805–1861* (Middletown, Conn.: Wesleyan University Press, 1988), which shows how and why Harvard was a partial exception to the Scottish orientation of most American colleges.

Among the primary French sources used were V. Cousin,

Oeuvres complètes (Paris: Ladrange, 1953–55), 16 vols. I used an American edition of his *Elements of psychology* (New York: Gould & Newman, 1838). The quote about intuition of the truth comes from V. Cousin, *Du Vrai, du Beau, et du Bien* (Paris: Didier, 1867), p. 38. Maine de Biran's *Oeuvres* were edited by P. Tisserand (Paris: PUF, 1920), 14 vols.; and I used Destutt de Tracy, *Elémens d'idéologie* (Paris: Charles M. Levi, 1824), 3 vols.

I also consulted E. Kennedy, *Destutt de Tracy and the origins of "ideology"* (Philadelphia: American Philosophical Society, 1978); M. Henry, *Philosophie et phénoménologie du corps: Essai sur l'ontologie biranienne* (Paris: PUF, 1965); F. C. T. Moore, *The psychology of Maine de Biran* (New York: Oxford, 1970); and the relevant sections of Emile Bréhier's *Histoire de la philosophie,* vols. 2 and 3 (Paris: PUF, 1932).

German traditional metaphysics presents a far more complex picture, because of Hegel's influence. Whereas Cousin and some of the right-wing Hegelians attempted to "synthesize" Hegel with Scottish philosophy, this synthesis was not characteristic of most German philosophy. For this period, and especially for the Scottish influence on Hegel, see L. Dickey, *Hegel: Religion, economics, and politics, 1770–1807* (New York: Cambridge University Press, 1987), and S. Hook, *From Hegel to Marx* (Ann Arbor: University of Michigan Press, 1962). D. Leary, "The philosophical development of the conception of psychology in Germany, 1780-1850," *Journal of the History of the Behavioral Sciences* 1978, 14, 113–21, is a useful overview focused on philosophy of mind. Despite Hegel's massive presence, many writers who were associated with medicine and the biological sciences and whom one well might consider to be philosophers or precursors to psychologists offered a *Naturphilosophie* that had strong affinities with traditional metaphysics. Some of the key texts in this tradition are J. F. Blumenbach, *The elements of physiology* (London: Longman, Rees, Orme, Brown, and Green, 1828); J. G. Fichte, *The vocation of man* (Indianapolis: Bobbs-Merrill, 1956); and F. W. J. Schelling, *Ideas for a philosophy of nature* (Cambridge: Cambridge University Press, 1988), 2d ed. T. Lenoir, in *The strategy of life: Teleology and mechanism in nineteenth-century Germany* (Boston: North Holland Publishers, 1982), begins to connect German work in the life sciences with philosophy. Similarly, F. Beiser's "Introduction: Hegel and the problem of metaphysics" in his *Cambridge companion to Hegel* (New York: Cambridge University Press, 1993) shows how much more of a naturalist Hegel was than is commonly realized.

Far too much has been and is still being written about Kant to enable an ordinary reader to make sense of it all. The discussion here relates primarily to the first and third of Kant's famous critiques: *The critique of pure reason,* translated by N. K. Smith (New York: Macmillan, 1929) and *The critique of judgment,* translated by W. S. Pluhar (Indianapolis: Hackett, 1989). For Scottish influence on Kant see M. Kuehn's *Scottish common sense in Germany, 1768–1800* (Montreal: McGill–Queen's University Press, 1987). For details on the early transmission of Kant's critical philosophy to the English-speaking world see G. Micheli, "The early reception of Kant's thought in England," in G. M. Ross and T. McWalter, eds., *Kant and his influence* (Bristol, Eng.: Thoemmes, 1991).

There are scores of books interpreting Kant's philosophy; however, what is relevant to the present discussion is not what Kant meant but what his readers took him to mean. On this subject there is only one place to begin: F. Beiser's *The fate of reason* (Cambridge: Harvard University Press, 1987) is a marvelously readable and useful introduction to the impact of Kant's *Critique of pure reason* on German philosophy before 1800. Beiser relates the various lines of interpretation that emerged from Kant's program, none of which stuck to Kant's combination of transcendental idealism and empirical realism.

The quote from Shelley about metaphysics comes from his "Treatise on morals" (around 1812-15) reprinted in D. L. Clark, ed., *Shelley's prose: Or, the trumpet of a prophecy* (New York: New Amsterdam, 1988), p. 185. Shelley's allusion to Kant comes from his farcical "roast" of Wordsworth, Coleridge, and others, "Peter Bell the Third":

> All Peter did on this occasion
> Was, writing some sad stuff in prose.
> It is a dangerous invasion
> When poets criticise: their station
> Is to delight, not pose.
>
> The Devil then sent to Leipsic fair,
> For Born's translation of Kant's book;
> A world of words, tail foremost, where
> Right-wrong-false-true—and foul and fair
> As in a lottery are shook,
>
> Five thousand crammed octavo pages
> Of German psychologics—he
> Who his *furor verborum* assuages
> Thereon, deserves just seven months' wages
> More than will e'er be due to me.

From D. Reiman and S. Powers, eds., *Shelley's poetry and prose* (New York: Norton, 1977), p. 340. (Born's translation was of Kant's works into Latin.)

James Mackintosh's discussion of "metaphysics" can be found in his *Dissertation on the progress of ethical philosophy chiefly during the 17th and 18th centuries, prefixed to the Encyclopaedia Britannica,* which is reprinted in *Miscellaneous works of Sir James*

Mackintosh (Philadelphia: Hart, 1853), p. 95. Charles Darwin's notebooks on "Mind, metaphysics, and morals" are reprinted in Howard Gruber, *Darwin on man* (New York: Norton, 1974).

James Stirling was one of the earliest British academics to "discover Hegel." He was also an acute critic of Hamilton and the received doctrine of mind. Stirling's *Sir William Hamilton: Being the philosophy of perception, an analysis*—the quotation is from p. 32—(London: Longmans, 1865) was overshadowed by Mill's massive *Examination of Sir William Hamilton's philosophy* published that same year. Still, there is much of value to be gleaned from Stirling's slim but insightful text.

The only general history of phrenology I know of is G. Lanteri-Laura, *Histoire de la phrénologie* (Paris: PUF, 1970). Roger Cooter's *The culture of popular science: Phrenology and the organization of consent in nineteenth-century Britain* (New York: Cambridge University Press, 1984) is an attempt as much to study intellectual public relations as to study phrenology and suffers from this divided focus. I believe that Geoffrey Cantor has refuted the hypothesis that phrenology was by and large associated with the radical movements of the period between 1815 and 1848; see G. N. Cantor, "A critique of Shapin's social interpretation of the Edinburgh phrenology debate" and also "The Edinburgh phrenology debate: 1803–1828," *Annals of Science,* 1975, 33, 245–56, 195–218. For the best statement of this "social" thesis concerning phrenology, see S. Shapin, "Phrenological knowledge and the social structure of early nineteenth-century Edinburgh," *Annals of Science,* 1975, 33, 219–43 (a reply to Cantor).

It is important to distinguish among the leaders of the phrenological movement and especially to note that Spurzheim, after he separated from Gall, tended to integrate his phrenology with traditional metaphysics much more than Gall. George and Andrew Combe in Scotland and Orson Fowler, among others, in America took this one step further (as did Dods) and argued that phrenology would become a pillar of Christianity. None of the churches was buying, however, and despite the immense popularity of both the Combes, Fowler, and others, they never became widely accepted by mainstream religious groups. Primary sources used were G. Combe, *The constitution of man considered in relation to external objects* (New York: Samuel Wells, 1869), 20th(!) ed. This was among the most popular nonfiction books published in nineteenth-century America. Combe's pious tract is a classic of American populist thought: for Combe, phrenology is the best new science, a science which shows that the Bible (received Christianity) is the best guide to morals. The wide interest in Combe's views shows how broadly based traditional metaphysics was until the last quarter of the nineteenth century. At the back of my copies of Dods and Combe are dozens of advertisements for books on phrenology and mesmerism, including many works of popular psychology (on character building, making your marriage work) and texts claiming to reconcile these scientific advances with Christian dogma.

I have used the American edition of Gall: F. J. Gall, *On the functions of the brain and each of its parts* (Boston: Marsh, Capen, & Lyon, 1835), 6 vols., and also his early *Philosophisch-medizinische Untersuchungen über Natur und Kunst im kranken und gesunden Zustande des Menschen* (Vienna: R. Grasser, 1791). T. L. Hoff's excellent essay, "Gall's psychophysiological concept of function: The rise and decline of 'internal essence,'" *Brain and Cognition*, 1992, 20, 378–98, shows how much historical discussion of Gall's work is fundamentally confused with regard to his central concept of "function." For anyone interested in phrenology, this is a must-read, and it is also an excellent example of why it helps to know some psychology when researching the history of psychology.

For Spurzheim I have also used American editions: J. G. Spurzheim, *Phrenology in connection with the study of physiognomy* (Boston: Marsh, Capen, & Lyon, 1834); *Phrenology, or the doctrine of mental phenomena* (Boston: Marsh, Capen, & Lyon, 1835); and *The natural laws of man* (New York: Fowler & Wells, n.d. [1846?]). In this last text Spurzheim comes very close to both the views and the procedure of George Combe.

CHAPTER 3: FRANKENSTEIN'S SCIENCE

The best secondary source on Erasmus Darwin is Desmond King-Hele's biography, *Doctor of revolution* (London: Faber & Faber, 1977), and his edition of *Darwin's correspondence* (New York: Cambridge University Press, 1981). Darwin's own works are eminently readable and well worth perusing, although his poetry occasionally calls for heroic endurance. Darwin's *Zoonomia* is his most comprehensive work, first published in two volumes in 1794–96 (London: J. Johnson) and reprinted several times in both England and the United States. We need a study of how influential this work was across Europe, especially in Italy and Germany. In *The temple of nature: Being the origin of society* (London: J. Johnson, 1803), Darwin lays out his evolutionary views. *The botanic garden* (London: J. Johnson, 1789–91), 2 vols., was perhaps his most popular work.

Thomas Brown's *Observations on the* Zoonomia *of Erasmus Darwin* (Edinburgh: Mundell & Sons, 1798) was written when Brown was just eighteen, but it contains many of his later ideas. His attack on Darwin takes as a starting point Hume's critique of the concept of causation (see p. xvi). In 1805 the first version of Brown's *Inquiry into the relation between cause and effect* was published (I used the American edition of 1822, published by M. Newman at Andover, Mass.), in which he defended Hume against charges of atheism. Brown's idea was to use Hume's supposedly atheistic theory of causation to prove that Darwin's theory was both atheistic and wrong. Following this endeavor, Brown was elected to the professorship of moral philosophy at the University of Edinburgh, where he gave the lectures that were posthumously published as *Philosophy of the human mind* (Philadelphia: J. Griggs, 1824), 3 vols. In the intervening years he had written *The Paradise of coquettes* (Philadelphia: M. Carey, 1816) and *Bower of spring, with other poems* (Philadelphia: M. Thomas, 1817) and, I believe, several other collections of poems.

Kant's attack on Priestley can be found in his *Critique of pure reason* (p. 592 of the Kemp-Smith translation, cited in Chapter 2). For Priestley's own views see J. Priestley, *An examination of Dr Reid's* Inquiry into the human mind on the principles of common sense (London: J. Johnson, 1774), and *Disquisitions relating to matter and spirit* (London: J. Johnson, 1777). For a sampling of Priestley's ideas, see J. A. Passmore, ed., *Priestley's writings on philosophy, science, and politics* (New York: Collier, 1965).

I cite Blake from D. Erdman's *The poetry and prose of William Blake* (Garden City: Doubleday, 1965) and am indebted to Erdman's *Prophet against the empire* (Princeton: Princeton University Press, 1954) and E. P. Thompson's *Witness against the beast* (New York: New Press, 1994) for interpretation of Blake. I cite Heine's *Seraphine* in the fine translation by Hal Draper: *The complete poems of Heinrich Heine* (Boston: Suhrkamp/Insel, 1982), p. 332. I cite Hoffmann from *The golden pot and other tales*, trans. R. Robertson (New York: Oxford University Press, 1992). For Shelley I used P. B. Shelley, *The complete poetical works of Percy Bysshe Shelley* (Boston: Houghton Mifflin, 1901); D. H. Reiman and S. Powers, eds., *Shelley's poetry and prose*

(New York: Norton, 1977); and D. L. Clark, ed., *Shelley's prose: Or, the trumpet of a prophecy* (New York: New Amsterdam 1988).

The best version of the William Lawrence story comes from A. Desmond, *The politics of evolution: Morphology, medicine, and reform in radical London* (Chicago: University of Chicago Press, 1989). See also P. G. Mudford, "William Lawrence and *The natural history of man,*" *Journal of the History of Ideas,* 1968, 29, 430–36. For the European political background see R. R. Palmer, *The age of democratic revolution* (Princeton: Princeton University Press, 1964), 2 vols., and D. Emerson, *Metternich and the political police: Security and subversion in the Habsburg monarchy* (The Hague: M. Nijhoff, 1968 [see under the earlier heading "General Studies"]). For a study of the important radical publisher Richard Carlile, see J. H. Wiener, *Radicalism and free thought in nineteenth-century Britain: The life of Richard Carlile* (Westport: Greenwood, 1983).

If I had to cite a single work on Shelley that best situates him intellectually it would have to be Richard Holmes's *Shelley: The pursuit* (Harmondsworth, Eng.: Penguin, 1974). Enthusiasts will want to read K. N. Cameron's monumental two-volume biography: *The young Shelley* (New York: Macmillan, 1950) and *Shelley: The golden years* (Cambridge: Harvard University Press, 1974). Desmond King-Hele has long emphasized both the influence of Erasmus Darwin on Shelley and the way Shelley used poetry to convey his scientific ideas, and I am indebted to him for this important insight. King-Hele's own book, *Shelley: His life and work* (Teaneck, N.J.: Farleigh-Dickinson University Press, 1970), 2d ed., however, is marred by a tendency to overintellectualize Shelley's thought. In particular, King-Hele seems eager to downplay some of the more radical social and political ideas found side by side with scientific thought in Shelley's texts. Nevertheless, all of King-Hele's writings on this subject are essential for tracing the scientific aspects of Shelley's work, especially D. King-Hele, *Erasmus Darwin and the Romantic poets* (New York: St. Martin's, 1986) and "Shelley and Erasmus Darwin," in K. Everest, ed., *Shelley revalued: Essays from the Gregynog conference* (Totowa, N.J.: Barnes & Noble Books, 1983).

For general background on both Percy and Mary Shelley and the influence of Hartley, Priestley, and others on British thought in the two decades after the French Revolution, see William St. Clair's *The Godwins and the Shelleys* (Baltimore: Johns Hopkins University Press, 1989). The best edition of Mary's masterpiece is M. Shelley, *Frankenstein: Or, the modern Prometheus*, edited by J. Rieger (Chicago: University of Chicago Press, 1982)—quotations pp. 47, 98, 103–4, 107. The secondary literature on this remarkable woman is beginning to explode. I found A. K. Mellor's *Mary Shelley: Her life, her fiction, her monsters* (New York: Routledge, 1989) far and away the most useful for understanding the scientific background of *Frankenstein*. Mellor is particularly good at elucidating the Darwinian context of Mary Shelley's thought. E. W. Sunstein's *Mary Shelley: Romance and reality* (Baltimore: Johns Hopkins University Press, 1989) is a more generally rounded biography but does not seem to take Shelley as seriously as a thinker as one might wish. Although I do not here deal with the gender issues raised by *Frankenstein* (an acute study of the womb envy of scientists), I cannot resist mentioning Brian Easlea's excellent *Fathering the unthinkable* (London: Pluto, 1983), which includes a provocative reading of *Frankenstein* as a critique of patriarchal science.

M. H. Abrams's *Natural supernaturalism* (New York: Norton, 1971) is a major influence on this entire chapter. F. Ewen's helpful *Heroic imagination: The creative genius of Europe, 1815–1848* (Secaucus, N.J.: Citadel Press, 1980) deserves to be better known than it is. Ewen is especially good at showing inter-connections between Romantic literature and science in writers like Balzac, Heine, and Hoffmann.

CHAPTER 4: THE BREAKDOWN IN THE CONCERT
OF EUROPEAN IDEAS

Dugald Stewart's *Dissertation, exhibiting a general view of the progress of metaphysical, ethical, and political philosophy since the revival of letters in Europe, part 1* is reprinted in volume 6 of his *Collected works* (Cambridge: Hilliard & Brown, 1829). This dissertation was prefixed to the *Encyclopaedia Britannica* in 1819. Part 2 was never completed. Robert Whytt's *Works* (Edinburgh: Hamilton, 1768) have unfortunately not yet been reprinted since his son collected them. F. Fearing's *Reflex action* and Ruth Leys's *From sympathy to reflex* help situate this "Scottish school" in context (both cited under "General Studies").

Thomas Brown's *Observations on the* Zoonomia *of Erasmus Darwin* (Edinburgh: Mundell, 1798) has been cited in the bibliographical notes to Chapter 3. *Observations on the nature and tendency of the doctrine of Mr Hume concerning the relation of cause and effect* (Edinburgh: Mundell, 1805), which began as a pamphlet, was expanded to book length for the second edition (1806) and then was further expanded and retitled *Inquiry into the relations of cause and effect* (Edinburgh: Tait, 1818). I have, as mentioned earlier, used an American edition of his 1820 publication, *Philosophy of the human mind* (Philadelphia: J. Grigg, 1824), 3 vols. The quotations are from Lectures 11, 20, 22, and 25. See also D. Welsh, *Account of the life and writings of Thomas Brown, M.D.* (Edinburgh: Tait, 1825), and J. A. Mills, "Thomas Brown on the philosophy and psychology of perception," *Journal of the History of the Behavioral Sciences*, 1987, 23, 37–49, and "Thomas Brown's theory of causation," *Journal of the History of Philosophy*, 1984, 22, 207–29. James Mills's statement about unwitting feelings and J. S. Mills's note are both taken from *Analysis of the Phenomena of the human mind* (see notes to Chapter 7), p. 42.

References to Maine de Biran are given in chapter 2. Schopenhauer's main work, the remarkable *World as will and representation,* trans. E. F. J. Payne (New York: Dover, 1964 [1819]), is one of the most lively pieces of metaphysical writing ever produced and is highly recommended. The prolegomenon to this work, *The fourfold root of the principle of sufficient reason,* trans. E. F. J. Payne (LaSalle, Ill.: Open Court, 1974 [1813]), gives a clear and concise overview of Schopenhauer's theory that perception is the result of the brain or mind's inferring the causes behind the sensory effects. In one form or another, not always that found in Schopenhauer's work, this theory has dominated thinking about perception ever since; see N. Pastore, *Selective history of theories of visual perception, 1650–1950* (New York: Oxford University Press, 1971), and E. S. Reed, *James J. Gibson and the psychology of perception* (New Haven: Yale University Press, 1988). Schopenhauer's "On the will in nature" is available in an English translation by K. Hillebrand, in *Two essays by Arthur Schopenhauer* (London: Bell, 1907). B. Magee's *The philosophy of Schopenhauer* (New York: Oxford University Press, 1983) is useful in helping to pull the diverse strands of Schopenhauer's work together. But Schopenhauer is among the clearest and best organized philosophers and therefore is easily approached directly. What readers might need to help them is a background in the natural science of the period between 1810 and 1830, in which Schopenhauer was steeped. This neither Magee nor any other commentator supplies.

Alexander Bain's two great works are *The senses and the intellect* (New York: Appleton, 1860) and *The emotions and the will* (New York: Appleton, 1888), both of which appeared in several editions and underwent important changes. (Those cited here are the 2d ed. and 3rd ed., respectively.) W. B. Carpenter's *Mental physiology* (New York: Appleton, 1891 [1874]) grew out of his *Principles of human physiology* (I used the 1847 American edition published by Lea and Blanchard of Philadelphia). It is worth noting that already in my 1847 edition there are two appendixes: one attacking phrenology as ill-founded, the other attempting to make sense of "mesmeric phenomena." Carpenter's essays, including his speculations on the correlation of natural forces, can be found in the collection of essays edited by his son, *Nature and man* (London: Kegan, Paul, & Trench, 1888). William James revived a number of Carpenter's ideas about action, especially about "automatic actions" (in other words, those which occur without our paying much attention to them), and thus further popularized many of these ideas. It is therefore interesting to note that at Christmastime in 1857, Henry James, Sr., asked William Carpenter's advice on purchasing a microscope for his eldest son, William.

The popularity of Carpenter's ideas—and of his text—is shown by the central role that a passage from Carpenter's *Physiology* plays in Wilkie Collins's immensely popular mystery *The moonstone* (New York: Collier, 1958 [1868]), p. 382. Collins also cites Elliotson and Combe to help explain a trance state in one of the novel's protagonists. Like his friend Dickens, whom Elliotson had taught to hypnotize people, Collins was extremely interested in questions of psychological science. Collins's novel of 1872, *Poor Miss Finch* (New York: Oxford University Press, 1995), revolves around Berkeley's theory of vision and the problems that (according to the theory) would be faced by someone who has been blind all her life and then regains her sight.

CHAPTER 5: THE BRIEF LIFE OF
NATURAL METAPHYSICS

The influence of Johannes Müller's *Handbuch—The elements of physiology*, trans. J. Baly (London: Murray, 1838; quotations pp. 1073, 3n.)—was pervasive in Europe until the 1850s. No scholarly studies of Müller in English exist, though W. Bernard, "Spinoza's influence on the rise of scientific psychology: A neglected chapter in the history of psychology," *Journal of the History of the Behavioral Sciences*, 1972, 8, 208–15, corrects the common misconception that Müller was some kind of Kantian.

For the Galvani-Volta controversy see M. Pera, *The ambiguous frog* (Princeton: Princeton University Press, 1993). J. Heilbron's *Electricity in the seventeenth and eighteenth centuries* (Los Angeles: University of California Press, 1979) is indispensable for following the ins and outs of early theories of electricity and magnetism.

Although Herbart was a major influence on educators throughout the Western world until 1900, few modern studies on him have appeared. I consulted J. F. Herbart, *Lehrbuch zur Psychologie* (Königsberg, East Prussia: Unzer, 1834), and C. De Garmo, *Herbart and the Herbartians* (New York: Scribners, 1895).

References to Schopenhauer are given in the bibliographic notes to the preceding chapter. The anonymous essay that launched Schopenhauer to European fame was "Iconoclasm in German philosophy," *Westminster Review*, 1853, 59, 202–12. James Sully's *Pessimism* (London: Kegan Paul, 1877) is an acute contemporary response to Schopenhauer's naturalistic pessimism, as is Charles Renouvier's essay of 1892, "Schopenhauer et la métaphysique du pessimisme," reprinted in S. Donailler, R.-P. Droit, and P. Vermeren, eds., *Philosophie, France, XIXe siècle* (Paris: Livre de Poche, 1994).

Fechner was a prolific and astonishingly diverse writer. His adopted persona, Dr. von Mises, wrote satires, whereas Fechner himself wrote scientific essays, such as his *Elemente der Psychophysik* (Leipzig: Voss, 1860), metaphysical essays, and indescribable admixtures of the two, such as G. T. Fechner, *Zend-Avesta, oder Über die Dinge des Himmels und des Jenseits* (Leipzig, Voss, 1851), and the selections reprinted in *Life after death* (New York: Pantheon, 1943). A very useful overview of Fechner's later views on psychophysics can be found in his "My own viewpoint on mental measurement," *Psychological Research*, 1987 [1877], 49, 213–19. Every student of Fechner will want to peruse his *Nanna, oder Über das Seelenleben der Pflanzen*. First published in 1848, this is the book that brought Fechner "back to life" from a horrible depression and psychosomatic blindness. His doctor during this affair was Lotze. My copy of the third edition of the book has an introduction by Kurt Lasswitz, the historian of atomism (Hamburg: Voss, 1903). W. Woodward's "Fechner's panpsychism: A scientific solution to the mind-body problem," *Journal of the History of the Behavioral Sciences*, 1972, 8, 367–86, is the only serious modern study of the relationship between Fechner's "science" and his "philosophy."

Lotze was a commanding figure in philosophy and psychology until approximately World War I. Nevertheless, modern writers have tended to ignore him, as they have ignored Herbart and Müller. His main works were R. H. Lotze, *Medicinische psychologie, oder Physiologie der Seele* (Leipzig: Weidmann, 1852); *Microcosmos: An essay concerning man and his relation to the world* (New York: Scribners, 1887), 2d ed.; and *Metaphysics* (Oxford: Clarendon Press, 1887), 2d ed. Some of the better secondary sources are O. Kraushaar's two papers: "Lotze's influence on the psychology of William James," *Psychological Review*, 1936, 43, 235–57, and "Lotze's influence on the pragmatism and practical philosophy of William James," *Journal of the History of Ideas,* 1940, 1, 439-58; T. M. Lindsay, "Rudolf Hermann Lotze," *Mind,* 1876, 1, 363-81; and G. Santayana's Ph.D. dissertation, *Lotze's system of philosophy* (Bloomington: Indiana University Press, 1971). W. R. Woodward's "From association to Gestalt: The fate of Hermann Lotze's theory of spatial perception, 1846-1920," *Isis,* 1978, 69, 572-82, somewhat oversimplifies the complex of psychological and metaphysical issues which Lotze's theory of local signs addressed. The local sign theory was appropriated by empiricists in their debate with nativists, but Lotze's motivations for the theory had little to do with this debate, a fact that is obscured in Woodward's paper.

Lotze's critique of Müller's "keyboard" metaphor for explaining the cerebral control of movement was taken up only in the 1930s, by Nicolas Bernstein, a Soviet physiologist. Bernstein's work, although now recognized as a major breakthrough, was little known in the West and was suppressed in the USSR until the 1960s. A good introduction to Bernstein's life and work is M. Latash and M. Turvey, eds., *Bernstein on dexterity* (Mahwah, N.J.: Erlbaum, 1996). My essay in this book, co-written with Blandine Bril, explains how Bernstein refuted the "cerebral habit" theory of motor learning.

Chapter 6: 1848 and All That

Jerome Blum's posthumous *In the beginning: The advent of the modern age. Europe in the 1840s* (New York: Norton, 1994) is an excellent overview of the social, political, economic, and cultural change of the 1840s. The early chapters of Herbert Schnädelbach's *Philosophy in Germany, 1831–1933* (New York: Cambridge University Press, 1984) make the point that much philosophical writing and thinking occurred outside the universities in the 1840s. Similarly, William Johnston's *The Austrian mind: An intellectual history, 1848–1938* (Berkeley: University of

California Press, 1972) tracks many diverse strands of thought, only a few of which obtained representation in the Austrian universities.

I used the following books and articles for information about changes in curriculum in universities and the early professionalization of physiology, psychology, and philosophy: J. Ben-David, "Social factors in the origins of a new science" and "Universities and academic systems in modern societies," in his *Scientific growth: Essays on the organization and ethos of science* (Berkeley: University of California Press, 1991); L. S. Jacyna, "Medical science and moral science: The cultural relations of physiology in restoration France," *History of Science,* 1987, 25, 111–46; J. E. Lesch, *Science and medicine in France: The emergence of experimental physiology* (Cambridge: Harvard University Press, 1985); J. Schiller, "Physiology's struggle for independence," *History of Science,* 1968, 7, 64–89; J. S. Jacyna, "Principles of general physiology: The comparative dimension of British neuroscience in the 1830s and 1840s," *Studies in the History of Biology,* 1984, 7, 47–92. There are very few studies of nonacademic science, but S. Sheets-Pyenson, "Popular science periodicals in Paris and London, 1820–1875," *Annals of Science,* 1985, 42, 549–72, provides a wealth of information.

Interestingly, a number of neurophysiologists in midcentury consciously decided to go back to late-eighteenth-century theories of mind-brain relations. This trend is reflected in the reprinting of two important essays by European contemporaries of Whytt, who offered theories similar to his: G. Prochaska, "A dissertation on the functions of the nervous system," and J. A. Unzer, "The principles of physiology," both published in T. Laycock, ed., *Unzer and Prochaska on the nervous system* (London: Sydenham Society, 1851).

Adam Crabtree's *From Mesmer to Freud* (New Haven: Yale University Press, 1993) gives a thorough account of the undermining of the physicalist theory of mesmerism in the 1830s and 1840s. See also the collection of James Braid's essays in A. E. Waite, ed., *Braid on hypnotism: The beginning of modern hypnosis* (New York: Julian Press, 1960). Ann Braude's *Radical spirits: Spiritualism and women's rights in nineteenth-century America* (Boston: Beacon, 1989) is still a good place to begin studying the history of spiritualism. It is surprising that the great American successes of spiritualism, phrenology, and faith healing in the nineteenth century have not been compared with the success of psychology as an American institution in the twentieth century. On the beginnings of the split between psychology and these other fields see T. and G. Leahey, *Psychology and its occult doubles: Psychology and the problem of pseudoscience* (Chicago: Nelson Hall, 1983), and D. J. Coon, "Testing the limits of sense and science: American experimental psychologists combat spiritualism, 1880–1920," *American Psychologist*, 1992, 47, 143–51.

For Helmholtz's role in the institutional development of psychology, see: R. S. Turner, "Helmholtz, sensory physiology, and the disciplinary development of German physiology," in W. Woodward and M. Ash, eds., *The problematic science: Psychology in nineteenth-century thought* (New York, Praeger, 1982), and also Turner's *In the eye's mind* (Princeton: Princeton University Press, 1994).

The history of the Metaphysical Society is recounted in A. W. Brown, *The Metaphysical Society: Victorian minds in crisis* (New York: Columbia University Press, 1947). Some representative essays by members of the Metaphysical Society and their circle: W. K. Clifford, *Lectures and essays* (London: Macmillan, 1879), 2 vols.; F. Pollock, *Spinoza: His life and philosophy* (London: Kegan Paul, 1880); J. Tyndall, *Fragments of science* (New York: D. Appleton, 1898), 2 vols.; A. Bain, "The intellect, viewed physiologically" and "The feelings and the will, viewed physiologically," *Fortnightly Review* 1865, 3, 575–88, 735–48; see also Bain's *Mind and body: The theories of their relation* (London: Henry King, 1873), 2d ed. These various writings are striking for their uniform commitment to some form of a dual aspect theory of the relationship between mind and body, and the authors' conviction—often poorly articulated—that such a dual aspect theory somehow provides a safe haven for religion. C. D. Cashdollar's *The transformation of theology, 1830–1890: Positivism and Protestant thought in Britain and America* (Princeton: Princeton University Press, 1989) shows the significant intertwining of liberal Protestant theology and what was loosely called positivism in the latter part of the 1800s. Paul Carter's *The spiritual crisis of the gilded age* (Dekalb: Northern Illinois University Press, 1971) traces American reactions to positivism, reactions which in many ways ran parallel to those of members of the Metaphysical Society.

The best overview of the positivistic trend across Europe in the mid-1800s is still Mandelbaum's *History, man, and reason* (see under the earlier heading "General Studies"). See also W. M. Simon, *European positivism in the nineteenth century* (Ithaca: Cornell University Press, 1963). The best way to get a feel for how the young *non*-Comtean positivists of the 1850s viewed the world is to read the two most articulate spokesmen for this position: H. Taine, *Les philosophes français du XIXe siècle* (Paris: Hachette, 1857), and H. T. Buckle, *History of civilization in England* (New York: D. Appleton-Century, 1939), 2d ed., 2 vols., originally published in 1859–61. Similarly, although there is no systematic historical review of the *Materialismusstreit* (materialism conflict) in the German-speaking world of the 1850s, a careful reading of Lange's *History of materialism and criticism of its present importance* can illustrate how this new generation of positivistic dual aspect theorists thought their views would save religion against the materialist onslaught. F. Gregory's *Scientific materialism in 19th-century Germany* (mentioned earlier) is a good study of the so-called vulgar materialists. For a contemporary pamphlet see M. J. Schleiden, *Über den Materialismus der neueren deutschen Naturwissenschaft* (Leipzig: Egelmann, 1863).

Fred Wilson's studies of Mill emphasize both his relations and his disagreements with Comte and other positivists. See F. Wilson, "Mill and Comte on the method of introspection," *Journal of the History of the Behavioral Sciences*, 1991, 27, 107–29 and *Psychological analysis and the philosophy of John Stuart Mill* (Toronto: University of Toronto Press, 1991).

Wundt is perhaps the most studied personage in the history of psychology. Part of the reason for this is that thanks to the influence of Wundt's Anglo-American apostle E. B. Titchener, many American psychologists mistakenly allied Wundt with the positivists as opposed to the natural metaphysicians. Recent scholarship has not only shown how wrong this was but has also traced the roots of some of these misconceptions: A. Blumenthal, "A reappraisal of Wilhelm Wundt," *American Psychologist*, 1975, 30, 1081–88, and "Wilhelm Wundt: Psychology as a propadeutic science," in C. Buxton, ed., *Points of view in the modern history of psychology* (New York: Academic Press, 1985); K. Danziger, "The positivist repudiation of Wundt," *Journal of the History of the Behavioral Sciences*, 1979, 15, 205–30; "The history of introspection reconsidered," *Journal of the History of the Behavioral Sciences*, 1989, 16, 241–62; "Wundt and the two traditions of psychology," in R. Rieber, ed., *Wilhelm Wundt and the making of scientific psychology* (New York: Plenum). Wundt's writings are diverse and went through many editions. I used: W. Wundt, *Beiträge zur Theorie der Sinneswahrnehmung* (Leipzig: Winter, 1862); *Vorlesungen über die Menschen- und*

Thierseele (Leipzig: Voss, 1863), 2 vols.; *Grundzüge der physiologischen Psychologie* (Leipzig: Englemann, 1874); and "Über psychologische Methoden," *Philosophische Studien,* 1883, 1, 1–40.

For an overview of the neo-Kantian movement see: T. E. Willey's *Back to Kant: The revival of Kantianism in German social and historical thought* (Detroit: Wayne State University Press, 1978) and also Lange's *History of materialism.* The Lange quote comes from K. Kuhnke, *The rise of neo-Kantianism* (New York: Cambridge University Press, 1991), p. 151. Kuhnke is particularly good at describing the role of the neo-Kantians (not the positivists) in promoting the idea that philosophy, and in particular epistemology, was or should be a kind of "science of science."

By the 1860s and 1870s the debates over materialism were common knowledge all across Europe. This is well illustrated by the following passage from *Anna Karenina* (first published in 1877). Levin goes to visit his brother and finds that "a well known professor of philosophy was with him, who had come especially from Kharkov to settle a dispute that had arisen between them on an important philosophical question. The professor was engaged in a fierce polemic against the materialists, and Sergius Koznyshev, who followed the polemic with interest, on reading the professor's last article had written to him reproaching him with having conceded too much to the materialists; and the professor had come at once to talk the matter over. The question was the fashionable one, whether a definite line exists between psychological and physiological phenomena in human activity; and, if so, where it lies?" (cited from p. 23 of the L. and A. Maude translation of *Anna Karenina* [New York: Oxford University Press, 1980]).

Ellenberger's *Discovery of the unconscious* (cited earlier) is essential background reading for the study of the unconscious. L. L. Whyte's *The unconscious before Freud* (New York: Basic Books, 1960) is useful on the connections between Leibniz, Whytt, and later writers. No one else, to my knowledge, has noted how interest in the unconscious increased markedly in the decades following 1848. A partial exception is K. Danziger, "Mid-nineteenth-century British psycho-physiology: A neglected chapter in the history of psychology," in W. Woodward and M. Ash, eds., *The problematic science: Psychology in nineteenth-century thought* (New York: Praeger, 1982).

Four major texts of the 1860s focus on the importance of unconscious mental processes in the shaping of the human mind. The background to this flowering of the unconscious mind in the 1860s is reviewed in E. S. Reed, "Theory, concept, and experiment in the history of psychology: The older tradition behind a 'young science,'" *History of the Human Sciences*, 1989, 2, 333–52. There are four key texts. The first is John Stuart Mill's *An examination of Sir William Hamilton's philosophy* (Toronto: University of Toronto & R. Kegan Paul, 1979 [1865]), which is the most explicit statement by an associationist of the need for postulating unconscious mental processes to generate a coherent associationist psychology. There, and also in his commentaries appended to James Mill's *Analysis of the phenomena of the human mind* (London: Longmans, Green, Reader, & Dyer, 1869), 2 vols., John Stuart Mill developed his hypothesis that some or all unconscious processes are similar to inferences. The second key text is Hippolyte Taine's *De l'intelligence* (Paris: Vrin, 1869), which also integrates the concept of unconscious mental processes with associationism but introduces a broader concern with the formation of the self, along with the idea that individual cultures in some way encourage different specific patterns of association of ideas in the formation of self. The third text is E. S. Dallas's extraordinary *The gay science* (London: Chapman & Hall, 1866), 2 vols., which really deserves a separate study. Dallas integrates ideas from mainstream philosophy and psychology with early research on the psychology of sleep, dreaming, drunkenness, and mesmerism. He therefore treats the unconscious as a kind of well of motives and images and as a source of ideas and inferences. He relates this complex unconscious to the analysis of literature and art in a text that was a full century ahead of its time. Finally, the fourth key book on the unconscious from the 1860s is Eduard von Hartmann's *Philosophy of the unconscious* (New York: Harcourt, Brace, 1931 [1869]), 3 vols. Von Hartmann uses the apparatus of naturalistic metaphysics (extensive discussions of biology and physiology, logico-mathematical arguments, etc.) to draw a picture of the unconscious as an entire sphere of life, of which we only catch glimpses in our ordinary mental activities.

Americans were not far behind in the study of the unconscious. A remarkable essay by Oliver Wendell Holmes, Sr., anticipates William James and the British school of the unconscious in "Mechanism in thought and morals: Address to the Phi Beta Kappa Society at Harvard College, June, 1870," in *Pages from an old volume of life: A collection of essays, 1857–1881* (Boston: Houghton-Mifflin, 1899). Holmes asserts that for a part of our lives we are engaged in habitual or automatic actions of which we are largely unconscious. Therefore, if we can guide these "mechanistic" behaviors to useful ends, we should do so.

The controversy between Bailey and John Stuart Mill was stimulated by S. Bailey, *A review of Berkeley's theory of vision, designed to show the unsoundness of that celebrated speculation* (London: James Ridgeway, 1842). Mill reviewed this work in "Bailey on Berkeley's theory of vision," in J. Robson, ed., *Essays on philosophy and the classics* (Toronto: University of Toronto and Routledge & Kegan Paul, 1978 [1842]—quote, p.). It is useful to compare Mill's comments in his critique of Bailey with his comments on Berkeley himself in "Berkeley's life and writings" in the same volume (11) of Mill's *Collected works; A system of Logic* is vols. 6-7. Bailey's most systematic work is his *Letters on the philosophy of the human mind* (London: Longman, Rees, Orme, Brown, and Green, 1855, 1858, 1863). In it he clearly describes both Hamilton's inconsistency and his undermining of the Scottish "realist" position. (It is therefore a shame that Mill did not pay sufficient attention to this text when writing his own critique of Hamilton.) Unfortunately, Bailey agrees with enough of what Dugald Stewart, Thomas Brown, and William Hamilton say about Reid to decide that the latter was no realist himself! (This interpretation is made possible by the quasi-Berkeleian position Reid adopts in *Inquiry into the human mind* [1764] unlike in his more radical *Essays* of the 1780s.) But Bailey is admirably clear about his own realism and continues his campaign of pointing out the nonexistence of many of the hypothetical mental entities required by associationist theory. The contrast between perception as unconscious inference and perception as direct observation of the world is brought out in an exchange of papers between Richard Gregory and Eleanor and James Gibson. Both Gregory's "Seeing as thinking" and the Gibsons' "The senses as information-seeking systems" appeared in the *Times Literary Supplement* 1972 and are reprinted in E. J. Gibson's *An odyssey in learning and perception* (Cambridge, Mass.: MIT Press, 1991).

C. S. Sherrington's review of muscle sense in E. A. Schafer's *Textbook of physiology* (Edinburgh: Pentland, 1900), 2 vols., is the best guide to this important topic. The idea that muscles might be "sentient" is an old one that only gradually evolved into the modern idea that muscles might include a neurally based sensory system—even though there are no conscious sensations associated with that system. Arguments over these ideas often reveal deep-seated assumptions about the nature of sense perception, the relation of mind to body (and the relation of mental states to action), and methodological issues (how we can know about this sensory system). This topic deserves far more detailed attention than I give it here. K. Figlio's "Theories of perception and the physiology of mind in the late eighteenth century," *History of Science,* 12, 1975, 177–212, and K. Danziger's "Origins of the schema of stimulated motion: Towards a pre-history of modern psychology," *History of Science,* 21, 183–210, begin to tell this fascinating story.

CHAPTER 8: THE APOTHEOSIS OF POSITIVISM

It is remarkable how invisible Lewes is in the standard histories of British philosophy. Someone who arguably did more than even Coleridge or Carlyle to bring European ideas to the British continent and who sparked the late Victorian revival of interest in Spinoza and dual aspect theories surely merits at least some discussion. Yet John Passmore's much-admired *A hundred years of philosophy,* for example (London: Duckworth, 1957), has only three perfunctory cites to Lewes, and no discussion of his contribution whatsoever.

R. Ashton's *G. H. Lewes: A life* (New York: Oxford University Press, 1991) is now the best introduction to the life of this important thinker. Ashton focuses mostly on Lewes's biography and especially on his relations with Marian Evans (George Eliot), but she gives good brief sketches of many of Lewes's ideas. The only thing that is missing is a sense of how central Lewes in fact was to the development of both physiology and psychology in Britain—understandable with an author trained in English literature like Ashton. What is less understandable is that historians of science and philosophy have failed to accord Lewes the respectful attention that students of George Eliot have! Some other important essays on the role of scientific and Lewesian ideas in George Eliot's work are: R. Greenberg, "Plexuses and ganglia: Scientific allusion in *Middlemarch*," *Nineteenth-Century Fiction*, 1976, 30, 33–52; M. Mason, "*Middlemarch* and science: Problems of life and mind," *Review of English Studies*, 1971, 22, 151–69; and S. Shuttleworth's interesting book, *George Eliot and nineteenth-century science: The make-believe of a beginning* (New York: Cambridge University Press, 1981). Shuttleworth is one of the few modern writers to refer to Dallas's *Gay science* (see p. 21).

Lewes's works were numerous (Ashton gives the most complete bibliography available). I used the American edition of his multivolume *Problems of life and mind: First series, Foundations of a creed; Second series, The physical basis of mind; Third series, The study of psychology* (Boston: 1874–79). James Osgood published all but the last series, which was put out by Houghton-Mifflin. Lewes's *Life and works of Goethe* is available in an Everyman edition. Lewes's *Biographical history of philosophy* (in some editions just called *History of philosophy*) was widely published on both sides of the Atlantic and went through perhaps as many as half a dozen significantly different editions. I have used *Biographical history of philosophy* (Manchester, Eng.: Routledge, 1893), 8th ed. The changes to successive editions of the book were mostly amplification, but Lewes also devoted considerable energy to rewrites, especially to toning down his allegiance to Comte and clarifying his conception of a non-Comtean positivism. This secular positivism, if I can use that term, was immensely influential in the 1870s and 1880s all across Europe. Lewes was by no means its only spokesperson, but he was an important figure in the movement.

Lewes's story about the club for studying Spinoza is worth quoting at length:

> About thirty years ago a small club of students held weekly meetings in the parlour of a tavern in Red Lion Square, Holborn, where the vexed questions of philosophy were discussed with earnestness, if not with insight. The club was extremely simple in its rules, and quite informal in its proceedings. The members were men whose sole point of junction was the Saturday meeting, and whose sole object was the amicable collision of contending views, on subjects which, at one time or other, perplex and stimulate all reflecting minds. On every other day in the week their paths were divergent. One kept a second hand bookstall, rich in free-thinking literature; another was a journeyman watchmaker; a third lived on a moderate income; a fourth was a bootmaker; a fifth "penned a stanza when he should engross;" a sixth studied anatomy and many other things, with vast aspirations, and no very definite career before him. Although thus widely separated, these divergent paths converged every Saturday towards the little parlour in Red Lion Square, and the chimes of midnight were drowned in the pleasant noises of argument and laughter: argument sometimes loud and angry, but on these occasions always terminating in laughter which cleared the air with its explosions. Seated around the fire, smoking their cigars and pipes, and drinking coffee, grog, or ale, without chairman or president, without fixed form of debate, and with a general tendency to talk all at once when the discussion grew

animated, these philosophers really did strike out sparks which animated each other's minds. . . .

[Among the debaters was] a German Jew, named Cohn, or Kohn, whom we all admired as a man of astonishing subtlety and logical force, no less than of sweet personal worth. He remains in my memory as a type of philosophic dignity. A calm, meditative, amiable man, by trade a journeyman watchmaker, very poor, with weak eyes and chest; grave and gentle in demeanour; incorruptible, even by the seductions of vanity; I habitually think of him in connection with Spinoza, almost as much on account of his personal characteristics, as because to him I owe my first acquaintance with the Hebrew thinker. (From G. H. Lewes, "Spinoza," *Fortnightly Review*, 1866, 4, no. 22, 385–406)

I wonder whether Kohn still frequented Red Lion Square twenty five years later, when William Morris lived there.

For the development and spread of positivism, see Mandelbaum's *History, man, and reason* (under "General Studies") and also W. M. Simon, *European positivism in the nineteenth century* (Ithaca: Cornell University Press, 1963). Some of the more articulate thinkers who deepened and extended Lewes's "secular positivism" were the scientists associated with the Metaphysical Society discussed in Chapter 6. F. Pollock's *Spinoza: His life and philosophy* (London: Kegan Paul, 1880) was not only one of the first books in English on Spinoza, but is essentially just a fleshing out of Lewes's interpretation of Spinoza as a proto-positivist.

Comte's *Cours de philosophie positive* began appearing in 1830 and continued for the next two decades. I have used the six-volume posthumous edition put out by the Société Positive in

Paris, 1896. A condensed version of the *Cours* was translated by Harriet Martineau into English, in part under Lewes's aegis, and published as *The positive philosophy of Auguste Comte* (London: J. Chapman, 1853). Chapman was one of Lewes's publishers, and an intimate of Lewes, Spencer, and Marian Evans (George Eliot). The quote from Spencer used here comes from D. Duncan, ed., *The life and letters of Herbert Spencer* (London: Williams and Norgate, 1911), p. 81.

Thomas Henry Huxley's influential version of the dual aspect theory can best be found in his address to the British Association for the Advancement of Science in 1872, "On the hypothesis that animals are automata," reprinted in *Methods and results* (New York: Appleton, 1896); and also in his *Hume: With helps to the study of Berkeley* (New York: Appleton, 1902 [1879]). Both these books amply attest to Huxley's phenomenalism and antimaterialism, the criticisms of his contemporary enemies notwithstanding.

For the Lewes scholarship in physiology at Cambridge, see E. M. Tansey, " 'The science least adequately studied in England': Physiology and the G. H. Lewes studentship," *Journal of the History of Medicine and Allied Sciences*, 1992, 47, 163–86. James's review of Lewes's *Physical basis of mind* is from the *Nation*, 1877, 25.

CHAPTER 9: THE ANOMALOUS MR. DARWIN

A. Desmond and J. Moore, *Darwin* (London: Michael Joseph, 1991), is the most authoritative biography to date, and D. Kohn, ed., *The Darwinian heritage* (Princeton: Princeton University Press, 1985), is a convenient summary of much of the vast secondary literature on Darwin. I would however take the idiosyncratic view that the best place to begin studying Darwin is with two other books: M. Ghiselin, *Triumph of the Darwinian method* (Chicago: University of Chicago Press, 1984 [1969]), and Mea Allan, *Darwin and his flowers: The key to natural selection* (New York: Taplinger, 1977). Both these books have the great virtue of providing clear and comprehensive overviews of all of Darwin's work, especially his work after 1859 and the publication of *The origin*. Understandably, many biographers and historians focus on the period prior to *The origin*. Interesting as this is from a human point of view, it tends to distort Darwin's remarkable achievement: the amazing breadth and depth of his revolutionary contributions. I have tried to add my little bit to this historical review of Darwin's accomplishments in E. S. Reed, "Darwin's worms: A case study in evolutionary psychology," *Behaviorism*, 1982, 10, 165-85; and also in chapter 2 of my *Encountering the world: Toward an ecological psychology* (New York: Oxford University Press, 1996). Darwin's *Works* were published by John Murray in Britain and D. Appleton in the United States in the nineteenth century, and have been recently reissued in twenty-nine volumes in London by Pickering & Chatto (1986).

Especially important for the history of psychology are Darwin's books on inheritance, human evolution, and behavior. These can be found in the recent Chatto and Windus reissue, but I used: *Variation of animals and plants under domestication* (New York: Appleton, 1896 [1868]), 2 vols.; *The descent of man and Selection in relation to sex* (New York: Appleton, 1902 [1871]), 2d ed.; *The expression of the emotions in man and animals* (Chicago: University of Chicago Press, 1965 [1872]); *The formation of vegetable mould through the action of earthworms* (New York: D. Appleton, 1904 [1881]).

Robert Boakes's *From Darwin to behaviorism: Psychology and the minds of animals* (New York: Cambridge University Press, 1984) is far and away the best introduction to the history of animal behavior. It has a good review of Spalding's work, including a photograph of Lady Amberley, Spalding's research assistant. Spalding's most important psychological papers were: "Instinct: With original observations on young animals," *Macmillan's*, 1873, 27, 282–93; reprinted with a note by J. B. S. Haldane in *British Journal of Animal Behavior*, 1954, 2, 2–11 (I have cited from Haldane's edition); "Instinct and acquisition," *Nature*, 1875, 12, 507–8; "The relation of mind and body (Review of Bain's *Mind and body*)," *Nature*, 1873, 7, 178–79; Review of Spencer's *Principles of psychology*, in *Nature*, 1873, 7, 198–200, 356–59; Review of Lewes's *Problems of life and mind*, in *Nature*, 1874, 10, 212–13.

Although Haldane—one of Britain's most distinguished scientists—officially "rediscovered" Spalding and published his main work in 1954, P. Gray again "rediscovered" Spalding in the 1960s—see "Douglas Spalding, the first experimental behaviorist," *Journal of General Psychology*, 1962, 67, 299–307—and two decades later Boakes re-re-rediscovered him in his aforementioned book. This neglect is all the odder as Spalding's work is discussed at considerable length in the chapter on instinct in William James's *Principles of psychology*. It is arguable that two of Spalding's discoveries—the phenomena of imprinting and of critical periods—are among the most important in the history of psychology, and his experimental methods of approaching them are still followed. A systematic study of the lack of impact of Spalding's work on developmental behavioral science is in order.

CHAPTER 10: THE GENERATION OF 1879

The date 1879 has been widely used to mark "the founding of experimental psychology" largely under the influence of Boring's *History of experimental psychology* (see under "General Studies"). Boring, a student of Titchener, the positivist disciple of Wundt, emphasized Wundt's laboratory and its research and downplayed Wundt's other interests. The best place to begin reassessing Boring's biases and their consequences for later students of the history of psychology is K. Danziger's "The history of introspection reconsidered," *Journal of the History of the Behavioral Sciences,* 1980, 16, 241-62. Danziger's book *Constructing the subject: Historical origins of psychological research* (New York: Cambridge University Press, 1991) is a detailed review of the social setting of Wundtian psychology and its transformation, especially in the United States. R. O'Donnell's *The origin of behaviorism, 1880–1920* (New York: NYU Press, 1985) focuses entirely on the transformation of "the new psychology" into something rather different after it reached America.

It is very useful to read some of the contemporary propaganda about the new psychology in order to see how the intellectual arguments for experimentation on mental life—bringing experiment into the preserve of philosophers and moralists—was promoted. Some of the most interesting literature of this type includes G. S. Hall's *Aspects of German culture* (Boston: James R. Osgood, 1881) and Cardinal Mercier's extraordinary *The relation of experimental psychology to philosophy* (New York: Benziger Brothers, Printers to the Holy Apostolic See, 1902), which tries to appropriate the experimental approach to psychology for a Thomistic view of the world, and the Frenchman Théodule Ribot's twin attacks on what he perceived to be the moribund state of French psychology: *English psychology* (London: Henry King, 1873) and *German psychology today* (New York: Scribners, 1886), both of which are unashamedly "boosterish" about positivism and early experimental psychology.

In this account I have relied heavily on W. Carl's *Frege's theory of sense and reference: Its origins and scope* (New York: Cambridge University Press, 1994) because it seemed to me to give the most balanced presentation of Frege's difficult-to-understand views about the nature of the objects to which propositions refer. G. P. Baker and P. M. S. Hacker's *Frege: Logical excavations* (New York: Oxford University Press, 1984) makes a case for Frege's being not just a realist but a Platonist. I think this goes too far, but the book is useful for showing just how strong an argument one can make for this position. In all cases, I have used modern English translations of Frege: *The basic laws of arithmetic,* trans. M. Furth (Berkeley: University of California Press, 1964); *The foundation of arithmetic,* trans. J. Austin (New York: Oxford University Press); *Conceptual notation and related articles,* J. Bynum, ed. (New York: Oxford University Press, 1972); *Logical investigations,* P. Geach and R. Stoothoff, eds. (New York: Oxford University Press, 1977).

Interestingly, one of the first English-language journals devoted exclusively to what we would now call philosophy was the *Journal of Speculative Philosophy,* which was started in 1867 by William Torrey Harris and other so-called St. Louis Hegelians. Thus, a group of nonacademics in the middle Southwest of the United States in the difficult years after the Civil War managed to start the first American philosophical journal, nearly a decade before the founding of *Mind* (1876) in civilized England. (For more on these thinkers, see W. H. Goetzmann's anthology with commentary, *The American Hegelians: An intellectual episode in the history of Western America* [New York: Knopf, 1973].) *Mind* itself, under its first editor, G. C. Robertson, was quite evenly divided between psychological and philosophical writings. The last quarter of the nineteenth century was perhaps the heyday in the English-speaking world of serious intellectual journalism. First-rate intellectual work was published, among other places, in *The Atlantic* and *Harpers* in the United States, in *The Fortnightly Review, Macmillan's,* and *The Nineteenth Century* in Britain, and in *La Revue des Deux Mondes* in France. Yet here again, historians of both philosophy and psychology have not explored these sources in any systematic way, nor even asked the more fundamental question of why discussions of rather technical philosophical and scientific issues were sufficiently popular to be given significant space in the popular media.

On the history of logic, the best overview is W. & M. Kneale, *The development of logic* (New York: Oxford University Press, 1962). I have used Hilary Putnam's introduction to the new edition of C. S. Peirce's 1898 lectures on *Reason and the logic of things* (Cambridge: Harvard University Press, 1992) as a guide to Peirce's place in the history of symbolic logic. The citations to Peirce are all drawn from N. Houser and C. Kloesel, eds., *The essential Peirce: Vol. 1, 1867–1893* (Bloomington: University of Indiana Press, 1992). The quotation about syllogisms comes from his "Grounds of validity of the laws of logic," p. 63 (which first appeared in *Journal of Speculative Philosophy,* 1869, 2, 193–208). The quotation about the faith of the logician comes from "On the Algebra of Logic," p. 202.

Bertrand Russell's early ideas on the importance of logic to philosophy are collected in his *Principles of mathematics* (New York: Norton, 1938 [1903]). For the background on Russell's thinking and for his idea of logic as the method for a new kind of philosophy (which ultimately came to be called analytic philosophy), see N. Griffith, *Russell's idealist apprenticeship* (New York: Clarendon, 1991) and P. Hylton, *Russell, idealism, and the emergence of analytic philosophy* (New York: Oxford University Press, 1991).

For the Austrian school, Barry Smith's outstanding *Austrian philosophy: The legacy of Franz Brentano* (Chicago: Open Court, 1994) is now the definitive text in English. See also J. MacNamara and G.-J. Boudewijnse, "Brentano's influence on Ehrenfels's theory of percepual gestalts," *Journal for the Theory of Social Behavior,* 1995, 25, 401–18. B. Smith and D. W. Smith's *Cambridge companion to Husserl* (New York: Cambridge University Press, 1995) is also very useful. I found R. Tieszen's chapter on Husserl's mathematics particularly helpful. M. Farber's detailed study of Husserl's prephenomenological writings, *The foundations of phenomenology* (New York: Paine-Whitman, 1962), is particularly useful on Husserl's antipsychologism. Husserl's *Logical investigations* was written and rewritten between 1897 and 1913. John Findlay's English translation is of the revised edition (Routledge & Kegan Paul, 1973). It was in the process of revising *The investigations* that Husserl deepened and clarified his concept of a "new science" on which he could base his philosophy. This new science he then dubbed phenomenology. See his "Ideen zu einer reinen Phänomenologie und phänomenologischen Philosophie," *Jahrbuch für Philosophie und phänomenologische Forschung,* 1913, 1, 1–323. It is not coincidental that this text was published as the opening part of a new journal, nor that the title of the journal emphasized research.

Daniel Wilson's *Science, community, and the transformation of American philosophy, 1860–1930* (Chicago: University of Chicago Press, 1990) offers a useful account of the pressures many turn-of-the-century thinkers faced to become more specialized. The author reports, for example, on an important exchange in the *Nation* in 1876 between G. Stanley Hall and William James, in which Hall condemned the American teaching of philosophy as unnecessarily encumbered by religious constraint and James pointed to science as a possible way of eliminating the constraint (pp. 40–41). Wilson recounts many details about the founding of the *Philosophical Review* at Cornell in 1892 (pp. 54–55, 104) and also the origin of the American Philosophical Association in 1901, nearly a decade after the founding of the American Psychological Association (pp. 99, 109). (Note that Hall's *American Journal of Psychology* was founded in 1887, five years before the *Philosophical Review.*) Even though psychology had a clear institutional head start, Wilson still uses the misleading rhetoric about psychology's "emergence" from philosophy's shadow! What, then, are we to make of Arthur Lovejoy's presidential address to the American Philosophical Association, in which Lovejoy urged that philosophy become more like a science, as psychology had done so successfully (pp. 143–45)?

CHAPTER 11: WILLIAM JAMES

James's equivocal position has only been hesitantly acknowledged by psychologists or philosophers. Philosophers have tried to downplay James's commitment to naturalism and science. Psychologists have tried to downplay the fact that this commitment, as James understood it, included an openness to polytheism and spiritualism. (Incidentally, James was strongly opposed to pantheism, especially the kind of pantheism with which many positivists dallied.) Despite the considerable secondary literature, almost no attention has been devoted to the polytheistic motivations animating a significant portion of James's work. One important exception is A. Funkenstein, "The polytheism of William James," *Journal of the History of Ideas,* 1994, 55, 99–111, which is, however, sketchy.

Harvard University Press has issued *The works of William James,* which is now the definitive scholarly edition. The majority of these texts have also been reprinted in the Library of America's edition of James's writings, which is more accessible. I have therefore cited from the first volume of these, William James, *Writings: 1878–1899* (New York: Library of America, 1984), for all the quotes here except those from "Are we automata?" and "The spatial quale," which are not included in this edition but can be found in W. James, *Essays in psychology* (Cambridge: Harvard University Press, 1983). "The Ph.D.

octopus" can be found in the second volume of the Library of America edition (William James, *Writings, 1902–1910* [New York: Library of America, 1984]).

F. M. Turner, *Between science and religion: The reaction to scientific naturalism in late Victorian England* (New Haven: Yale University Press, 1974) shows the significant intertwining of religious and theological concerns in the development of British science at the turn of the century. His chapters on A. R. Wallace, F. W. H. Myers, and James Ward are excellent introductions to the role psychology (and also psychic research) played in reconciling the scientific and religious views of many people in the late 1800s. Much of James's work occurred in a similar context. In particular, James was very sympathetic to the work of Myers, whose studies of the occult and of psychic phenomena are usually ignored in histories of psychology or philosophy.

The secondary literature on James and his family is vast, but unfortunately, very little of it has focused on his relationship with psychologists and psychology as an emerging science. One exception to the rule is D. Bjork's *The compromised scientist: William James in the development of American psychology* (New York: Columbia University Press, 1983), which describes James's rather equivocal relationship with the nascent American Psychological Association and its main proponents. R. B. Perry's *Thought and character of William James* (see the bibliographic notes to Chapter 1) is still the most reliable overview of James's ideas. In "The psychologist's fallacy as a persistent framework in William James's psychological theorizing," *History of the Human Sciences,* 1995, 8, 61–73, I try to give a thumbnail sketch of James's psychological concerns. G. Myers's *William James* (New Haven: Yale University Press, 1986) should be used with caution. E. Taylor's *William James on exceptional mental states* (New York: Scribners, 1983) is the best review of James's thinking about psychic phenomena. And now see also Taylor's *William James: On consciousness beyond the margin* (Princeton, N.J.: Princeton University Press, 1996). In *Science and religion in the era of William James: The eclipse of uncertainty, 1820–1880* (Chapel Hill: University of North Carolina Press, 1995) P. J. Croce so overemphasizes the loss of certainty that he often loses sight of James, who was never centrally concerned with issues of certainty or skepticism. F. O. Matthiessen's *The James family* (New York: Knopf, 1947) is still worth reading, and G. W. Allen's *William James* (New York: Viking, 1967) is still the standard biography. The quotation from Henry James comes from his *Autobiography,* ed. F. Dupee (London: W. H. Allen, 1956), p. 147.

INDEX

Abercrombie, John, 36–37, 60, 234
Abrams, M. H., 16, 54
Action: as secondary to will, 116; in Bain's theory of perception, 76–77
"Active Powers of the Mind," 22
Agape, 55. *See also* Eros; Love
Amberley, Lady, 179–80
Amberley, Lord, 179–80
Ampère, André-Marie, 83
Animal electricity, xi, 4
Animal magnetism, xi, 4, 120; materialist psychology influenced by, 38, 82–83; in theories of the unconscious, 127, 129; psychological basis of, 113–15
Apperception: in Wundt's theory of perception, 123
Associationism: role of sensation in, 29–30, 72, 75, 76, 133–35; doctrine of the association of ideas in, 38–39; in Shelley's *Frankenstein,* 52; laws and dispositions of the human mind in, 60–61; role of volition in, 76, 77, 116, 212; critiques of, 81; compared with Lotze's theory of local signs, 104; the logical unconscious in, 131–35; in the "new psychology," 203–4. *See also* Association of ideas; Bain, Alexander; Brown,

Thomas; Condillac, Etienne de; Hartley, David; Hume, David; Mill, James; Mill, John Stuart; Priestley, Joseph; Principles of association
Association of ideas, 29, 31, 38–39, 41; doctrine of, 29–30, 39
Atheism: and scientific psychology, 9
Atomism, 98; attacks on, 208–9
Attention: in theories of mind, 31

Bailey, Samuel, 135–41
Bain, Alexander, 145, 148, 150; on motor theory of perception, 76–77, 78; on belief, 77; on sense of effort, 86; on voluntary action, 93, 94, 104; on volition, 116, 118; relationship to Spalding, 179, 182
Baldwin, James Mark, 6–7, 216, 227, 230
Balzac, Honoré de, ix, 11, 58
Bell, Charles, 17, 234
Bell-Magendie Law, 17
Bentham, Jeremy, 12
Berkeleian philosophy, 33, 37
Berkeley, George, 62, 63–64, 67, 71, 133, 135, 139
Bichat, F. X. J., 44
Binet, Alfred, 80, 184
Blake, William, 41–42, 241

Blum, Jerome, 109
Boring, E. G., 146, 172, 224–25
Boscovic, Rudiger, 36–37
Bouterwek, Frederic, 111
Braid, James, 79, 114
Brentano, Franz, 186, 198; critique
    of psychological science, 99, 158;
    on phenomenological descrip-
    tion of mental states, 153, 154,
    195, 196–97
British Idealism, 112
Brown, Thomas: associationism of,
    30, 65–66, 72–74, 79, 104, 134,
    139; critique of fluid material-
    ism, 40–41, 65; career of, 64–65;
    on muscle sense, 64–74, 86, 116;
    on spatialization of the mind,
    93; on volition, 116
Büchner, Ludwig, 8, 9, 149, 231–32
Byron, George Gordon, Lord, 50

Career psychology: development
    of, xi
Carlile, Richard, 48
Carlyle, T., 12
Carpenter, William B., 77–80,
    120–21, 139, 150
Cartesian philosophy, 6, 32, 36,
    118–19, 194
Cause and effect, laws of: in
    psychology, 45
Censorship: of early materialist
    psychology, 43–45, 47–48
Cerebral reflex, 79
Charcot, Jean-Martin, 80
Cheyne, George, 61
Clifford, William K., 120, 160, 161
Cohn (friend of G. H. Lewes), 147
Coleridge, Samuel Taylor, 11, 12,
    15, 27, 149

Collins, Wilkie, 80
Combe, Andrew, xi, 239
Combe, George, xi, 77, 114, 239,
    240
Comte, Auguste, 8, 145, 148, 158,
    224
Condillac, Etienne de, 31, 32, 133,
    136, 233
Congress of Vienna, 14
Conscience, 121
Consciousness, theories of, 31, 36,
    152
Continental rationalists, 32
Cousin, Victor: career of, 30–32,
    111, 147, 235; eclecticism of, 32,
    35; intuitionism of, 33–36, 52, 99,
    120; works of, 234–35
Cullen, W., 225
Cullen family, xiii
Cultural transformations: influ-
    ence on emergence of scientific
    psychology, 109–11

Dallas, Eneas S., 142
Darwin, Charles: attacks on theo-
    centric science, 2–3, 100–101,
    159, 173–76; psychological writ-
    ings of, 23, 167, 170, 176–78;
    on theory of natural selection,
    100–101, 169, 170, 172–76, 177;
    career of, 168–72; experiments
    of, 171–72, 177–79; on emotional
    expression in man and animals,
    176–78; Spalding compared
    with, 179–83
Darwin, Erasmus, xi–xii, xv, 173;
    career of, 14–16, 48, 49; poetry
    of, 14, 15, 39, 58, 70, 174; ma-
    terialism of, 18, 19, 27, 39–43,
    44, 49–51, 54, 57, 65, 83–84, 98,

151; on diet, 40, 47; influence of Shelley on, 45; associationist ideas of, 51, 52, 77, 93; on sexual love, 55, 56, 57; on perception, 70; on sense of effort, 86-87

Davy, Humphrey, 15

Descartes, René, 25, 91, 200

De Vaux, Clotilde, 148

Developmental critical period (Spalding), 181

Deviance: associationist explanation of, 17

Dewey, John, 216, 230

D'Holbach, Baron, 33, 48

Dickens, Charles, 113, 163, 219

Diderot, Denis, 33, 233

Diet: and mental health, 47

Disease: as imbalance of electrical forces, 4; as psychosomatic, 39

Dr. Jekyll and Mr. Hyde, 164-66

Dods, John Bovee, 1-2, 3-4, 7, 10, 111

Donders, Franciscus, 108

Dostoevsky, Fyodor, ix, 163

Doyle, Sir Arthur Conan, 115

Dreaming: dissolution of volition in, 80; unconscious mind in, 119, 120

Dual aspect theory of mind and body, 95, 98, 155, 156-57

Dualism: of conscious and unconscious mind, 7, 118-19, 164; Cartesian, 6, 19

Du Bois Reymond, Emil, 89, 98, 160, 232

Durham, W., 89

Ehrenfels, Christian von, 195, 197

Electrical psychology, 1-2, 3-4. *See also* Dods, John Bovee

Electrical stimulation: as cure for disease, 4

Eliot, George. *See* Evans, Marian

Elliotson, John, 113

Empirical realism: of Kant, 63

Empiricism, 32, 135-37

Empiricist psychology: versus nativist psychology, 52. *See also* Empiricism

Engels, Friedrich, 111, 185

Enlightenment, 31. *See also* Condillac, Etienne de; Maine de Biran, François-Pierre

Enthusiastic intuition, 34

Erkenntnislehre ("science of science"), 124-26, 159-60, 161, 186

Eros, 15, 56-57; versus agape, 55

Erotic experience: evolutionary significance of, 55-58, 120

Erotic view of the world: in Shelley's poetry, 55-58

Evans, Marian (George Eliot), 49, 88, 149, 152

Evil: as external to core self, 6, 7; relativity of, in *Frankenstein,* 53. *See also* Deviance

Evolutionary theory, 169, 172, 175, 176. *See also* Natural selection

Experimental psychology: establishment of, 5, 144, 184-86, 201; metaphysical concerns of, 117; goals of, 122-24, 143, 144-45, 154-55, 184-86. *See also* "New psychology"; Psychophysics; Reaction-time studies

Externalism: historical, xii-xiii

Faculty psychology, 27-28, 34. *See also* Metaphysics: traditional

Faraday, M., 83
Fechner, Gustav, xv, 86; on dual aspect theory of mind and body, 95, 98; on concept of "world soul," 97–98, 129; psychophysics of, 96–98, 102, 107, 117, 123, 129, 153
Ferrier, David, 4
Feuerbach, Ludwig, 47, 48, 111
Fichte, Immanuel, 34, 111, 112, 127
Fiction: as medium for underground psychology, 49. See also *Dr. Jekyll and Mr. Hyde; Frankenstein; Master Flea*
Fluid materialism, 14; implications of, 16, 41–42, 43; censorship of, 16, 43–44; description of, 38–42, 43–44; expressed in works of literature, 51, 57, 58
Fluid theory of electricity, 14
Force: concept of, xi. *See also* Vital force
Frankenstein: materialist psychology in, 45, 50–56, 58
Franklin, Benjamin, 14, 38, 83
Free action (Carpenter), 78
Free will: Schopenhauer on, 88; as introspective phenomenon, 121
Frege, Gottlob, 126, 153, 185, 189–95
Freud, Sigmund: criticism of new psychology, 20; on the unconscious, 120, 127, 142, 166–67; positivism of, 156, 159
Fritsch, Gustav, 4
Functional psychology, 177
Fused sensation, 74

Gall, Franz Josef, 28, 77
Galton, Francis, 184

Galvani, Luigi, x–xi, 38
German idealism, 31. *See also* Transcendental idealism; *and individual philosophers*
Gestalt psychology, 195–97, 198
Gibson, Eleanor, 135
Gibson, James J., 135, 137
Goethe, J. W. von, 145, 149
Gray, Asa, 101, 176, 204
Greaves, James Pierrepont, 147
Gregory, John, 61

Habitual action, 93–94
Haldane, J. B. S., 182
Hales, Steven, 61
Hall, G. Stanley, 216
Hall, Marshall, 123
Haller, Albrecht von, xv
Hamilton, William, 33, 35, 111, 134, 233, 234, 238
Hartley, David: associationism of, 38–39, 51, 52, 77, 93, 133; physiological theories of, 61, 93, 98; on volition and moral judgment, 77
Hartmann, Eduard von, 123, 141, 142, 162
Hegel, G. W. F.: career of, 31–32, 111, 112; Lewes's discussion of, 145, 147, 148
Hegelian philosophy, 35, 88
Heine, Heinrich, 46–47
Helmholtz, Herman von: on Müller, 84, 89, 91; positivism of, 98; psychophysics of, 107–8, 117–18, 200; on doctrine of unconscious inference, 118, 132, 135, 140, 142, 143, 162, 188, 189, 195
Herbart, Johann Friedrich, 84, 85, 98, 102, 129

Hering, Ewald, 143, 161, 189
Hertz, Heinrich, 98, 100, 161
Hitzig, Edward, 4
Hobbes, Thomas, 185
Hobsbawm, Eric, 110
Hodgson, Shadworth, 157
Hoffmann, E. T. A., 16, 49–50
Hume, David, 11, 62, 64–65, 157, 158, 200
Humean philosophy, 33, 88
Hunt, Leigh, 49, 147
Husserl, Edmund, 156, 187, 189–90, 195, 198–99
Huxley, T. H., 33, 120, 150; phenomenalism of, 33, 121, 158, 160–61, 162; automatism of, 151, 152, 156, 157, 178, 181; on evolution, 169
Hypnotism, 79–80, 114, 115, 120, 128. See also Animal magnetism; Suggestibility

Ideas: Darwin's theory of, 39–41; feelings associated with, 51. See also Association of ideas
Idéologues, 31. See also Condillac, Etienne de
Ideomotor Action, doctrine of (James), 105
Illuminism, 75
Illusory perception, 188–89
Indirect perception, 41
Inebriation: dissolution of volition in, 80; role of the unconscious in, 128
Insanity: as physiological disorder, 44; role of the unconscious in, 128
Internalism: historical, xii
Introspection: limitations of, 19, 80, 85, 104, 117–18, 138, 140, 187–88; natural metaphysicians on, 85; versus physiological analysis, 121, 122; role of, in traditional metaphysics, 127, 128; unconscious ideas inferred through, 129, 131, 138; use of, in experimental psychology, 143
Intuition: versus inference, 133–34, 162; of moral judgments, 35, 52–53
Intuitionism. See Cousin, Victor: intuitionism of
Irrationality: as external to core self, 7
Irrational unconscious. See Unconscious mind

James, Henry, 218
James, William, 120, 142, 182; on electrotherapy, 4; on criticism of the new psychology, 20, 21, 26, 195, 202–3, 209–10, 214–15, 219; on habitual action, 94; on doctrine of ideomotor action, 105; psychic research of, 119, 201; experiments of, 154; on relation between mind and body, 155–56, 158, 177; attacks on positivism, 158, 160; on sensations, 161; on the unconscious, 166–67; functional psychology of, 177; career of, 184–85, 201; attacks on theories of unconscious inference, 189; on stream of consciousness, 199, 201, 208–9, 211; perceptual theory of, 202–3, 210–11; on theory of conscious mind, 204–8, 216; on will, 213–15
Jefferson, Thomas, 52

Johnson, Samuel, 64
Jouffroy, Theodore, 111
Jung, Carl Gustav, 167
Jung-Stilling, Johann, 113
Just-noticeable difference (jnd), 96–97

Kant, Immanuel, 37, 72, 93, 112; on scientific study of the soul, 10, 13–14, 24–29, 45, 82; psychology of, 22–24, 35, 38, 90–91; influence of, on Maine de Biran, 31, 34; on human freedom, 45; against psychological materialism, 54, 82; on inability to prove existence of external world, 62–64, 66, 70; transcendental idealism of, 63, 69; on the noumenal world, 86, 128; on science, 124–26; Lewes's discussion of, 148; epistemology of, 153; on distinction between the noumenal and the phenomenal, 163; impact of, on modern psychology, 200
Kierkegaard, Søren, xi, 111, 163
King-Hele, Desmond, 42, 55
Knowledge, 116; logico-mathematical versus empirical, 195

Lange, Friedrich A., 7, 125–26, 160
Lavoisier, Antoine, xii
Lawrence, William, 44–45, 48, 50
Laycock, Thomas, 79, 150
Leibniz, G. W., 105, 130, 131, 132
Lewes, George Henry, 6, 13, 49, 107; career of, 11, 145–57; on Spinoza, 147; positivism of, 148–49, 155, 156; on dual aspect

view of mind and body, 149–50, 162, 151, 155, 156, 157; on spinal reflexes, 151, 154; automatism of, 152, 154; on analysis of sensations, 161; on Spalding, 182
Liebig, Justus, 146
Linnaeus, C., 14
Lipps, Theodore, 200
Local signs, doctrine of (Lotze), 104–6
Locke, John, 22, 25, 33, 34, 62
Lockean philosophy: and Enlightenment, 31, 32, 33, 34; and associationism, 38
Logic: and psychologism, 186–94
Logical unconscious, 131–32, 141, 162
London Metaphysical Society (1869–80), 120
Lotze, Rudolf Hermann, 2, 78, 86, 98, 106, 107, 116, 123, 152, 154; career of, 102; attack on vitalism, 102–3; on theory of local signs, 103–6
Love, 56–57. See also Agape; Erotic experience
Löwenheim, Leopold, 191

Mach, Ernst, 100, 143, 158, 161, 195, 196, 197
Mackintosh, James, 23
Magendie, François, 17
Magnetism: use of magnets to influence soul, 16; magnetic crisis, 83; magnetic sleep, 83, 114; psychological basis of, 113
Maine de Biran, François-Pierre, 31, 34, 52, 75–76, 84, 116
Manning, Archbishop, 120–21
Marriage of Heaven and Hell, The

(Blake): materialist psychology in, 41–42

Martineau, Harriet, 148

Marx, Karl, 111, 185

Master Flea (Hoffman): materialist psychology in, 49–50

Materialism, 8, 9, 32–33, 37, 62, 65, 125, 174. *See also* Fluid materialism; Materialist psychology

Materialist psychology, 16, 19, 38, 39, 40–41, 52, 53, 58. See also *Frankenstein; Marriage of Heaven and Hell, The; Master Flea*

Meinong, Alexius, 195, 197, 198

Mental philosophy: as science of the mind, 35; British, 82

Mental states: as natural entities, 176; in simple animals and plants, 177. *See also* Mind-body relationship

Mercier, Cardinal, D., 185

Mesmer, Franz Anton, 16, 38, 44, 82–83

Mesmerism, xi, 1, 3, 44, 112, 127, 128, 142; psychological basis of, 113–14

Metaphysics, 22–23; traditional, 27–29, 34–36, 60–61, 80, 81–82, 84, 99, 111; natural, 107, 108. *See also* Faculty psychology

Metternich, K., 38

Mill, James, 12, 60, 74, 76, 77, 116, 133, 139, 210, 212–13

Mill, John Stuart, 12, 75, 76, 179, 182, 210, 212; on science, 124, 148; and theory of the logical unconscious, 131–43, 162, 164, 179, 182, 187

Mind: Condillac on, 31; Darwin on, 40; theories of, 36–37. *See also* Mind-body relationship

Mind-body relationship: nineteenth-century conception of, 3–5, 29; pantheistic view of, 48; materialist view of, 50; as mutual influence, 61; Lotze on, 103; Taine on Spinoza's views of, 100–111; positivist view of, 157, 160–61

Moral philosophy: as psychology, 3, 22, 35; and intuitionism, 36; versus natural philosophy, 82; role of introspection in, 127

Moral sense, 52–53

Motor theory of perception: Brown's, 72–74; Bain's, 76–77, 78; Carpenter's, 77, 78

Müller, Johannes, 17, 18, 98; on vital force, 17, 84, 91–92, 102; on doctrine of specific nerve energies, 84, 90–91, 94, 101–2, 103–5, 107–8; metaphysics of, 86, 89–95; on habitual action, 94; and reflex function, 122–23

Muscle sense: Brown's invention of, 66–67, 70–72, 74, 80, 81, 86

Nativism: perceptual, 135; Kant's epistemology as, 153

Natural metaphysics, 81–85, 122, 123, 126, 141, 144. *See also* Fechner, Gustav; Lotze, Rudolf Hermann; Schopenhauer, Arthur

Natural philosophy: censorship of, 14; as natural science, 22

Natural selection: Darwin's theory of, 100–101, 169, 170, 172–76, 177; Wallace's theory of, 172

Natural supernaturalism, 16, 54, 55–56
Natural unconscious. *See* Unconscious: natural theories of
Necessity, doctrine of (Shelley), 45
Neo-Kantianism, 112, 124, 125–26. See also *Erkenntnislehre*
Neurophysiology, 13
Neurosis: as neural processes, 150. *See also* Dual aspect theory of mind and body
"New psychology": emergence of, 5, 8, 13, 185; positivism of, 19; defense of indirect perception, 41; scope of, 122, 123, 144–45. *See also* Experimental psychology
Newtonian science, 24, 25, 36–37
Nietzsche, Friedrich, 111, 142, 163, 185
Noumenal world, 85, 86, 87, 88, 92, 128, 129, 163
Novel: as medium for psychological theories, ix, 58

Obsessive thinking, 114. *See also* Suggestibility
Organic happiness, 55, 56. *See also* Erotic experience
Oxygen, theory of, xii, 13

Paley, W., 89
Panphenomenalism, 121, 161. *See also* Positivism
Panreflex theory of mind, 150
Pantheism, 48
Pavlov, Ivan, 145
Peirce, Charles, 126, 154, 185, 186, 189–95

Pflüger, Eduard, 107
Phenomenalism, 33, 121, 141
Phenomenal world, 85, 87, 129, 163
Phenomenology, 195, 197, 199, 200
Phrenology, xi, 1, 3, 4, 28–29, 44, 65, 112, 113–14, 148
Physiological psychology, 4
Piaget, Jean, 94
Plato, 56
Platonism, 56, 88
Pneumatology, 22; distinguished from natural science, 82
Poe, Edgar Allan, 16
Poetry, 57–58
Porterfield, William, 61
Positivism, 103, 108; emergence of, 8, 23, 85, 156; in new psychology, 19, 98, 111, 124; scientific, 99–100; Comtean, 99, 148–49, 158; Spencerian, 99; and panphenomenalism, 121–22, 161; versus natural metaphysics, 126, 141; and the unconscious, 151–52, 164, 167; dual aspect, 155, 156–60; sensationalism and, 162; and evolutionary psychology, 167, 175–76
Pragmatism, 77, 112
Precognition, 119
Pre-established harmony (Leibniz), 105
Presentism, xii
Priestley, Joseph, xii, 38, 39, 41, 54
Principles of association, 65, 74
Psychic research, 119
Psychoanalysis, 80
Psychologism, 187–200 *passim*
Psychophysics, 96–97, 100, 107, 117, 122, 123

Psychosis, 150. *See also* Dual aspect theory of mind and body

Puységur, A. M. J., 83

Queen Mab, 45–48

Reaction-time studies, 122–23, 143

Reflex theory, xiv. *See also* Sherrington, Charles

Reid, Thomas: on scientific study of the soul, 10, 13–14, 23–29, 34, 36, 45, 62–63, 82; psychology of, 26–27, 33–35, 37, 38, 41, 65–66, 72–74, 90, 93, 134, 135–36, 138; critique of associationism, 29–30; critique of Lockean epistemology, 31–34, 35; empirical ethics of, 52–53

Religion: and development of psychology, 1–4, 5–11, 12, 13–17, 217–220

Ribot, Théodule, 156, 185

Robertson, Croom, 185

Romanes, George J., 170

Royer-Collard, Paul, 31, 34

Russell, Bertrand, 180, 187, 191

Schelling, Friedrich, 31, 83, 102, 112, 127

Schopenhauer, Arthur: on will, 75–76, 84, 86–88, 91, 116, 127, 142; life of, 86, 88–89, 94–95, 111, 115, 141, 142; on aesthetics, 87–88

Science of the mind, 35. *See also* Mental philosophy; Moral philosophy

Scientific psychology: critique of, 10, 13–14, 23–29, 34, 36, 45, 62–63, 82; emergence of, 112, 186–87. *See also* Experimental psychology; "New psychology"

Sechenov, Ivan, 145

Sensationalism, 63, 71, 72, 141, 164

Sensation and perception, 29–30, 65–66, 72–76; distinction between, 26–27, 33, 133–40; role of active attention in, 31

Sensory isolation experiments (Spalding), 181

Sensory threshold. *See* Fechner, Gustav: psychophysics of

Sentient principle. *See* Whytt, Robert: sentient principle of

Seraphine (Heine), 46–47

Sexual love, 55–56

Sexual selection, 170, 175, 177

Sheehan, James, 12

Shelley, Mary, 15, 16, 27, 45, 50–54, 57–58, 83, 202, 218

Shelley, Percy Bysshe, ix, 15, 19, 49, 50, 107, 144, 147; on scientific views expressed in *Queen Mab,* 15, 47–48; on erotic view of world, 15, 55–59, 120; on metaphysics, 22–23, 27, 90; on doctrine of necessity, 45; materialist psychology of, 45–46, 50; on diet, 47

Sherrington, Charles, xiv–xv, 155

Sin, 6

Skinner, B. F., 94

Soul: immortal, 4, 113; location of, 5–6, 18; materialism of, 16, 41–42, 54, 174, 183; and volition, 78; natural science of, 82, 83, 85, 86, 107; local signs theory of, 103, 104–6; as unconscious mind,

Soul: immortal (continued)
119, 121, 143; weaknesses of, 128,
143; and dual aspect theory of
mind and body, 147, 183
Soul psychology, 119-20
Spalding, Douglas, 179-83
Specific nerve energies, doctrine
of, 84, 90-91, 93-94
Spencer, Herbert: positivism
of, 8, 9, 99, 159; on will, 116,
118; career of, 146, 150; pan-
phenomenalism of, 161, 162; on
evolutionary theory, 169, 172,
173, 176, 181-82
Spinal reflex. *See* Lewes, George
Henry: on spinal reflexes;
Whytt, Robert: on discovery of
spinal reflexes
Spinoza, Baruch, 48, 49, 89-91, 95,
111, 147, 148, 162
Spiritualism, 3, 7, 9, 16, 34, 74, 79,
114, 120, 141, 142
Stendhal, 58
Stevenson, Robert Louis, 164-66
Stewart, Dugald, 30, 31, 32, 34, 36,
37, 52, 60-61, 64, 99, 125
Stimulus, xiii, 26
Stimulus threshold (Fechner),
96-97
Stirling, James, 26
Strauss, D., 48
Stream of consciousness, 199
Studies of reflex function, 122-23
Stumpf, Karl, 161, 195-98
Subthreshold phenomena, 18, 19
Suggestibility, 79-80, 83, 114, 119;
and unconscious mind, 128
Sully, James, 185
Supernatural unconscious, 128-29,
141

Swedenborg, Emanuel, 75
Symbolic logic, 195, 200

Taine, Hippolyte, 110-11, 142, 161
Telepathy, 119
Titchener, Edward B., 124
Trances, 119, 129
Transcendental idealism, 63. *See
also* German idealism; Kant,
Immanuel
Trialism, 118-19
Tyndall, John, 150, 156, 161, 179

Unconscious cerebration, 79, 139
Unconscious inference, 118, 132,
187-89
Unconscious mind: dualism of
conscious mind and, 7, 19, 20,
118; fluid materialism of, 43; as
soul, 119, 120; study of, through
introspection, 122; theories
of, 127, 128-29, 130-43 *passim;*
supernatural theories of, 128-29,
141, 142; natural theories of, 128,
129, 142; the logical unconscious
as, 131-43; as irrational, 164-67
"Underground Psychology," 14, 18,
51
Universals, 33-34

Vision, 138
Vital force, x-xi, 17, 78; as will, 84.
See also Vital principle
Vital principle: of animate matter
(Müller), 91-92
Volition: as consciousness, 31; as
free action, 78; dissolution of,
79-80; and psychological theory,
115-17, 118. *See also* Will
Volta, Alessandro, x-xi, 38

Voltaire, 48

Wallace, Alfred Russel, 115, 172, 175
Weber, Ernst H., 96, 102, 107
Weber Fraction, 96, 100
Wedgewood, Josiah, xii
Wertheimer, Max, 196
Whewell, William, 35, 111, 124
Will: as mental force, 84, 85, 92-93; in Schopenhauer's philosophy, 86-88; consciousness of, 115-17, 123. *See also* Volition
Woehler, Friedrich, 91
Wordsworth, William, ix, 12, 15
World soul (Fechner), 97-98, 129
Whytt, Robert: career of, xiii-xv, 61; invention of *stimulus* concept, xiii; on discovery of spinal reflexes, xiii, xv, 5-6, 130, 151; sentient principle of, xiii, xiv; on distributed soul, 6, 15; on relation of mind to body, 61-62; on motor activity, xiv, 76; on existence of unconscious feeling, 130, 131, 151
Wundt, Wilhelm: on sense of effort, 86-87; career of, 89, 144-45, 154, 156, 184, 185, 200; metaphysical views of, 98; experimental research of, 117, 122, 123-24, 143; on volition, 116-17, 123; on unconscious inference, 118, 119, 132, 142, 143, 195; on apperception, 123-24; on laws of sentience, 153; on sensations, 161, 196, 197